Cricket's Dawn That Died

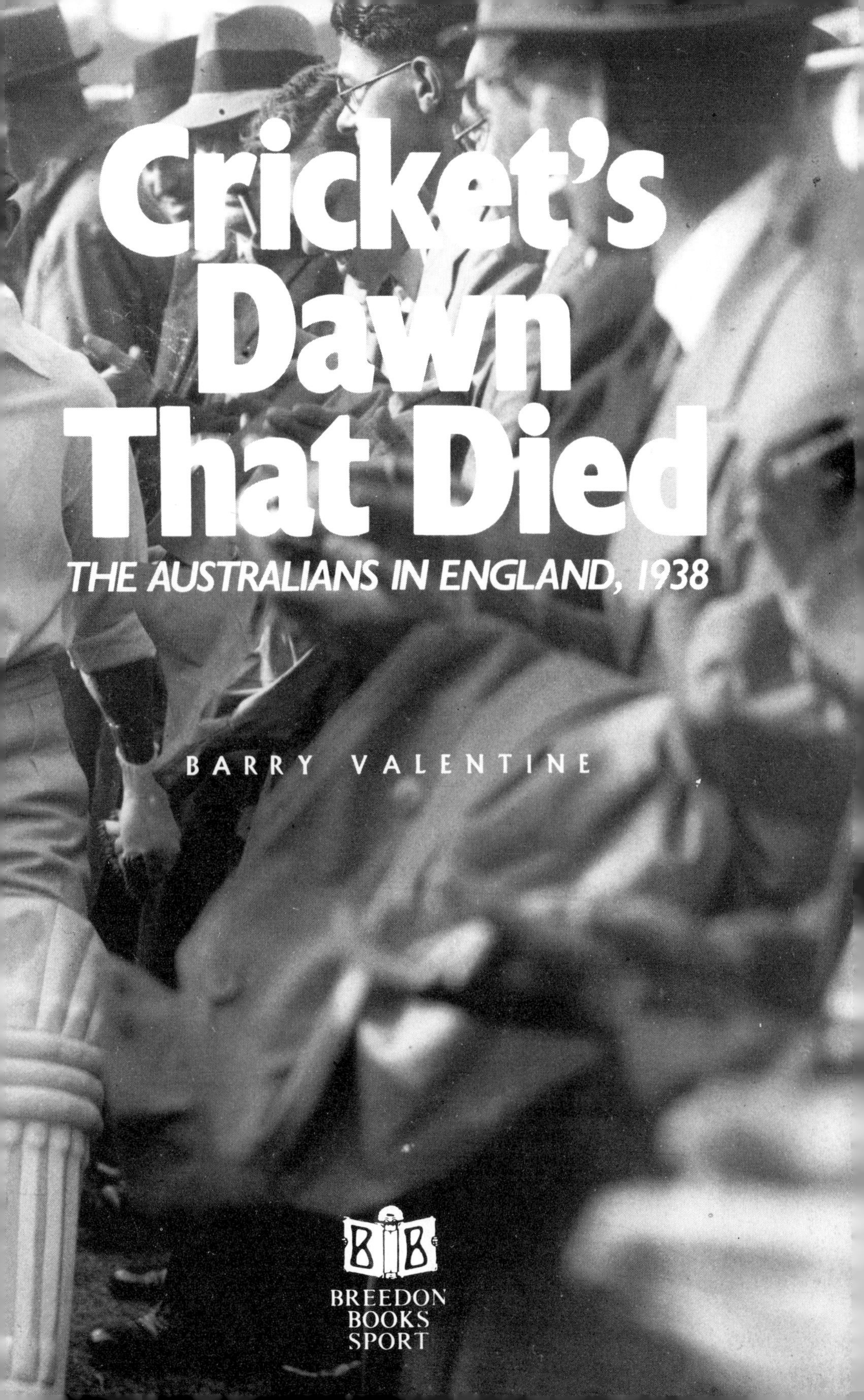

Cricket's Dawn That Died

THE AUSTRALIANS IN ENGLAND, 1938

BARRY VALENTINE

BREEDON
BOOKS
SPORT

First published in Great Britain by
The Breedon Books Publishing Company Limited
44 Friar Gate, Derby DE1 1DA
1991

ISBN 0 907969 83 6

Printed and bound in Great Britain by The Bath Press Limited, Bath and London.
Jacket printed by Arkle Print Ltd of Northampton.

Contents

A Note About The Scorecards

THE scorecards of first-class matches are taken from the 1939 *Wisden* and can therefore be assumed to be reliable. The second-innings batting orders in all matches have been added from contemporary daily newspapers. The fall of wickets come mostly from Australian daily newspapers. For the Gentlemen v Players match at Lord's, the original score-book held in the MCC Library yielded the additional details of batting times and boundary hits.

It should be remembered that in 1938, extras conceded by no-balls and wides were not debited in the bowling analysis. In scores and averages, the prefix 'Mr' is used to indicate amateur status.

* (Against a name) — captain.
† (Against a name) — wicketkeeper.
* (Against a figure) — not out or unfinished partnership.

Test Scorecards and Averages

THE official Test score-books of W.H.Ferguson, the famous Australian scorer and baggage-master, are preserved in New South Wales Cricket Association Library and from them I was able to reconstruct the Test Matches ball-by-ball. Hence the expanded score-cards of the Tests which give the same sort of extra detail that one sees in newspapers and cricket magazines about Tests today. These extra data are, I hope, largely self-explanatory. The bowling column gives the cumulative analysis of each bowler at each interval and at the end of the innings. It also states the number of times a bowler was called for a no-ball (whether hit for runs or not) and wide. The 'Timetable of the Innings' marks the time, score and over of the innings at which various events took place: the fall of each wicket, intervals and stoppages in play, and the passing of the team total 50, 100, 150 etc; in the final column is the score of the not out batsmen at each interval and at the fall of a wicket.

It would seem from the lay-out of Ferguson's score-books that he did not keep the books up to date as play went on but rather recorded the match in some sort of ball-by-ball form, transferring the details to the official score-book at intervals. The transcribing produced occasional errors which I had to try to correct to conform to the final certified scores. Consequently, the figures for balls received by each batsman cannot be guaranteed to be absolutely correct, but I am satisfied that the margin of error is not more than 2%.

The following points should be noted about the Test scores and about the Test averages and Epitome of the Test Series:
'runs' in a team innings includes extras.
'runs' scored by a batsman or conceded by a bowler excludes all extras.
'balls' includes no-balls (whether hit for runs or not) and excludes wides.
'Overs' excludes no-balls and wides.

In the extras column, 'NB' (no-balls) means the number of runs accruing to the total as extras from no-balls and thus excludes runs hit by the bat.

Anywhere else, a reference to 'NB' or 'no-balls' means the number of times that a bowler was called for a no-ball, whether hit for runs or not.

In the extras column 'W' (wides) means the number of runs accruing to the total from wide deliveries.

Anywhere else, 'W' or 'wides' means the number of times that a delivery was called wide.

In the Test Averages and Epitome, distinguish between '15.50 overs' and '15.5 overs'. The former means 15½ overs; the latter means 15 overs 5 balls. Similarly, '15.33 overs' means $15\frac{1}{3}$ overs, and '15.3 overs' means 15 overs 3 balls.

Foreword

TIME marches on. When I finished the main text of this work in June 1990, no one foresaw how relevant the issues and events of 1938 and 1939 would seem in the light of new international problems; still less would one have guessed that this Foreword would be written at a time of war.

I considered amending the opening words about the state of contemporary Europe, but decided to leave them as they stand, for who knows what will be happening in the world when the book reaches the bookshops?

War and the threat of it is an unavoidable backdrop to the chronicle of the 1938 cricket season, but this book dwells mainly on the happier struggles of bat against ball. Had it not been for the coming war in 1939, the season might be seen as the dawn of a new era for English cricket, as the early 1940s might have been for Australia. What grand battles the two countries would have had in 1940-41 and 1942! A new era did begin in 1938 in that television cameras appeared for the first time at a cricket ground. Cricket was transmitted live to a few thousand people, but alas, none of it was recorded for us to see today.

The best excuse, if one is needed, for this book is that no full account of the Australian tour of England in 1938 has ever appeared in 53 years. Neville Cardus' daily newspaper reports on the Test Matches were included in a post-war collection of his writings. Jack Fingleton, in a book of his, mainly about 'Bodyline', has published excerpts from his tour diary. These *(The Essential Neville Cardus* and Fingleton's *Cricket Crisis)* were priceless sources of inspiration and information for me. They and most of the other books, magazines and newspapers to which I have resorted are listed in the Bibliography at the end. Especially valuable were the 1939 *Wisden,* the books of Jack Pollard, books by and about Bradman, Hutton, Compton and Hammond, the monumental *Who's Who of Cricketers,* Michael Marshall's *Gentlemen v Players,* and Alan Gibson's little biographies over the years in *The Cricketer.*

The story of the 1938 season is told, I hope, simply, with no pompous 'message' or judgements in hindsight, no phoney nostalgia. I hope readers will understand the rather quaint use of the prefix 'Mr' to distinguish amateurs from professionals. This is merely to follow the convention of the time, not to suggest that the former are held in higher esteem.

My thanks are due to Mr Ross Dundas, librarian of the New South Wales Cricket Association, for promptly and kindly sending me copies of the Test scorebooks of the official Australian scorer; to Mr Stephen Green and his staff who make the MCC Library such a welcoming place for the cricket researcher; and to my publisher for assiduous work in putting my efforts into such an attractive and well-appointed form.

Barry Valentine   Belfast   February 1991

Cricket in 1938

AT THE moment when I write these words, fingers crossed and wood touched, Europe has achieved a degree of political freedom unprecedented in its history. A process which began in Portugal in 1974 has swept aside fascist and communist totalitarianism everywhere except Albania. The prospect in 1938 was not so happy. Portugal, Italy and every Eastern European state, except Czechoslovakia, were held under right-wing dictatorships. In Spain, democracy was dying in a two-year-old civil war. They were sandwiched between two great monstrosities, the perverted nationalism of Hitler's Germany, pushing outwards, and the perverted socialism of Stalin's Russia, cruelly turned in on its own people. Apart from brutal internal repression and persecution of Jews and others, Germany had denounced treaties made by its pre-Nazi governments, re-armed illegally, re-occupied the demilitarized Rhineland, helped the fascist rebellion in Spain, made treaties with Italy and Japan (currently overrunning China), and now in early 1938, Hitler was starting to talk about 'the Germans beyond the Reich' in Austria and Czechoslovakia.

The National (in reality Conservative) Government of Mr Neville Chamberlain was pursuing a policy of quiet diplomacy and even quieter rearmament and his attempted rapprochement with Italy caused the resignation of the young Foreign Secretary, Anthony Eden, who joined the Parliamentary rump of Churchill's anti-appeasers. Chamberlain was a member of a famous political family, schooled in Victorian morality and reasonableness, horrified by the senseless suffering of World War One, a good reforming administrator and confident communicator on the newsreels, but lacking the ruthlessness and resolution that were necessary in the dangerous international situation.

Britain was a homogeneous society, with few racial or ethnic problems and enjoying a period of internal peace and order not seen before or since. The crime rate was low, organized crime was small-scale, senseless violence, hooliganism and vandalism were almost unknown. Murders were few enough that each case aroused, with the added *frisson* of hanging, great public interest. There was little political unrest — some minor riots by the unemployed, trouble aroused by Sir Oswald Mosley's Blackshirt pro-Nazis. The IRA seemed dormant.

Yet there were deep divisions of class and breeding which could not yet be breached. It was difficult to rise from a poor background to wealth and those who did were fully never accepted by the upper classes. Accent, family and schooling counted more than money. For the rich it was holidays on ocean liners, town houses, country weekends, chauffeured Rolls-Royces, dressing for dinner. For the growing middle class, the suburban semi-detached, the radio, the new small car in the garage, lovingly polished, the family holiday in Torquay or Scarborough. For the urban poor, bread and margarine, shared baths in a tub in front of the smokey coal fire, outside toilets, kids sleeping three in a bed, damp, rats, rickets and hairlice, and Dad's cough no better from the dust in the factory.

An unskilled worker earned £3-4 a week, a man on the 'dole' with a wife and family less than £2 a week. Unemployment had been slowly declining towards 1,600,000, partly because of re-armament, but the recovery had not noticeably spread to Scotland, Wales and the North, and in 1937-8 the figures for unemployed were starting to rise again. Ten pounds a week was a good wage for a clerical worker and £2,000 a year was a top-class income. In 1938, the budget raised income tax to 5s 6d in the pound. A good suburban semi-detached house could be got for £1-a-week mortgage and a small saloon car for £300. Bed and breakfast in a top London hotel was not much more than £1 a night, 5s in a good hotel. *Wisden Cricketers' Almanack* cost 5s for the limp edition. A new cricket book (of which there were not many published around this time) ranged from 2s 6d to 8s 6d. Admission to a Test match would be 2 or 3s. A professional playing for England received £50 per Test, plus third-class railway fare and payment of his hotel bill.

On the face of it Britain was at the height of its international power, with an Empire and dominions covering one-third of the world. But the days of imperial rule in India were clearly coming to an end and the burdens of rule were beginning to tell. In Palestine, which Britain held under a mandate from the League of Nations, the immigrant Jewish population and the native Arabs were in violent conflict.

It was a fast changing world. A person in late middle age could remember a time when there were no 'movie' cinemas, no 'talkies', no radio, no cars, no aeroplanes or airships, no television, no fascism, no communism. Television had started in 1936 and only a few enthusiasts with money and an address in the London area would even consider it. Radio was reaching the majority of homes: the BBC National Programme, the Regional, and the continental stations. On it were heard the staid sombre news programmes, the 'talks' and plays, the Sibelius concerts from the Queen's Hall and the dance bands — Henry Hall, Ray Noble, Geraldo and his Goucho Tango Orchestra, crooner Al Bowlly, and a new sound from America, the Glenn Miller Orchestra. Music-hall was dying and being replaced by variety, summer shows and pantomime. Cheeky Max Miller, little Arthur Askey, the anarchic Crazy Gang, laconic Rob Wilton. On the stage were the light musical comedies of Nöel Coward, the romances of Ivor Novello, Lupino Lane's 'Me and my Gal' and its famous *Lambeth Walk.*

The United States of America was a far-off country, with President Roosevelt leading a recovery from the Depression. But for most, America meant one thing — the weekly visit to the Picture Palace to see the new Hollywood 'movie', with Gable, Garbo, Fred Astaire, Dick Powell, Tyrone Power, Bette Davis, Laurel and Hardy or the Marx Brothers. British films could not quite compete, although they had classic actors like Olivier and Vivien Leigh, Gielgud, Robert Donat, light-hearted singers like Gracie Fields and George Formby from the northern working classes, evergreen singer-dancer Jessie Matthews, and bumbling Will Hay. People got their news from the solemn tones of the BBC news bulletin and from the hectoring, propagandist-sounding newsreels of *Pathé News* or *Gaumont British.* For any sensitive or analytical reporting of the world's troubling events, one had to read the newspapers, the quality Press, the *Times, Daily Telegraph, Manchester Guardian,* or the 'populars', the *Express, Mail, Mirror, News Chronicle* or *Daily Herald,* or the new magazine *Picture Post.*

This, then, was something of the society that the Australian cricketers were coming to in 1938. They were coming from an independent country, the Commonwealth of Australia, which still firmly regarded itself as a son of the British Empire with ties of affection which even the Bodyline Controversy of 1932-3 had not disturbed. Australia had been helped through the Depression of the early 1930s by British loans and was now in good health. The Prime Minister was J.A.Lyons, leader of the conservative United Australia Party. Both he and his leading minister, R.G.Menzies, the Attorney-General, were firm lovers of Britain and of cricket.

The Game

Although it is a game fond of tradition and continuity, cricket has changed greatly in the 50-odd years since the era which this book is about. There were fewer Tests, fewer international tours, more county cricket, no limited-over or knock-out competition, no commercial sponsorship, bigger crowds, players whose approach was simpler, more casual even, seeking to enjoy and entertain; yet with subtleties of spin bowling and weather-affected wickets that are virtually lost to the modern player. Bats were lighter, balls had less pronounced seams, no batsman or fielder wore a helmet. There were fewer fast bowlers, fewer medium-pace seamers, more bowlers who relied on swing in the air, and more spinners. Until the 1950s, there were comparatively few successful off-spinners; the great bowlers were leg-break and googly men or orthodox slow left-armers, largely due, no doubt, to the pre-1935 lbw law. Spinners relied more on the weapons of flight and deception than they do today, hoping for stumpings and catches from mistimed shots, rather than bat-pad catches from defensive shots. Fielders never came nearer than four to five yards from the bat. Players took less time on the field agonizing over tactics, they just got on with the game. Bowlers bowled their overs at about 20 per hour and needed no fines or statutory minimum limits to encourage them to do so. Batsmen were expected to score at around three runs per over, which was 60 per hour, a run a minute. Players did not dawdle or glare at each other, or jump on top of each other when they got a wicket.

The standard of play may have been lower than today, at least in so far as most counties used only native English players. Some counties were much more of a push-over than any county today, and also countries such as West Indies, India and New Zealand were only beginning to develop in international cricket. Certainly, catching in the outfield and ground fielding have improved immeasurably as a result of limited-over cricket. It was an era of prodigious batting achievements by some of the greatest batsmen the game has ever seen, and if no rain was about, then sweating bowlers were the toilers of the game. There was a widespread view that batsmen had it too easy on the well-prepared batting strips which groundsmen vied with each other to provide. Spectators were much quieter and more polite (English crowds being much quieter than Australian). They applauded loudly where appropriate, barracked occasionally, but otherwise sat in respectful concentrated silence. There was no chanting or heckling or carrying of banners or running on to the playing area or mobbing players at the end of a match. Jackets, shirts and hats were worn, even in high summer. Because of the better behaviour and less stringent safety regulations, the grounds held much bigger capacity and it was normal for hundreds to sit on the grass behind the boundary rope.

Cricket both reflected and transcended the class divisions in English society. The old-style aristocracy and upper middle class were in control of the administration of cricket. Those classes produced the amateurs, or 'Gentlemen', who played the game up to the very highest level as a hobby. Fewer and fewer could afford to play regular first-class cricket every year, unless supported by benevolent employers who gained vicarious goodwill from their cricketers' fame. It was still the invariable convention, on the verge of breaking down, that counties and the Test side be captained by an amateur, even if he was not otherwise worthy of a place in the side. But the tradition, particularly marked in Yorkshire, of appointing a figure-head of moderate playing ability was dying out by the early 1930s. Amateurs of reasonable ability were courted by the more impecunious counties, whose finances did not stretch to ten or 11 paid cricketers for every fixture.

The bulk of the best cricketers, especially bowlers, were professionals, or 'Players'. A county pro was not highly paid but earned more than most industrial or agricultural workers and had a relatively pleasant and healthy life, although for four months he had to play six days a week with some long train journeys and early-morning arrivals at hotels. In a reasonably well-off county such as Nottinghamshire, for example, young Arthur Jepson started on a 22-week contract in 1937 at £1 10s a week plus £9 for each home match played and £11 for each away match played. [1] Men such as Jack Hobbs, Herbert Sutcliffe and Frank Woolley had, by their ability, their grace and dignity, so increased the standing of the professional that the public was starting to question whether any real distinction should be made between those who were paid for their cricket and those who were not. However, there was no great wish to abolish the distinction because, unlike other sports such as tennis, amateurs and professionals played freely with and against each other on the same fields, and the annual battle at Lord's, Gentlemen v Players, was a popular and important event. In countries outside England, all cricketers were amateurs, playing much less domestic cricket, although some like Learie Constantine played for money in English league cricket in the North.

The Laws

Until 1947, cricket was played under the Third MCC Code of 1884 as amended over the years. It is worthwhile to look at those aspects in which the laws differed markedly from the Laws of today.

Before 1935, a batsman could not be out lbw unless the ball would have hit the wicket, hitting him in front of the stumps and having pitched in line of wicket to wicket. By an experimental rule of that year, made permanent in 1937, he was also out if the ball pitched outside the line of the off-stump. The rule was the same whether or not the batsman was attempting a stroke.

A bowler was no-balled if, at the time of releasing the ball, his back foot was not grounded behind the bowling crease. The new ball could be claimed at the start of the innings and thereafter when at least 200 runs had been scored since the last new ball. In the wake of the Bodyline Controversy, a new rule allowed the umpire to warn

[1] Interview with Stephen Cantle, *Wisden Cricket Monthly* November 1983.

Yorkshire's Herbert Sutcliffe, one of the great players of the inter-war period who had done so much to increase the standing of the professional cricketer. Although he had been Yorkshire's permanent opener since 1919, many considered him to be still good enough to open for England in 1938.

a bowler and ultimately take him off for 'persistent and systematic bowling of fast short-pitched balls at the batsman standing clear of his wicket'. But there was, as yet, no limitation of the number of fielders on the leg-side.

A fielder could touch or lean against the boundary when catching or fielding the ball.

The wicket was deemed to be down if a bail was dislodged from its groove, even if it had not fallen to the ground.

No declaration could be made on the first day of a match of three or more days, and the follow-on was enforceable with a lead of 150 runs. No side could forfeit an innings. There was no mimimum number of overs to be bowled in a day or in the last hour of a match; fielding sides were trusted not to slow things down. If an over commenced before the scheduled end of a session of play, that over could be completed.

The wicket could be covered to protect it from rain during the 24 hours before the match was due to start, but not at any time thereafter (except, in county matches, on a Sunday). But the outfield and part of the wicket up to three and a half feet beyond each popping crease could be covered at any time. Thus, covering of the run-ups, allowed since 1913, meant that fast bowlers could operate immediately after rain. The rule banning the covering of wickets was of vital importance to the complexion of the game. The disadvantages were that it allowed the weather to play a crucial role in bringing victory to one side, and that it might extend the delay before conditions were fit for play. On the other hand it brought greater variety; the character of the pitch could vary from hour to hour as it dried out. Where a lot of time was lost, the eccentricities of the wicket could speed up the fall of wickets and thus bring about an exciting result, rather than a futile stalemate. A wet wicket would usually be lifeless when play started but the drying sun and wind would bring moisture to the surface and give pace and bounce to the pace bowlers and spin to the spinners. The wicket could not be rolled or treated during a match, save that the batting side could require it to be rolled and dusted at the end of a day's play or at the start of an innings. Under an experimental rule for 1938, the umpires could allow the wicket to be rolled or otherwise dried, solely to make it fit for play after rain.

The normal hours of play in county cricket were 11.30am to 6.30pm on the first two days and 11.30am to 6.00pm on the third. By agreement of both captains, an extra half-hour could be played on the second day to achieve a finish. On the third day, either captain could demand a further half-hour beyond the scheduled finishing time. Lunch was from 1.30pm to 2.10pm; tea usually from 4.15pm to 4.30pm. Often, if either side had a long journey to play the next day, they would arrange for an early finish in the third day (say, 4.30pm, which meant a potential finish at 5.00pm.) with longer hours on the first two days. Normal hours for the Australian tour matches were 11.30am to 6.30pm on the first two days, 11.30am to 5.30pm on the last.

For the 1938 Test, the hours of play for every day were: 11.30am to 1.30pm; lunch; 2.15pm to 4.30pm; tea; 4.45pm to 6.30pm. (The tea interval was subject to variation if, for example, a side had one wicket to fall at 4.30pm).

County and tour matches were played on Saturday-Monday-Tuesday and Wednesday-Thursday-Friday. Four-day Tests were played on Friday-Saturday-Monday-Tuesday. (Sunday was of course *hors de combat* for all but a few charity and benefit one-day games.

The Fight for the Ashes

When World War One ended, England held the Ashes, but the legendary Australian side of Warwick Armstrong soon changed that. J.W.H.T.Douglas's MCC touring team of 1920-21 was by no means a poor side but they lost every one of the five (timeless) Tests. The defeated and the victorious came to England on the same ship and Australia triumphed again in that bone dry summer of 1921. The first three Tests, at Nottingham, Lord's and Leeds, the Australians won with ease. In the last two, at Manchester and The Oval, England made a better fist of resisting the bowling of Gregory and Macdonald and secured two draws. (Tests in England were limited to three days.) When Arthur Gilligan took MCC to Australia in 1924-5, the two sides were much more even; England were unlucky to lose four Tests but took great heart from an innings victory in the Fourth. Herbie Collins brought Australia back in 1926; the first four Tests were drawn, the First Test at Nottingham a near wash-out, the Second Test at Lord's a high-scoring stalemate, the Third Test at Leeds saved after England were in trouble, the Fourth Test at Manchester ruined by rain. For the deciding , timeless, Test at The Oval, England brought in a bright young captain, Percy Chapman, and won an absorbing contest to recover the Ashes amidst great public rejoicing.

Chapman's star-studded 1928-9 side beat Australia by 4-1 and the young Wally Hammond seemed to be the best batsman in the world, even though Australia had discovered a new prospect called Bradman.

In 1930, a rebuilt Australian side was led by Bill Woodfull. The Tests were extended to four days. England won a low-scoring First Test at Nottingham, but the Second Test, at Lord's ushered in a change in the character of Test cricket for the next decade. England won the toss and made 425 in a day and a bit. The only worry was whether they could force a win. Enter Don Bradman to play the first of his great Test innings, a faultless 254, and Australia won by seven wickets. In the Third Test at Leeds he scored 309 in a day, England followed-on but rain saved them from probable defeat. Rain took half the time at Manchester, another draw. In the deciding Oval Test (timeless), England started with 405 but still lost by an innings and 39 runs. Bradman scored 232 but after a break for rain, Larwood got the ball to lift for a short while and Bradman's unease was plain. The seed of an idea was planted that grew into bodyline bowling. The single-minded Scot, Douglas Jardine, no lover of Australian crowds, led the MCC in 1932-3 and used Larwood, Voce and Bowes in a system of planned short bowling aimed a the batsman's body with a crowded leg-trap. It helped England to regain the Ashes by 4-1, but so great was the antagonism of Australian players and public that it put the 1934 tour in jeopardy.

The MCC oligarchy were discenchanted with bodyline when they saw it in practice at home in 1933, and withdrew their whole-hearted support for Jardine, who saved embarrassment in the spring of 1934 by suddenly announcing (by a cable to a newspaper) his resignation as England captain. Larwood and Voce were not selected for the Tests and the 1934 series was a re-run of 1930, even to the extent that the captain Woodfull regained the Ashes again on his birthday at The Oval. Only in the tourists' match against Nottinghamshire did they encounter bodyline bowled by Voce and they threatened to pull out of the game; Voce had diplomatic shin trouble in the second innings. Australia won the First Test at Nottingham by 238 runs in a low-scoring match. It was the only time in an Ashes Test before 1947 when Bradman did not contribute a century in a Australian win. England squared the series at Lord's, thanks to Verity's spin on a drying wicket. The Manchester Test produced a heatwave and too many runs for England to secure a victory. In the Fourth Test at Leeds, Bradman ended a run of low scores with 304 and England were almost counted out when rain on the last day saved them. In the timeless Oval Test, England just crumbled under the weight of Australia's total of 701.

England's captain in 1934 was Bob Wyatt, a loyal supporter of Jardine in the Bodyline Tour. For the 1936-7 series, England picked G.O.Allen to lead. Australian-born, popular there, his refusal personally to bowl short for Jardine was remembered. No-one gave much for his chances. With help from the weather, he trounced Australia in the first two Tests. The English public reeling from the abdication of King Edward VIII, were astonished. Bradman, at the start of his Test captaincy career, faced the biggest crisis of his life. The Third and Fourth Tests swung to and fro but superior luck and tactics gave Australia the victories. Australia won the Fifth Test by an innings and, although the tour had restored goodwill and broken all attendance records, Allen was heartbroken at having the prize snatched from his grasp.

The Australians

There was always something special about a season in Australia which preceded a tour to England. The Australians had beaten South Africa and West Indies at home in the early 1930s and, thanks to the bowling of Clarrie Grimmett and without Bradman, had trounced South Africa on a tour there in 1935-6. In 1937-8, four States competed for the Sheffield Shield — New South Wales, Victoria, South Australia and Queensland, who played each other twice. The season began with a testimonial match in which Grimmett, the veteran leg-spinner, came on and bowled Bradman with his fourth ball. The persistent, diminutive South Australian, born in New Zealand, had formed a great partnership with Bill O'Reilly but had been passed over in the 1936-7 Tests. He was hopeful of a place on the boat to England and was not alone in that view. He was second to O'Reilly in the Shield averages, with 30 wickets (av. 22.86). O'Reilly was in a class of his own and his 14 for 98 for NSW against South Australia helped his State to win the Shield for the first time in four years. Bradman, of course, headed the batting averages, averaging 98.30, playing for South Australia. Ian Lee, 24-year-old Victorian left-hander, was next with 477 runs (av. 59.62).

By winning on the first innings at Sydney, on 21 to 25 January, NSW clinched the title over Victoria and young Sid Barnes made a timely 110. The touring team, selected by Bradman, E.A.Dwyer and W.J.Johnson, was announced on 27 January. There was no doubt about the captain, Bradman. McCabe was appointed vice-captain. Let us now look at the 16 chosen tourists, grouped in categories, together with a few of those unlucky to be left behind.

Opening Batsmen

John Henry Webb (Jack) FINGLETON (New South Wales). Born at Waverley on 28 April 1908. A political and legal reporter with a Sydney newspaper, son of a member of the State Parliament (who was not wealthy and who died young) and son-in-law of the State Chief Justice. An evocative and witty writer and talker, who rarely showed those characteristics at the crease. He was a fluent, painstaking right-hand batsman who recognized his limitations at Test level and showed inexhaustible patience. He bore the brunt of bodyline in 1932-3, was dropped, missed the 1934 tour but got back in with the retirement of Woodfull and Ponsford. He had a very short backlift, a sound defence, with a possible weakness early on against the outswinger. He was fit, disciplined, a brilliant outfielder and fearless close in at short leg to the spinners. In the Sheffield Shield in 1937-8, he made 494 runs (av. 54.88). After the war he became Australia's greatest cricket writer. A thin, cheerful face with receding hair.

William Alfred (Bill) BROWN (Queensland). Born at Toowomba on 31 July 1912. Played his early cricket in New South Wales. He was a surprise and very successful tourist in 1934, scoring a century in the Lord's Test. Then a job as a car salesman took him back to his native state where he became a Queensland Cricket Association coach. Attractive to watch, a poised and orthodox right-hand bat, always a careful starter, with a preference for the on-side. Whether scoring quickly or slowly, he never drew attention to himself. Probably the second most dependable batsman in the side. A keen physical trainer and good field who usually stood beside Fingleton at short leg. In Queensland's poor 1937-8 season he scored only 203 runs (av. 29.00) so some thought him lucky to make the tour. He came back to England with the great 1948 team and when he got a chance was as good as anyone. Tall and neat in appearance.

Clayvel Lindsay (Jack) BADCOCK (South Australia). Born at Exton, Northern Tasmania, on 10 April 1914, he crossed the straits to play for South Australia as a teenager and his brilliance, confidence and footwork saddled him with the name 'the Tasmanian Bradman'. He had an old-style upright stance but was short and stocky with dark Latinate features and a boyish sense of humour. He made a century in Australia's big total in the Final Test 1936-7 and scored 360 runs (av. 36.00) in the 1937-8 Sheffield Shield. Great things were expected of him in 1938, whether opening or down the order. He acquired the nickname 'Musso' on the voyage. In 1941 lumbago forced his retirement and he returned to his farm in Tasmania.

The choice of these three openers meant there was no room for Ian Lee or Keith Rigg, the successful Victorian opening pair.

Middle-order batsmen

Donald George (Don) BRADMAN (South Australia). Born at Cootamundra, New South Wales, on 27 August 1908 and brought up in the country town of Bowral, near Sydney. He made his debut for New South Wales in his teens but moved to South Australia in 1935, when he got a position in a stockbrokers' firm in Adelaide. His right-handed batting had by then rewritten the ground rules of Test cricket. In the 1930s he was the most famous sportsman in the British Empire, the greatest cricketer of his time, the greatest batsman of all time. What made this quiet unassuming small and unprepossessing figure so great? His physical co-ordination, quick footwork, intelligence and lightning quick brain, which enabled him to place the ball exactly where he wanted it — *ie* where the fielder was not. Thus he was able to score runs at the speed of a slogger whilst taking no more risk than a stonewalling defender. He made a point of never hitting the ball in the air until he had made as many runs as he wanted. He was said to have a weakness against

Bill Brown, a successful tourist on the Australian's last visit to England in 1934.

Jack Badcock, 'the Tasmanian Bradman' of whom great things were expected on the 1938 tour.

fast short-pitched bowling and against top-class spin on a drying wicket, but that probably meant that he was reduced to the level of the best of the rest. Not physically strong (he nearly died of appendicitis in 1934), Bradman was a compact and wiry figure and one of the smartest outfielders. He took over the Australian captaincy in 1936-7, lost his first two Tests abjectly but recovered to win the series. With his astute and organized mind and a strong but scrupulously fair drive to win every match as emphatically as possible, he settled well into the role. His tally for 1937-8 was 983 runs (av. 98.30). Back trouble nearly ended his career in 1946 but he came back for one final round of triumphs and was knighted upon his retirement in 1948. To some of his teammates he was 'Braddles'; to the vast public he was just 'The Don'.

Stanley Joseph (Stan) McCABE (New South Wales). Born at Grenfell on 16 July 1910, where his father was a barber, he went to St Joseph's College Sydney. After a few games for the State, the selectors spotted his class and sent him to England in 1930 and again in 1934. Both tours were reasonably successful. McCabe was an orthodox right-hand bat, who always carried the attack to the bowler. Short and slight of build with strong arms and wrists, he was a great hooker and when the mood took him he could murder an attack in a way that Bradman never could, as he did in two legendary Test innings, in 1932-3 and 1935-6. A neat figure, almost bald (nicknamed 'Napper' after Napoleon for reasons too complicated to explain here), he was a versatile fielder and accurate bowler at brisk medium pace. He had given up a job as an insurance clerk for cricket and now ran a sports store in Sydney. In 1937-8 he scored 416 runs (av. 46.77) and took seven wickets (av. 21.71). He had foot trouble throughout his career and did not reappear after the war. He died in a fall from a cliff in 1968.

Arthur Lindsay HASSETT (Victoria). Born at Geelong on 28 August 1913, Lindsay Hassett was the smallest first-class cricketer in Australia, at 5ft 6in and 10st. He went to the famous Geelong Grammar School and became an accountant. Before the war he was an aggressive, cheeky right-hand batsman, quick on his feet, and a good deep field, a witty, happy cricket with a penchant for practical jokes. He entered first-class cricket in 1935-6 and had no Test experience. In the 1937-8 Shield he scored 298 runs (av. 42.57). After the war, having led Australia in the Victory Tests of 1945, he schooled himself to play the sheet-anchor role and succeeded Bradman to the captaincy. His brother played tennis and cricket for Victoria.

Arthur Gordon CHIPPERFIELD, (New South Wales). Born at Ashfield, Sydney, on 17 November 1905 and the oldest member of the party, he made his first-class debut only in 1933-4 and was a surprise choice for the 1934 tour. In his first Test he ate lunch on 99 not

Arthur Chipperfield, at 33 the oldest member of the Australian touring party.

Lindsay Hassett, the smallest first-class cricketer in Australia, an aggressive batsman and fine outfielder.

out and got out without addition. Arthur, or 'Chipper', was stocky, bald, a solid, enthusiastic right-hand bat and a slow right-arm bowler. He owed his selection to his deceptively casual ability as a slip fielder, although A.G.Moyes thought he tended to stand too fine. In 1937-8 he made 210 runs (av. 21.00) and took 1-68. He was a good table-tennis player and adept at copying the signatures of his fellow players, a useful man for answering requests for autographs.

Sidney George BARNES, (New South Wales). Born at Charters Towers, Queensland, on 5 June 1916, he was the youngest tourist. His father was already dead when he was born on an impoverished sheep farm in the outback. When he was a baby his family moved to Sydney. He was now in the motor trade and was fixing a motor-bike in the back garden when his brother relayed the news of his selection from the radio. A very promising attacking off-side right-hand bat, he came to England with only nine first-class matches in two seasons, but he was full of confidence, almost precocious, a character who never let the petty rules of authority interfere with his enjoyment. In the 1937-8 Shield he scored 492 runs (av. 44:72) and took 1-34 with leg-breaks. After the war he became a prolific opening bat. Selected for a Test in 1951-2, the Board of Control vetoed him and although he cleared any slur on his character in a libel action, he was never selected again. He took his own life in 1973.

The unluckiest to be left at home was Ross Gregory, a surprise omission, the Victorian who scored 151 delightful runs in two Tests in 1936-7 and who probably should have been preferred to Chipperfield. Also disappointed were Raymond Robinson (New South Wales), temporarily with South Australia, a forceful bat who played one Test in 1936-7, and Rex Rogers, a hard-hitting left-hander from Queensland.

All-rounders

Mervyn George WAITE, (South Australia). Born at Kent Town, Adelaide, on 7 January 1911, he had been around since 1930-31 without playing a Test. A 'bits 'n' pieces' man, a useful right-hand bat and accurate medium pace or off-break bowler and a safe field, he was a member of the Adelaide Oval staff. In 1937-8 he scored 300 runs (av. 33.33) and took 15 wickets (av. 23.66). Waite was an Australian Rules footballer and nicknamed 'Dango'.

Edward Clive Stewart WHITE, (New South Wales). Born at North Sydney, on 17 April 1913, son of a State cricketer. He was a right-handed batsman who, after entering Shield cricket in 1933-4, developed more as a medium to slow left-arm bowler with subtle variation of pace. He was 6ft tall, fair and slim, a curiously anonymous man with an unobtrusive schoolmasterish appearance, who worked in a

Eddie White, right-hand batsman and left-arm medium-slow bowler.

'Dango' Waite, an all-rounder from South Australia who had been around since 1930-31 but still had to make his Test debut. He is wearing the traditional Australian 'baggy' cap which, for some reason, the 1938 tourists did not sport.

stockbroker's office. In 1937-8 he scored 142 runs (av. 20.28) and took 9 wickets (av. 28.00).

Left behind was Morris Sievers of Victoria, who had played three Tests in 1936-7 but had a poor 1937-8 season.

Fast bowler

Ernest Leslie (Ernie) McCORMICK, (Victoria). Born at North Carlton, Melbourne, on 16 May 1906, he was rumoured to be Australia's fastest since Gregory and Macdonald. Bradman certainly had high hopes of him, saying on arrival in England that McCormick was the fastest bowler in the world. He had one of the longest run-ups in the game — 30 yards — and steamed in with his long arms held stiffly by his side, making the most of his 6ft height in swinging over his right arm. He was not averse to dropping a few short, but bore no malice and had a great sense of humour. He was very fast at the start of an innings, as in Brisbane 1936-7 when he took three wickets in four overs. But his ferocity flagged in a second or third spell, perhaps because of incipient lumbago. 'Goldie' was a Melbourne jeweller and played a bit of baseball. In 1937-8 he took 13 wickets (av. 35.00) and hit 33 runs (av. 8.25) with his low order left-hand batting.

It was eloquent of the state of Australian cricket that there was really only one other pace bowler who might have made the team: 'Ginty' Lush of New South Wales, who was close to a Test place in 1936-7 but who appeared only once in the 1937-8 Shield.

Spin bowlers

William Joseph (Bill) O'REILLY, (New South Wales). Born at White Cliffs on 20 December 1905. Nicknamed 'Tiger', he was the son of a school teacher and became one himself. O'Reilly hailed from a town north of Sydney and played club cricket against the young Bradman in the 1920s. He made his State debut as early as 1927-8, was ignored for a few years, but from 1932-3 until the war he was the linchpin of the Australian attack. He stood 6ft 3in tall and was lanky and short of hair. He bowled right-arm leg-breaks and googlies at near medium pace and had the priceless quality of combining accuracy and subtlety with a lot of spin, bite and bounce. He tended to 'roll' the leg-break and reserved his most venomous spin for the top-spinner and googly. He could blast the batsman out with the unexpected vicious leg-break or 'kicker', which would be popped up into his close-in leg-trap. He hated batsmen like any Trueman or Larwood did. In his younger days he was a successful athlete and his springy run-up owed something to the 'hop, skip and jump'. On the unsmiling Test wickets of the 1930s he was consistently the world's best wicket-taker and is arguably the greatest spinner of all time. Occasionally he would swing lustily as a low-order left-hand bat. His 1937-8 figures

Ernie McCormick, with one of the longest run-ups in the game he was said to be the fastest bowler in Australia since Gregory and Macdonald. Don Bradman pinned high hopes on him in 1938.

Bill O'Reilly, on the unsmiling wickets of the 1930s he came to be regarded as arguably the greatest spin bowler of all time, bowling leg breaks and googlies at near medium pace.

were 33 wickets (av. 14.06) and 75 runs (av. 10.71). After the war he played one more Test then became a pungent journalist before retiring in his 80s.

Leslie O'Brien FLEETWOOD-SMITH, (Victoria). Born at Stawell on 30 March 1910, 'Chuck' was the son of a local newspaper owner from a town in Victoria. A right-arm pace bowler at college, when he broke his right arm he tried bowling with the other hand and found that he could impart a huge spin. He was one of the first exponents of the 'chinaman', the left-arm wrist spun off-break and its googly. He was tall, well-built and handsome, with black hair and moustache coiffured in the manner of a 1930s dance band conductor. He bowled slow-medium off a short, casual run and spun the ball so much that it hummed in flight. An unplayable ball might steal in amongst a succession of long hops and full tosses. He first played for Victoria in 1931-2. Hammond made it his business to knock him out of the reckoning for the 1932-3 Tests. He toured England successfully in 1934 but without playing in a Test. In 1936-7 he took some of the vital wickets which won the Ashes. He was a confirmed number-11 batsman, right handed, and a good short leg and slip. In 1937-8 he took 32 wickets (av. 25.84) and scored one run in three innings. He worked in the advertising department of a Melbourne newspaper. A happy social life took its toll and when he died in 1971, he was out of work and fighting his way back from alchoholism. An archetype of his era, like airships and the *Lambeth Walk*, and the only 'hyphenated' Australian Test cricketer.

Francis Anthony (Frank) WARD, (South Australia). Born in Sydney on 23 February 1909, he played for St George's Club, Sydney, but when Grimmett was away on tour to South Africa in 1935-6 he took his chance to move to South Australia. He was a good, persistent right-arm leg-spinner who could spin the ball hard but lacked the touch of genius to get the best batsman out, perhaps due to his quiet modesty of character. He was favoured by Bradman and chosen ahead of Grimmett for the 1936-7 Tests and 1938 tour. He was of medium height, of agricultural visage, not enhanced by a broken nose sustained when attempting to hook G.O.Allen at Brisbane 1936-7. He was a tail-end batsman who could stick around in a defensive mode, and an adequate fielder. The firm for which he worked as a salesman promised him one guinea for every wicket he took in the Tests. In the 1937-8 Sheffield Shield he took 25 wickets (av 27.88) and hit 125 runs (av. 15.62).

Ward's preference over Grimmett was a great surprise and disappointment to many in Australia and England, including O'Reilly, who thought he bowled better with Grimmett at the other end. However, Bradman and the other selectors thought that Grimmett

Frank Ward, a leg spinner who was chosen ahead of Clarrie Grimmett, much to the disappointment of many in Australia and England.

'Chuck' Fleetwood-Smith, one of the first exponents of the 'chinaman' and an archetype of the 1930s.

was a liability in the field and that the younger Ward was a quicker taker of wickets than the accurate, insidious Grimmett.

Wicketkeepers

Benjamin Arthur (Ben) BARNETT, (Victoria). Born at Auburn on 23 March 1908, he was from Hawthorn in East Melbourne and first played for Victoria in 1929-30. He was a surprise choice as running mate for Bert Oldfield in 1934. Now he came to England as first choice, although still without Test experience. Not an outstanding wicketkeeper, but a good taker of spin and a hard hitting and capable left-hand bat. A popular tourist with a pleasant face and crinkle-cut hair. An amateur conjurer and actor, he worked for a Melbourne insurance office and played Australian Rules football. In 1937-8 he scored 199 runs (av. 33.16), caught 10 and stumped 5. After the war he emigrated to England and played for Buckinghamshire.

Charles William WALKER, (South Australia). Born at Hindmarsh, Adelaide, on 19 February 1909, the 6ft 3in tall reserve wicketkeeper made his debut for the State in 1928-9 and was the unexpected deputy to Oldfield on the 1930 tour, but dropped out of the reckoning after that and had never played a Test. He had a cheery face with wavy brown hair and was a solid right-hand bat. A furniture salesman, nicknamed 'Chilla', he might have fared better but for an unfortunate liability to bone injury in the fingers, which he tried to protect with special gloves. In 1937-8 he made 95 runs (av. 11.87), caught 6 and stumped 7 before dropping out with an injured finger near the end of the season. When war came he joined the RAAF and was posted missing in action over Germany in 1942.

There was some disappointment that Bert Oldfield's reign as the gentleman behind the stumps was over. But the most inexplicable omission was that of Don Tallon, the Queensland 'keeper who was in a class of his own and at that time an excellent batsman. It is believed that all three selectors voted for him: Bradman along with Walker, Dwyer and Johnson with Barnett. For some reason their consultations resulted in him being left out, perhaps because of an unjustified fear that he could not keep so well to the spinners. Australians who saw him after the war must have kicked themselves that he was not given a chance in 1938.

'They also serve. . .'

Mr W.H.(Bill) Jeanes, secretary of the Australian Board of Control, was the manager, making his first tour as such. Dr Roland Pope of Sydney, who played for New South Wales and in one Test in 1884-5, was a kind of camp follower, making the tour at his own expense, an unofficial team doctor and confidant. A.G.(Johnnie) Moyes, a former South Australian state player, who was a close friend of Bradman, who confided

Ben Barnett, Australia's first-choice wicketkeeper in 1938, although still without Test experience.

Reserve wicketkeeper 'Chilla' Walker, who was unlucky to suffer from bone injuries to his fingers.

his views to him, came as correspondent of the *Sydney Sun.* Joining them was the famous scorer and baggage master W.H.(Bill) Ferguson. The selectors on the tour were Bradman, McCabe and Barnett.

It was a good team, strangely lacking a specialist left-handed batsman, but neither then nor in the perspective of history was it a great side. Sir Pelham Warner, chairman of the England selectors, commented: "They are not invincible. We have a chance". R.W.V.Robins said: "My honest opinion is that we shall beat them." They were a young side, even by Australian standards, although if hair on top of the head were to decide the fate of the Ashes, they would not be over confident. Five of the team had Irish ancestry: O'Reilly, Fleetwood-Smith, McCabe, McCormick and Barnes.

All the tourists were passed fit except Badcock, but he was alright after a fortnight's rest. On 25 February 1938, some 5,000 people saw them off from Melbourne on the *SS Orontes* to Tasmania, where they played two three-day games against the island, winning by 386 runs and by 485 runs. Then it was on to Western Australia where, on 18-21 March, they beat the State by an innings and 126 runs. Neville Cardus saw Bradman's 102 at Perth and wrote that he displayed faults of technique that were new but that he was still good for his familiar yield of centuries. On 21 March, the party was delayed by huge crowds with streamers and this made them two hours late at Freemantle for the voyage across the Indian Ocean.

The news from Europe was troubling. In February, Hitler had started to stir up feeling of Austrian Nazis and of German speakers in the democratic Czechoslovakia towards union, *Anschluss,* with the *Reich.* The Austrian Chancellor, Kurt Schuschnigg, defiantly announced a plebiscite of his people on 9 March. The Nazis stampeded him into resigning and replaced him with Herr Seys-Inquart, who cancelled the plebiscite and invited German troops in. Hitler drove in triumph through his native country and on 14 March, Anschluss was proclaimed to cheering crowds in Vienna. In Spain the fascist leader, General Franco, launched a major assault on the Republican Government forces in Catalonia. On 24 March, the British Prime Minister pledged support to France and Belgium.

The Australians, meanwhile, arrived at Colombo, Ceylon, and stopped for one day on 30 March to play against the colony. Australia made 367-9 dec (Badcock 116, Hassett 116), Ceylon 114-7 (Chipperfield 4-24). On 5 April the *Orontes* docked at Aden. Stanley McCabe had a sore but improving throat. On 9 April they got off at Suez and whilst the ship cruised up the canal, they dashed to Cairo to play against Gezira Sporting Club. On 13 April they stopped at Naples and went to see Pompei. The manager, Bill Jeanes, had lumbago and walked with a stick, prompting Ernie McCormick to remark:

"Bill, old boy, I can hardly tell you from the ruins." In Naples harbour there were 116 ships on naval exercises.

On 14 April the Australian party stopped at Villefranche in the south of France and were entertained at Nice Lawn Tennis club, where King Gustav of Sweden was playing. Four truants went on a tour of the Riviera by bus. One Italian passenger took Badcock for a compatriot and was highly displeased when Badcock seemed unwilling to converse in the language. And that is how he got the name 'Musso'. He and Sid Barnes became close friends on the tour and shared some unusual experiences: a near-riot in Cairo and an unfortunate experience with French champagne at Villefranche. Barnes began some physical exercise and as the ship approached Gibraltar, he got up one day at 6am and, clad in woollen sweat suit, jogged six times around the deck. For stretching exercises he jumped up to grab one of the steel ropes joining the sun awnings and his hand slipped. Barnes fell back and landed on his left hand. He bathed it in hot water for half an hour. But when sightseeing in Gibraltar, the wrist became sore and swollen. He said nothing until the ship embarked and then showed it to a passenger, a young Melbourne doctor called Norman Cust. He put the arm in plaster.

The English

Under Douglas Jardine's captaincy England had won every Test series between 1931 and 1933-4. When he resigned in the spring of 1934, the selectors fell back on R.E.S.Wyatt. The pugnacious, dedicated Warwickshire all-rounder proceeded to lose three Tests series in a row. After losing the Ashes in 1934 he took a fairly strong MCC team to the West Indies. In the first of the four Tests, at Barbados, England won a close-fought battle on a sticky wicket but lost the Second Test confortably. They were humiliated in the decider at Jamaica, where Wyatt retired with a broken jaw. In 1935, a good but not outstanding South African team led by H.F.Wade won the Lord's Test and could not be dislodged from their one-nil lead. English cricket was definitely in the doldrums. England dropped Wyatt and tried G.O.Allen as captain in the three Test against India in 1936, with a view to his leading Down Under. The Indians were weakly organized and England won two and drew one. Allen himself took 20 wickets. So he took MCC to Australia with his own country captain, R.W.V.Robins, as unofficial deputy and the gallant sortie just failed to bring back the Ashes.

Allen dropped out of regular cricket in 1937 and Robins was given the job in three three-day Tests against New Zealand. For the First at Lord's, England at last recalled Paynter and brought in Hutton and Jim Parks as openers. Hutton dragged a slower ball on to the stumps after 20 minutes without scoring. Hammond and Hardstaff put on 245 in 215 minutes. Paynter made 74 and England were all out for 424. New Zealand fell to 176-7 but Wallace, Moloney and Roberts led a recovery to 295. England went for quick runs on the final morning; Hutton was out for 1, but Barnett and Hardstaff added 104 in an hour and New Zealand were set 356 in four hours. Despite a chin injury, J.L.Kerr battled out the last two hours and they saved the game at 175-8.

At Manchester, Hutton, opening with Barnett, made exactly 100 and England scored 358-9 dec on the first day. Arthur Wellard reduced the visitors to 119-5, but Walter Hadlee counter-attacked with 93. Leading by only 77, England were 75-7 on the final morning. Then F.R.Brown was dropped four times and scored 57. New Zealand needed 265 to win. Vivien and Moloney opened with 50 but Tom Goddard (6-29) bowled them out for 134.

For the Final Test, England called in Austin Matthews of Glamorgan, Denis Compton and, when Paynter dropped out through injury, Cyril Washbrook. After a virtual washout on the first day, New Zealand scored 249 and Washbrook distinguished himself in the field. England lost three wickets for 36, then Compton and Hardstaff led a recovery in poor light and drizzle. On the third day, Compton went on to 65 before being unluckily run out at the non-striker's end when the bowler deflected Hardstaff's hard drive on to the stumps. Hardstaff made 103. At lunch England were 254-7 and Robins declared. England bowled out New Zealand on a turning wicket, but not in time to allow them to go for victory.

Apart from the emergence of Hutton, Compton and Washbrook, the 1937 Tests were of no great interest, but the season itself produced some herculean efforts. Hammond and Parks (who also took 100 wickets) passed 3,000 runs and a few others got close. Gover, Verity and Goddard (248) all passed 200 wickets.

In the 1937-8 winter, Lionel Lord Tennyson, England captain in 1921 and grandson of the poet, now 48 and overweight, led a good English side on an unofficial tour of India. The first of five internationals was held at Lahore, where India were twice got out cheaply by Gover's pace and Peter Smith's leg-breaks. Yardley drove well for 96 and Edrich hit two 50s in Tennyson's win by nine wickets. On the second day, the crowd poured on to the field and the pavilion clock dropped off because of a severe earthquake in the city. Play was held up for a few minutes. In the second 'Test' at Bombay, India were twice bowled out cheaply by Gover and Wellard, with Gibb taking six catches behind the wicket in the first innings. Edrich guided the English to a six-wicket victory with 86 not out, which, apart from 88 by 20-year-old Vinoo Mankad, was the only 50 of the match.

On a perfect wicket at Calcutta, India made 350, despite George Pope running through the tail. He also scored 41 not out in the visitors' total of 527. Then Wellard and James Langridge exploited a wearing track. England's XI needed 286 to win but only Hardstaff batted well and it was India who emerged victorious by 93 runs. In the fourth match at Madras, Mankad made 113 not out but, thanks to Pope's 5-51, India scored only 263. After overnight rain Tennyson's side were dismissed twice by Amar Singh, a Lancashire League pace bowler, and lost by an innings and 6 runs.

In the decider at Bombay, Amar Singh bowled England out for 130, but Wellard, Pope and great fielding kept the Indian lead down to one run. Edrich, Worthington and Pope then gave the English 287 to bowl at, and Pope and Wellard ensured that they won the match by 156 runs, and the series by 3-2.

It had been a good, well-contested series. Unfortunately, the authorities did not recognize the matches as official Tests, presumably because it was not an MCC party and because England were due to play India in 1939-40. Despite troubles in the nether regions connected with diet, the tourists had a happy and successful tour, especially Bill Edrich, Hardstaff, George Pope, Wellard, Gover (overcoming knee trouble), Worthington and Gibb. James Langridge and Yardley had done reasonably well. The disappointments were Ian Peebles, McCorkell of Hampshire, Jim Parks and Peter Smith.

The England selectors for 1938 were: Sir Pelham (Plum) Warner, the chairman and a former England and Middlesex captain, administrator, author, journalist and magazine-founder; Percy Perrin of Essex, one of the best batsmen never to play for England; and M.J.Turnbull and A.B.Sellers, respectively captains of Glamorgan and Yorkshire. The first consideration was the England captaincy. G.O.Allen was not certain to be playing regularly. Wyatt, who thought his Test career to be finished, had contracted to write on the Tests for the *Daily Mail.* He had spent an enjoyable winter in Argentina with Sir Theodore Brinckman's team. Walter Robins was a possiblility but might not be worth a place on playing ability alone. Whether by co-incidence or design, Walter Hammond had announced in the autumn of 1937 that he had accepted a job with a tyre company that would enable him to continue to play as an amateur. In February, Walter Robins had told the Press: "No cricketer would object to being led by such a great player as Wally Hammond." His county colleague, Charlie Barnett, later expressed the view that Hammond's ambition to lead England had been aroused when Bradman took the Australian captaincy.

The Counties

The cornerstone of English first-class cricket was the County Championship, dominated for most of the decade by the northern sides, Lancashire, Derbyshire and, above all, Yorkshire. The southern challenge was led by Middlesex. Surrey were at a low ebb and other counties like Kent, Essex, Sussex and Gloucestershire had their moments but lacked the consistency to stay at the top. Since 1933 the counties had played an unequal number of matches and the positions were decided by points obtained as a percentage of points possible. A new system was introduced for 1938, which was relatively simple:

Each team played at least 24 matches.
12 points to the side winning outright.
6 points to each side in a tie.
4 points to the side leading on the first innings — such points to be retained only by the side which loses, ties or draws.
2 points to each side for a tie on first innings if the match is drawn.
8 points to a side winning on first innings if no play had taken place on the first two days.
If no result was achieved on the first innings, the match did not count as a match played.
Championship positions were decided by each county's total points obtained, divided by its number of matches played.

Derbyshire

A dour county, not wealthy, but rich in pace bowlers and all-rounders, Derbyshire rose steadily through the 1930s, won the title in 1936, and were third in 1937. They were the only county to break through the cartel of the traditional leading counties.

Their captain since 1937 was Mr Robin H.R.Buckston, born at Kensington, London, on 10 October 1908, an Etonian, son of G.M, the 1921 captain. He was a popular leader but a liability as a player, a moderate batsman and reserve wicketkeeper.

The leading bowler was ginger-haired W.H.(Bill) Copson, born in Stonebroom on 27 April 1908, an excellent right-handed fast-medium bowler with long arms and strong shoulders and a rather muscle-bound run-up, who had both swing and pace off the pitch. Copson toured Australia in 1936-7 without playing in a Test and his career was hampered by back trouble. He took up cricket during the 1926 Miners' Strike, bowling a batsman with the first ball he ever bowled in his life.

T.B.(Tommy) Mitchell, born in Cresswell on 4 September 1902, was an eccentric, bespectacled, stumpy-legged leg-spinner, who spun the ball a lot. Another former miner, he was discovered when the county team played Cresswell Colliery during the 1926 strike. He toured Australia in 1932-3 and took a couple of useful wickets in the one Test he played. In 1911, he had sung *Oh For the Wings of a Dove* when the King and Queen visited his school.

The Pope brothers from Chesterfield were the two leading all-rounders in the side. The younger, George H. born in Tibshelf on 27 January 1911, was a tall, thin fast-medium bowler who got lift, and a hard-hitting batsman. He had a good tour of India in 1937-8. Alfred V Pope was two years older, a more medium-pace bowler and not quite so good with the bat. George was balder but with caps on they were very hard to tell apart.

Denis Smith, born in Somercotes on 24 January 1907, was a prolific left-hand opening batsman, a tall, easy strokemaker and close fielder. Occasionally mooted for the Test side, he played twice in 1935.

T.Stanley Worthington, born in Bolsover on 21 August 1905, was a balding, 6ft-tall, broadly-built middle-order batsman and useful medium-pace bowler, a strong driver and puller, who toured Australia unsuccessfully under G.O.Allen. An electrician at Bolsover Colliery.

Others who were to play for the team in 1938 included Albert Alderman, a patient opening partner for Smith and notable deep fielder, and who also played League football for Derby County and Burnley; Leslie Townsend, a good driver and medium-pace off-spinner, who had played four Tests abroad; A.E.G. ('Dusty') Rhodes, a young first-change fast-medium bowler of slight physique, who started as a leg-spinner and who could bat a bit. And Harry Elliott, one of the best wicketkeepers in the County Championship, who had hardly missed a match since the mid-1920s and had played four Tests.

Essex

The nomad county, with no home ground, taking their tents to seven county grounds, Essex were a happy side with a strong amateur representation, capable of beating anybody, especially Yorkshire. They had done well in the 1920s and rose to sixth in 1937.

For 1938, Essex were to have a shared captaincy, led for the first half of the season by Mr Denys R.Wilcox. Born in Westcliff on 4 June 1910, he was a diminutive opening batsman, a master at Dulwich College. Then Mr T.N.(Tom) Pearce took over. Pearce was born in Stoke Newington on 3 November 1905, a consistent batsman and popular leader.

Mr Kenneth Farnes, born in Leytonstone on 8 July 1911, was one of the most imposing figures ever to play cricket, well-built at 6ft 5in tall, a shock of black hair and a face like a dance band crooner. He was England's fastest bowler, off a run of only 11 yards, with a grunt at the moment of delivery, and even faster when inspired or angry. After leaving Romford School in 1930 he packed in his job in a bank to have a go at first-class cricket. He went up to Cambridge in 1931, became a geography master at Worksop College and got into the Test team in 1934, taking ten wickets in the First Test, and was a virtually automatic choice thereafter. He was a confirmed number-11 batsman. School restricted his cricket for Essex but in 1938 he was available at the end of May. When war came he joined the RAF. Only a year after his well-written autobiography was published, in 1941 he died in an air crash on an exercise.

Morris Stanley Nichols, known as Morris, Stan or 'Nick', was born in Stondon Massey on 6 October 1900. He also opened the Essex bowling, an indefatigable right-arm fast bowler and effective and consistent left-handed hitter. Over 6ft tall with big feet, a nautical gait and an ungainly style in both batting and bowling, he schooled himself to bowl quick in his 20s and had amazing stamina; he moved the ball away in the air and could make it break back. He was the first man to the double in 1935, 1936 and 1937. He played Tests in 1930 and 1935.

Backing up these two bowlers was moustachioed Captain J.W.A. ('Steve') Stephenson of the Middlesex Regiment, born in Hong Kong on 1 August 1907, an arch enthusiast, a medium-pace bowler, a hard hitter, an athletic fielder, never quiet, never still. After taking 9-46 against the Players in 1936 he was close to selection for Australia.

T.P.B. (Peter) Smith was born in Ipswich on 30 October 1908, a debonair professional, an aggressive leg-spin bowler and low-order hitter, a product of Faulkner's School. In his action he had a peculiar sideways kick of the right leg in the follow through. In 1933 he rushed to play in The Oval Test to find that he was the victim of a cruel hoax, but he did play four Tests after the war. In his time he was a Post Office engineer and a Rhodesian 'Mountie'

The strong Essex attack also had Ray Smith, Peter's younger cousin, a medium-pace bowler. Then there were Reginald Taylor, a cultured but inconsistent right-hand bat and improving slow left-arm bowler; little Jack O'Connor, 40-year-old light-footed scorer of 1,000 runs in 15 consecutive seasons and bowler of teasing spinners. Former amateur Laurie Eastman, 41, was a tall and graceful opening bat and leg-spinner. His partner was A.V.'Sonny' Avery, small and stylish. Behind the wicket was expert stumper and soccer player Tommy Wade, who took it up in 1934 after failing as an off-spinner.

Glamorgan

The 'baby' county, having become first-class only in 1921, Glamorgan survived severe financial difficulties and with some fine cricketers rose to seventh place in 1937 under the forthright leadership of M.J.Turnbull. As club secretary he had undertaken an exhausting tour around Wales, appealing for funds and with the help of personal contributions from himself, John Clay and others, had turned a deficit of £5,000 into a surplus of £1,000.

Mr Maurice J.L.Turnbull, born in Cardiff on 16 March 1906, joined the side straight from Downside School in 1924. He was a single-minded and courageous captain and batsman. He was appointed an

England selector in 1938 and was an outside bet for the England captaincy — a little more consistency in his batting and he would surely have led the Test team already. He played Tests on tours to New Zealand and South Africa and wrote two witty books about them with M.J.C.Allom. He was a great believer in the amateur tradition, perhaps a little over-zealous in discouraging fraternization between the county amateurs and professionals. He had a cartilege operation in the spring of 1938. Turnbull also played nine rugby internationals for Wales. As a major in the Welsh Guards he was killed by a sniper's bullet in Normandy in 1944.

The other pillar of Glamorgan cricket was Mr J.C. (Johnny) Clay. Born in Bonvilston on 18 March 1898, he had played as regularly as his shipping business permitted since 1921, first as a fast bowler now as an off-spinner, taking 170 wickets in 1937, and an adaptable batsman. He was over 6ft tall and thin, with a high arm action and deceptive flight. He captained the side before Turnbull and played a Test in 1935. In 1933 he took two wickets with underarm lobs.

Austin D.G.Matthews, born in Penarth on 3 May 1904, had come to his native county from Northants in 1937 when, as a very tall fast-medium bowler, he played one Test against New Zealand.

D.Emrys Davies, born in Llanelli, Carmarthen, on 27 June 1904, was a long-serving and dependable left-handed opening batsman and slow left-arm bowler. Despite his popularity, his benefit in 1938 raised only £688.

Believe it or not, he was not the only Davies in the side; there was David (Dai), also from Llanelli, a middle-order batsman, who, when batting with Emrys, liked to call for runs in Welsh. He was also a slow-medium bowler who was called up for his debut in 1923 after a night shift in a steel works; and Haydn G. Davies, another Llanelli man, was a very safe wicketkeeper. There were three Jones's, including W.E. (Willie), an attractive amateur left-hand bat and slow left-arm blower; and Eddie C., an off-spinner who was considered for a Test cap in 1937. It will come as no surprise to learn that none of these people were related to each other.

Other regulars were Arnold Dyson, Yorkshire-born tidy opening bat and close field; Cyril Smart, a naturally talented big-hitting batsman, who came to regular cricket too late; Tom Brierley, a wicketkeeper-batsman; Richard Duckfield, a middle-order batsman from Maesteg and Jack Mercer, a 43-year-old steady fast-medium bowler and fluent Russian speaker, who joined the county from Sussex in 1922. Waiting in the wings, as it were, was Mr Wilfred Wooller, a right-hand batsman and fast-medium bowler from the North Wales coast, a 25-year-old amateur who had played at Cambridge but who was more famous as a Welsh rugby international. After the war he was to step into the shoes of Turnbull and Clay.

Gloucestershire

The county of the Graces and now of Hammond, Gloucestershire were still one of the big name counties, although they had not won the Championship this century. Fourth in both 1936 and 1937, they had plenty of talented batsmen and two top-class spinners but were short on pace bowling.

The captain was Mr Basil O.Allen, born in Clifton on 13 October 1911, a sound defensive left-handed opening bat, brave close fielder and forthright leader.

Charles John Barnett, born in Cheltenham on 3 July 1910, son and nephew of leading Gloucestershire cricketers, was an aggressive right-hand opening batsman, established in the England side since his success in Australia in 1936-7. He first played for the county at the age of 16 and was a natural stroke-maker with a full swing of the bat, who got on with it from the moment the first ball was bowled. He had a slight limitation against the fast rising ball on the leg-stump. He also turned the arm over to advantage at medium pace.

Cornishman J.F. (Jack) Crapp, born in St Columb Major on 14 October 1912, was a gifted left-handed batsman and slip fielder, dark, taciturn, long-armed. George M.Emmett, born in Agra, India, on 2 December 1912, son of a soldier, qualified in 1936 after playing for Devon. He was a small, compact batsman, a good timer of the ball, although he had an arthritic knee. Both these men played for England after the war.

T.W.J. (Tom) Goddard, born in Gloucester on 1 October 1990, was a 6ft 3in tall, dark-haired character with huge hands and a 'Tommy Cooper' face. He had moderate success as a quick bowler in the 1920s, then became a prolific wicket-taker with his off-breaks, bowled mostly around the wicket. He was a grumbling but willing workhorse and an indefatigable and vehement appealer for lbw. He was the country's leading off-spinner in an era when that art was out of favour. He was unlucky not to have played in many Tests. His 1936 Benefit raised £2,097. In 1937 he took 248 wickets.

Of Mr Walter Reginald (Wally) Hammond, born in Dover, Kent, on 19 June 1903, much could be said. From a military family, he was brought up in Malta. Then his father died and his mother came back to England and he went to Cirencester Grammar School. His county career was delayed by the need to qualify, but he soon announced his unmistakable class as a young professional right-hand batsman. Illness on an MCC tour of the West Indies deprived him of his rightful place in the Tests in 1926. He bounded back with 1,000 runs by the end of May 1927. In 1928-29, harnessing his brilliance to the needs of timeless Tests, he became for the moment the greatest batsman in the world. In the 1930s he yielded that place to Bradman and possibly

Wally Hammond, whose change in status from professional to amateur made him the leading contender to captain England in 1938.

to George Headley, but unlike them he was near Test standard as a fast-medium outswing bowler and a brilliant, deceptively casual slip fielder. As a number three or four batsman he was very orthodox, majestic, powerful, unflappable, with no weakness or limit. In Tests he consciously eschewed the hook shot, substituting a horizontal-batted caress of the short ball down to fine leg. In the autumn of 1937, Hammond was offered a job with the London-based Marcham Tyres with a director's salary of £2,000 and with no restriction on his cricket. He accepted primarily for financial reasons but the change in status, and his tactical skill exhibited in captaining the Players at Lord's from 1935 to 1937, made him suddenly the chief contender to lead England. For all his brilliance and success there was a certain sadness and loneliness in the eyes of Walter Hammond, an unhappy marriage, a regret that whatever he did would be topped by his Australian rival, a shyness and moodiness of manner that became more marked in his career after the war, when fibrositis reduced him to mortal status.

Mr Beverley H.Lyon, born in Caterham, Surrey, on 19 January 1902, was a good right-hand batsman, who now played only occasionally but whose bold and innovative county captaincy up to 1934 was influential. He was one of the first to use the 'freak' declaration.

Goddard's spinning partner was R.A. (Reg) Sinfield, born in Stevenage, Herts, on 24 December 1900, a slow-medium off-spinner and cutter with a low, insidious action rather like Clarie Grimmett's. He was also a useful defensive batsman, who used to open the innings. He looked a bit like Jack Hulbert and Tommy Trinder. He always wore a cap when bowling. 1938 was his benefit year.

Others making up the team were Billy Neale, a steady batsman and occasional bowler, a farmer from Berkeley Vale; Colin Scott, slight fair-haired opening bowler, who made his debut in 1938; and Andy Wilson, a left-handed wicketkeeper batsman, a Londoner who had first played for Middlesex.

Hampshire

The county of the heroic Lionel Lord Tennyson had never won the Championship. They were a team of gallant triers, with no stars, that rarely strayed into the top half of the table. They were unlucky to be 14th in 1937.

The captain, having been vice-captain in 1937, was Mr C.G.A. Paris, born in India on 20 August 1911, educated at King's Canterbury, a nudging and pushing type of batsman. The captain in 1937, when he scored 316 against Warwickshire, had been Mr R.H. (Dick) Moore, who was born in Bournemouth on 14 November 1913.

Johnny Arnold, born in Cowley, Oxford, on 30 November 1907, was the county's best player, a light-footed opening batsman and cover field. He played for England against New Zealand in 1931. A double international, Arnold was also a left-winger for Fulham and England.

G.Stuart Boyes, born in Southampton on 31 March 1899, was the 'senior pro', a tall slow left-arm bowler and short leg who joined Hampshire from the Army in 1921.

Neil McCorkell was a small opening bat and wicketkeeper, who kept for the Players in 1936 and toured India in 1937-8. Left-hander Jim Bailey from Winchester, also a slow left-arm bowler, was playing in Lancashire League but in 1938 was called up to strengthen the batting. Other left-handed batsmen were South African Len Creese, good against fast bowling, strong off the back foot; A.E. (Sam) Pothecary, a good thrower from cover and D.F. ('Hooky') Walker[2], an RAF pilot who joined Hampshire as a professional in 1937. He died over Germany in 1941.

The pace bowlers included George Heath, who swung the new ball dangerously; Ossie ('Lofty') Herman, a tall, high in-swing bowler from rural Oxfordshire; and the Rev J.W.J. Steele, an Army chaplain who first appeared in 1938. Gerry Hill, from the New Forest, was an off-spinner and dogged bat.

Kent

The Garden of England produced an attractive and gifted side that did not quite mould together as a team. After the great winning years up to 1914, Kent had met with little success. In decline since 1935, they were 12th in 1937. They were capable of making large scores quickly but found difficulty in bowling out the opposition.

The 1938 captain was Mr F.G.H. (Gerry) Chalk, born Sydenham on 7 September 1910, a right-hand batsman. He took time off from his teaching at Malvern. Missing in action in 1943, his body and his 'plane were found in 1989.

Leslie Ethelbert George (Les) Ames, born in Elham on 3 December 1905, was schooled at Folkestone. He had dark skin, freckles and Romany blood but possessed a genuine Kent accent. Ames is one of the game's legendary wicketkeeper-batsmen. England's first-choice stumper since 1931, he was safe against fast bowling, and a very good taker of spin. He was also a class batsman, quick-footed and good against fast bowling. In 1938, he was just beginning to suffer from lumbago trouble.

Arthur E.Fagg, born in Chartham on 18 June 1915, was a consistent opening batsman, strong all round the wicket and the reserve wicketkeeper. He went to Australia with Allen's team but came home early with rheumatic fever and missed all the 1937 season.

Mr Bryan H.Valentine, born in Blackheath on 17 January 1908, was educated at Repton and Cambridge. He scored a lot of runs very quickly. He toured India in 1933-4 and was a top-class amateur footballer, tennis player and golfer.

[2] Not to be confused with the amateur D.F.Walker (Oxford University and Norfolk) who was also an RAF pilot. They were born and died within a year of each other, the latter over Norway.

For Frank E.Woolley, born in Tonbridge on 27 May 1887, the 1938 season was to be the farewell to a career which, from 1906, had seen him as Kent and England's great left-handed all-rounder. Any graceful, handsome left-handed batsman such as Graeme Pollock or David Gower is always compared to Woolley. He bowled little in the 1930s, but still fielded comfortably in the slips. He decided to end his days as an opening batsman.

In D.V.P. (Doug) Wright, who was born in Sidcup on 21 August 1914, England hoped to have found a match-winning counter to O'Reilly. As a young solicitor's clerk he went to Faulkner's famous Cricket School, where he took up leg-spin. Off a long, loping run he bowled leg-spin, googlies and top-spinners at medium pace and, on his day, could get anybody out. His turn and bounce usually missed everything. He was erratic in length and prone to bowl no-balls, but he was the man Bradman and the others least wanted to see in the England side.

Kent had also Peter Sunnucks, a bespectacled opening bat, Tom Spencer from Hastings, a right-hand bat and later Test umpire, and they could sometimes call upon Mr C.H. (John) Knott, a Tonbridge master who was a hard-hitting batsman, despite a short backlift. The bowling was opened by the bucolic Alan Watt, who had a fast, slinging action off a short run and was a six-hitting tailender, and Leslie Todd, a left-hander who did the double in 1936 and was a fluent, if moody, batsman who had visual difficulties since being hit between the eyes by Larwood in 1930; also, Norman Harding, a tall fast bowler who lacked robust health and died suddenly of polio in 1947. Then there was Claude Lewis, a slow left-armer who never established himself. When Ames was absent or playing only as a batsman, Mr Howard ('Hopper') Levett kept wicket. Levett, who would have walked into many county sides, toured India in 1933-4 and played four times for the Gentlemen at Lord's.

Lancashire

The Red Rose county had won the title only once in the 1930s but was one of the top four in the period. They possessed a good all-round side which produced several top-class performers and some characters as well, their doings chronicled in the *Manchester Guardian* by the greatest of all cricket writers, Neville Cardus. After winning in 1934, Lancashire came 4th, 11th and 9th. They had three fine pace bowlers but Wilkinson lacked support in the spin department.

The captain was Mr W.H.L.Lister, born in Formby on 11 October 1911, an amateur international footballer, who since he came to the side from Cambridge University in 1933, was usually the only amateur in the team. He was a batsman of no great ability.

J.L.(Len) Hopwood, born in Newton Hyde, Cheshire, on 30 October

1903, was a solid, defensive batsman who sometimes opened, a straightforward slow left-arm bowler with an attractive action, who did the double twice and played two Tests against Australia in 1934. He was a 1938 beneficiary.

Jack Iddon, born in Mawdesley on 8 January 1902, was a prolific all-rounder, a gifted right-handed bat — more cautious than he needed to be — and slow left-arm, who played five Tests in West Indies in 1934-5. He died in a road accident a month before cricket resumed in 1946.

Norman ('Buddy') Oldfield, born in Dukinfield, Cheshire, near Manchester, on 5 May 1911, was a slight figure but a strong cutter and a good deep field.

Eddie Paynter, born on 5 November 1901, had his birthplace of Oswaldtwistle stamped right through him. He was a middle-order left-hand bat now opening for the county, a classic quick-footed puncher and slasher. Small of stature, with sleek-backed hair and a toothy smile, Paynter had one shot all his own, a sort of pull-drive with both feet airborne. He left school at 12 to work in a cotton mill, then a brick yard. He was nearly 30 before he secured a regular county place and was one of England's batting heroes on the 1932-3 Bodyline Tour, but then was ignored by the selectors until 1937. His omission for 1936-7 was an act of unexplained lunacy that probably handed Australia the Ashes. In 1937 he scored 322 in a day at Hove. Paynter had the top joints of two fingers missing.

Opening the bowling were W.E. (Eddie) Phillipson, born in North Reddish, Cheshire, on 3 December 1910, a right-arm fast-medium swing bowler, and the red-haired R. (Dick) Pollard, born in Westhoughton on 19 June 1912, a willing fast-medium 'carthorse'. Both men were possible Test prospects.

Although he was to become familiar as opening partner to Len Hutton after the war, Cyril Washbrook, born in Blackburn on 6 December 1914, was the established county opener and had already made his Test debut in 1937. From Bridgenorth Grammar School he made his debut for Lancashire aged 18. He was a serious single-minded cricketer, not 'one of the lads', but with a reassuring hang-dog face, jug-like ears, determined jaw and slanted cap. He was short and neat, a great cutter and expert cover field.

L.L. (Len) Wilkinson was born in Northwich, Cheshire, on 5 November 1916, a promising lanky leg-spinner from Bolton with big hands and a fizzing leg-break and disguised googly.

Bill Farrimond was, for many years, the loyal reserve wicketkeeper, refusing offers from other counties. He had actually played in four Tests and who now finally got his chance with the retirement of George Duckworth. Merseysider Albert Nutter was a first change fast-medium pace bowler for whom 1938 was to be his first full season.

Leicestershire

The fox-hunting county was the first in modern times to have a regular professional captain, W.E.Astill, who led them to sixth place in 1935. Otherwise they abided naturally in the bottom half of the table and were 16th in 1937. They had four pace bowlers and no regular spinners.

Captain since 1936 (when he qualified) was Mr C. Stewart Dempster. Born in Wellington, New Zealand, on 15 November 1903, he was a world-class batsman who played ten Tests for his country. He had come to England on business and started in the Lancashire League and in Sir Julien Cahn's XI. Committments to Sir Julien still restricted his availability. He was short and stocky, a magnificent driver and a good cover.

Leslie G. ('Jinks') Berry, born in Dorking, Surrey, on 28 April 1906, went to live in Market Harborough as a child. As an opening right-hand bat he had been a perennial run scorer since 1924, one of the best who never played for England nor toured with MCC. He was a goalkeeper in the Football League for three clubs.

Veteran all-rounder George Geary, born in Barwell on 9 July 1893, was in his last year in county cricket and was to take the captaincy in July, when Dempster was unavailable. A tall medium-pace bowler, a great slip and a good bat, he took a few crucial wickets in his 14 Tests. He was one of 16 children of a shoemaker.

Opening the batting with Berry was Frank Prentice, a Yorkshireman; down the order came Norman Armstrong, a prolific sheet-anchor; and stylish George Watson, old boy of Shrewsbury who joined Leicestershire as a professional. The pace bowling was in the hands of Haydon Smith, a hard-working fast bowler, W.H. Flamson, who had a style similar to Geary, and the left-armer, Jim Sperry, a former miner. Fifty-year-old off-spinner Ewart Astill — although he looked younger — had been a regular since 1906 and was a veteran of nine Tests. At the other end of the spectrum, the wicketkeeper was 17-year-old George Dawkes, who was called up from club cricket in 1937 when the regular stumper was injured. Dawkes proved so good that he kept the job. For spin, Leicestershire had to look to the occasional appearance by Australian 'Chinaman' bowler Jack Walsh, a big spinner of the ball, who was retained by Sir Julien Cahn. His fellow Australian, all-rounder Vic Jackson, was qualifying for Leicestershire in 1938. Two batting newcomers for 1938 were Laurence Thrusting, a Londoner, and Maurice Tompkin, aged 19.

Middlesex

Middlesex were very much an 'establishment' county in 1938 and one of the major teams between the wars. After a bad spell in the early 1930s, they were runners-up in 1936 and 1937. They had several gifted amateurs to call upon for a few matches. On the professional side, some of the great names of the past had retired but there were some very promising young players making an impact.

Results had improved markedly since Mr R.W.V. (Walter) Robins — called 'Robbie' — had become captain in 1935. Born in Stafford on 3 June 1906, he was a daring, inspirational leader, ideal for county cricket. He was a leg-spin bowler with a hopping run-up and a big twist on the ball, an improvisor, often inaccurate but always liable to take a wicket. At number-seven or eight, he was a nimble-footed driver with a very high backlift, famous for his big charges down the wicket. He had played 19 Tests and, although not quite an established Test player, he was captain *in situ,* having taken over from Allen in 1937. Flexibility in human relationships was not his strong point.

Mr G.O.B. ('Gubby') Allen, born in Sydney, Australia, on 31 July 1902, of Eton and Cambridge, was a beau ideal of the amateur cricketer; of medium height, handsome, dark-haired, he bowled very fast with a classic side-on whole-hearted action and stroked the ball stylishly at number-eight in the batting order. His work in the City of London kept him from playing full-time but he was able to tour Australia under Jardine in 1932-3. Although refraining from any public dissent, he refused personally to use Bodyline tactics. He and Australia liked each other — although brought up in England, he had numerous relatives there — and was a very popular and diplomatic captain on the tour of 1936-7 when he so nearly won back the Ashes. He was a hopeful contender to lead England again in 1938. To the end of his long life he was associated with the game's administration in various ways and it is customary in all potted biographies to describe him as the *eminence grise* at Lord's.

Denis Charles Scott Compton, born in Hendon on 23 May 1918, was the beau ideal of the young professional, a man from humble circumstances whose natural ability and charm took him to the top. He became, in the austerity years after the war, the most popular cricketer in the country. He left school at 14 to join Middlesex and Arsenal. His unique, untutored unorthodox but basically sound style of batting announced itself at once on his debut in 1936 and within the year he scored 65 run out on his Test debut at The Oval. Compton was a 'lucky' cricketer. He had a relaxed, open right-hand stance, a casual grace of stroke and a very good eye. He was especially strong as a hooker and sweeper and a useful slow left-arm bowler, later taking up the 'Chinaman', and an enthusiastic, versatile fielder. An outside-left for Arsenal FC, he was nearly good enough to play for England — indeed, he won wartime caps — but the football gave him knee trouble later on. His reputation for quixotic running between the wickets does not seem to have arisen before the war. His brother, Leslie, also played for Arsenal and Middlesex.

William John (Bill) Edrich, born in Lingwood, Norfolk, on 26 March 1916, came to be regarded as a cricketing brother of Denis Compton, although his own Norfolk family had nearly enough talent to make a county XI. He qualified for Middlesex in 1937 and toured India under Lord Tennyson. Short at 5ft 6in, but well built, he was a strong, punchy batsman and a powerful hooker, either opening or at number-three. He was also a fearless close fielder and, off a short run, a tearaway fast bowler with a slinging action. Before the war his ability exceeded his temperament; after the war it was the other way round. He played the game of life hard, won the DFC for low flying daylight raids over Europe, was still playing for Norfolk at the age of 55, and at the age of 70, in the words of his fifth wife, he 'conked out'.

Mr Ian A.R.Peebles, born in Aberdeen on 20 January 1908, the son of a manse, who left a bank job at 17 to become secretary of the Faulkner Cricket School, was a very promising young leg-spinner, tall with an easy action. When still at Oxford University he was chosen for England in 1930 and caused problems even for Bradman. He played 13 Tests in all, but he overdid the googly and, partly as a result of a shoulder injury, virtually lost his leg-break. After the war, in which he lost any eye, he was a distinguished journalist and author.

W.F.F. (Fred) Price, born in Westminster on 25 April 1902, was a very experienced wicketkeeper who sometimes opened the batting. He toured the West Indies in 1929-30 without playing a Test. In 1937 he took a record seven catches in an innings. He was efficient, despite a certain flat-footedness.

J.M. (Jim) Sims, born in Leyton, Essex, on 13 May 1903, was a tall leg-spinner with a gaunt, pessimistic-looking face and a laconic sense of humour which materialized out of the side of his mouth. He toured in 1936-7, when he played two of his four Tests. He could also bat a bit. The man who said that leg-spinners were philosophers was probably a friend of 'Simmo'.

Also tall and deadpan, but different in every other way, was C.I.J. (Big Jim) Smith, born in Corsham, Wiltshire, on 25 August 1906. He stood 6ft 4in and weighed in at 17½st. Broad of shoulder and fair-haired, he was a village blacksmith type of figure, who joined Middlesex from Wiltshire when he was 27. Off a long run up he bowled a sharpish fast-medium, got lift and break-back and could swing the ball late. He had appeared in five Tests and was unlucky not to have played against Australia. People forgot his excellent bowling record because, as a number-ten batsman, he was a legend. All the bars would empty as he wandered unconcernedly out to the wicket. He had virtually one stroke — he plonked his left foot down the wicket and swung

Denis Compton, one of the young batsmen who appeared to herald a new dawn for English cricket.

mightily with the bat like a cleaver in the direction of long-on. The ball would go anywhere, depending on whether he middled it, edged it or missed it altogether. For as long as chance allowed him to stay in, he would treat the crowd to a succession of sixes and lofted shots, all played without a hint of exhilaration.

Also featuring for Middlesex were Jack Robertson, a promising stylish opening bat, who started in the club cricket at Turnham Green and was very successful after the war; and Syd Brown, a solid bat who later opened and a good deep field. Joe Hulme, a right-hand batsman who was a little too keen on dashing down the wicket, was an Arsenal and England footballer. Laurie Gray was a tall medium-fast opening bowler from Tottenham.

Northamptonshire

Poor Northants! They had not won a first-class match, even against a University, since 15 May 1935, came last every year since 1934 and struggled constantly to keep afloat financially. The best players, V.W.C.Jupp and E.W.Clark, were virtually retired and Fred Bakewell's hopes of a comeback after his road accident in 1936 were dashed.

The captain was Mr Robert P.Nelson, born in Fulham, London, on 7 August 1912, a noted schools cricketer who played for Middlesex and Cambridge University before joining Northants in 1937 when he became head of a local preparatory school. A gifted left-hand bat, he had to adapt his attacking game to the thankless task of leading the side.

The county's best player was Dennis Brookes, born in Kippax, Yorkshire, on 29 October 1915, an immaculate opening or number-three batsman. He was given a trial for the county in 1932 but it took two years for them to recognize his talent.

The other batsmen in the team were Mr A.W. (Alec) Snowden, a businessman whose appearances were restricted. He was an opening bat, hampered by a rugby injury, naturally left-handed but forced at school to bat right; Norman Grimshaw, a dour Yorkshireman; F.P.O'Brien, a hard-hitting New Zealander; Maurice Dunkley, a moderate 'agricultural' batsman; Henry Greenwood, a solid opener from Sussex who joined the county in 1938 and was available only in midweek; and Jack Timms, a lovely but inconsistent batsman, medium pace bowler and good field. S.M.Nasir-ud-din was to play a few matches for the county in 1938; he was the son of an Indian state ruler and privately educated in England.

The opening bowlers were Jack Buswell, a medium pacer with a long run, and Reg Partridge, a right-arm in-swinger of delicate health who sometimes bowled off-breaks. Eric Herbert was a stock medium-pacer. Ken James was a very good wicketkeeper and useful bat, a New Zealander who had toured England in 1927 and 1931. A third

New Zealander, leg-spinner Bill Merritt, was qualifying for Northants in 1938.

Nottinghamshire

Nottinghamshire was a mining county with a plentiful supply of pace bowlers and the birthplace of 'bodyline bowling', one of the traditional big guns, going back to the days of Shaw and Shrewsbury in the 1880s. Notts won the Championship in 1929 under the stern captaincy of Arthur Carr. They were tenth in 1937 with their batting strong but fast bowling in decline on the true, easy-paced wickets at Trent Bridge.

The captain since 1935 was Mr G.F.H.Heane, born in Worksop on 2 January 1904, a farming vet, gallant leader and excellent all-rounder, left-handed bat and right-arm medium pace with a good outswinger.

Joseph Hardstaff ('Young Joe') was born on 3 July 1911 at Nuncargate, the son of an England batsman. He was a class right-hand batsman with an upright stance, a handsome, graceful style and a consistent scorer, with a rebellious streak against the establishment. He was a regular in the England middle order from 1936.

Charles B.Harris, born in Underwood on 6 December 1907, was an unpredictable opening batsman, breaking out of his usual dour defence with burst of peculiar attacking shots, and an off-spin bowler. He was a practical joker and comedian who could sometimes be heard 'commentating' on himself while batting.

His partner and 'straight man' was Walter W.Keeton, born in Shirebrook, Derbyshire, on 30 April 1905, a sound batsman with plenty of strokes, a high scorer, a good outfield and a sort of 'lived-in' face. He had played one Test against Australia in 1934.

William (Bill) Voce, born in Annesley Woodhouse on 8 August 1909, was a tall, well proportioned left-arm bowler with a powerful and graceful, though slightly round-arm, action. He started his career as a slow bowler but then developed a fair pace. In a famous partnership for county and country, the bodyline tactic was developed, which Voce practised from round the wicket. He was an important component of the England attack in Australia in 1932-3. In 1934 he had bowled the Australians out in their county match in the first innings using bodyline tactics, which caused so much ill-feeling that he was diplomatically unfit for the second innings. In 1936, having given what MCC described as 'an entirely satisfactory statement', he was chosen to tour Australia again under G.O.Allen and he met with reasonable success using uncontroversial tactics. He had back trouble on that tour and a knee operation in 1937. He was not to be underestimated as a powerful low-order left-hand bat. Oddly enough he never played in a home Test against Australia.

Voce's legendary partner, Harold Larwood, was born in Nuncargate on 14 November 1904. One of the greatest fast bowlers in history, of medium height, he now rarely bowled at his fastest and rheumatism restricted his participation in 1938.

George V.Gunn was the last of the famous family of Notts professionals, a natural stroke player and leg-break bowler. David Jones, from Derbyshire, and Joseph Knowles were middle-order right-hand batsmen. Harold Butler was now Voce's opening partner with his windmill action; Arthur Jepson, the Port Vale goalkeeper, was a fast-medium bowler and useful tail-ender; Frank Woodhead was another pace bowler. Arthur Staples was a veteran all-rounder. The wicketkeeper was Arthur Wheat, a miner in winter.

Somerset

The south-western outpost of first-class cricket, a happy band, never flush with money, Somerset played as well and as cheerfully as they could. Normally low in the table, they came seventh in 1936 and 13th in 1937 and were unpredictable, capable of good runs of form. They had to play a lot of amateurs for economic reasons.

Mr Edmund F. ('Bunty') Longrigg, born in Bath on 6 April 1906, a left-handed bat and a solicitor, had taken over the captaincy from R.A.Ingle.

W.H.R. (Bill) Andrews, born in Swindon, Wiltshire, on 14 April 1908, was the junior partner in a famous opening bowling partnership. He had a high action with an in-swinger and a leg-cutter and he bowled a full length, hoping for edges into the leg-trap. He was also a good enough bat to do the double in 1937. An extrovert, undaunted by a slight stammer.

Somerset had a legendary opening batsman in Harold Gimblett, who was born in Bicknoller on 19 October 1914. In 1935, having being rejected after a net trial, he got an emergency call-up from his farm to play at Frome; coming in at 104-6, he scored 123 in 80 minutes and won the Lawrence Trophy for the fastest century of the season. Within a year he played for England against India. He made no compromises on his aggressive instincts and was always a close contender for Charles Barnett's role in the Test team, although he had yet to live up to his early promise. He was a good fielder in the slips or the outfield.

Mr R.J.O.Meyer, born in Clophill, Bedfordshire, on 15 March 1905, of Haileybury and Cambridge University, was a talented batsman and slow-medium bowler who had played occasionally for the county since 1936.

Arthur W.Wellard, born in Southfleet, Kent, on 8 April 1902, was a successful bowler for Bexley CC in his 20s, but Kent showed no interest in him. He qualified for Somerset in 1929 and was an instant success. He was an indefatigable classic outswinger at fast-medium pace with a sharp break-back who was not well served by the county's slip fielding cordon. Standing 6ft 2in tall, he was a very strong driver of the ball and specialized in towering sixes, hitting 72 in one season and twice hitting five in an over. Unlike Jim Smith of Middlesex, he also had a sound and solid batting technique. He played for England in 1937.

The other opening batsman was Frank Lee, who qualified in 1929 after a trial with Middlesex, a stubborn and prolific left-hander who devoted most of his energy to patting the pitch. H.F.T. (Bertie) Buse was a useful middle-order batsman and medium-pace bowler, an amateur who accepted professional terms for 1938. Horace Hazell was a burly rotund slow left-arm bowler. The county wicketkeeper was the small and skilful Wally Luckes (pronounced 'Luckees'), noticeable for his panama hat. Short of regular middle-order batsmen, Somerset were grateful to be able to recall — when available — for 1938, Mr M.D.Lyon (nicknamed 'Dar'), a barrister who had returned after serving as a magistrate in Gambia. He was a fine driver and brother of B.H.Lyon of Gloucestershire.

Surrey

One of the established, wealthy counties for whom many of England's greatest had appeared, Surrey had nevertheless not won the title since 1914 and tended to finish in the middle of the table, thanks to weakness of bowling on the beautiful Oval wickets. Their stalwarts, Hobbs, Sandham, Jardine and Fender, had all retired and they were now a youngish side, mostly professional. In 1937 they were eighth after a poor start.

Captaincy was in the hands of dashing, debonair, cravated Mr Errol R.T.Holmes, born in Calcutta, India, on 21 August 1905. Of Malvern and Oxford, he was a cavalier captain and a clasic driver who played five Tests for England. He led the non-Test MCC tour of Australasia in 1935-6 and had to decline an invitation to tour in 1936-7, due to business commitments which also restricted his appearances for Surrey. He was also a handy medium-pace bowler off a sprinting run-up.

Mr F.R. (Freddie) Brown, born in Lima, Peru, on 16 December 1910 was a brave 'bull-dog' of a cricketer, if slightly impetuous all-rounder, a hard hitter and big spinning leg-spinner. Having toured Australia in 1932-3, he had failed to live up to his early promise, possibly due to the fact that he could only appear for a few matches every season because of his job in the City. After the war he joined Northants and, at an age when most amateurs were retired, became a heroic England captain.

Laurie B.Fishlock, born in Battersea on 2 January 1907, was a successful left-hand opening batsman, a fleet-footed player of spin, a trained engineer, who had an unhappy tour of Australia in 1936-7. He was also a League soccer player.

A.R. (Alf) Gover, born in Epsom on 29 February 1908, was one of Surrey's greatest opening bowlers, very fast, tall and thin, using both swerve and seam. Gover, who had a run-up like a man running against a fierce head-wind, suffered a lot from dropped catches. Nevertheless, he exceeded 200 wickets in both 1936 and 1937, in which years he gained three Test caps. He went on Tennyson's tour of India in 1937-8 and suffered knee trouble there. He founded a famous cricket school after the war and turned his arm over till the age of 80.

R.J. (Bob) Gregory, born in Selsdon on 26 August 1902, was the other opening bat, a right-hander. He was also a leg-spinner and a fielder renowned for his long throw on the huge outfield at The Oval space. He toured India in 1933-4 but played no Tests. He was also a soccer full-back,

E.A. (Eddie) Watts, born in Peckham on 1 August 1911, was Alf Gover's opening partner and his brother-in-law, a hearty swing bowler, well built and good for a quick 50 runs with the bat.

When Holmes was absent, Surrey were led by Mr H.M. (Monty) Garland-Wells, a captain of similar style, a forceful middle-order batsman, an amateur international goalkeeper who was also involved in the dog-racing business. T.H.Barling was a consistent right-hand bat. The rest of the batting was in the hands of all-rounders: Fred Berry, a Yorkshireman, born in the town of Hirst and Rhodes; John Parker, tall upright, very orthodox, a specialist slip who suffered from back trouble; H.S. (Stan) Squires, an unflappable batsman, off-spinning breaker of partnerships and wearer of rimless spectacles; and E.W.Whitfield, in and out of the side since 1930, who was tried as a opening batsman in 1938. The 1938 beneficiary was E.W.J. (Eddie) Brooks, aged 39. A pioneer of the acrobatic style of wicketkeepers, he first came from Cheam CC in 1925 as a bowler.

Sussex

Many great players graced the country of the martlett bird, but they had never won the Championship. From a peak on the early 1930s, Sussex slipped to 14th in 1936 but were fifth in 1937. They were short of specialist bowlers, but rich in familial connections. Amongst the regular players were three pairs of brothers and a son of a former player.

The captain was Flight-Lieutenant A.J. (Jack) Holmes, born in Thornton Heath, Surrey, on 30 June 1899, a moderate batsman who inspired the side with his fielding. In World War One he had joined the Royal Flying Corps and now he was a mink farmer and RAF reservist.

Mr Hugh T.Bartlett, born in India on 7 October 1914, was a left-hand batsman who had been noticed by Frank Woolley when at Dulwich College. He played a few games for Surrey before going up to Cambridge and joined Sussex in 1937. He was 6ft 2in tall, tanned, fair-haired and was an exhilarating hitter of the ball with deceptively powerful arms and wrists, and a delight to watch in full flow. He was a notoriously poor starter and spent the winter of 1937-8 tuning up his defence. During in the war he was awarded the DFC.

The Langridge brothers were the backbone of the side. James, born in Newick on 10 July 1906, had six Tests behind him and would have had more but for Hedley Verity's presence. A slow left-arm bowler with a very genteel action, accurate and teasing, and a mainly dour defensive left-hand bat, James could be relied upon in a crisis. Six times he had performed the double. John G., born in Chailey on 10 February 1910, was a right-hander, an opening batsman with a two-eyed, angular stance and more fluency than his brother. He was unlucky not to have appeared in a Test. He had a long lease on the first slip position and 'c Langridge, John, b Langridge, Jas' was a recurrent entry in the scorecard. Both brothers overcame delicate health, John having tuberculosis when young.

James H.Parks, born in Haywards Heath on 12 May 1903, was an unspectacular middle-order batsman and slow medium off-cutter, but with a great heart and brilliant in the field. Left widowed with a baby son (who was later to play for Sussex and England), in 1937 he performed the unique feat of 3,000 runs and 100 wickets in a season and played in one Test. He was a member of Tennyson's tour of India. His fair-haired brother, Harry, was a consistent and cheerful bat and renowned deep fielder.

The Oakes brothers came from Horsham, both born on the edge of the cricket ground where their father was groundsman. Charlie was the elder and more gifted, a useful bat and big tweaker of top-spin and googly. Jack was born in 1916 (middle name 'Ypres'), an off-spinner and batsman.

George Cox Jnr was a brilliant right-hand bat with a slightly wobbly defence, a bowler of left-arm medium-pace 'floaters' and a cover fielder. His father was a county player and now the coach, who showed his son no favouritism.

The Cornfords were a *trompe-l'œil*: they were not related at all. Jim was a fast-medium opening bowler who modelled his action on Maurice Tate and who was thought never to have bowled a no-ball. Walter, or 'Tich', Cornford was the long-standing (or rather crouching) wicketkeeper of some class, only 5ft 3in tall, he stood up to the stumps for nearly all bowlers and was a willing nightwatchman.

Of the rest, Mr S.C. (Billy) Griffith was a very promising wicketkeeper-batsman, a teacher at Dulwich College, who had played for Surrey; H.E. (Jim) Hammond was a medium-pace all-rounder and forward for Fulham FC in the winter; Mr R.G.Stainton, the deputy captain, was a batsman and brilliant fielder; and John Nye, a fast opening bowler, proved penetrative but expensive.

Warwickshire

Warwickshire were an efficient batting side but lacking in penetrative bowlers. Former England captain, R.E.S.Wyatt, had led them to fourth place in 1934. At the end of the 1937 season, in which they were 11th, the county committee replaced him as captain, although he remained in the side.

The new captain was Mr Peter Cranmer, born in Acocks Green, Birmingham, on 10 September 1914. He was an unorthodox leader, a right-hand batsman who was at his best when quick runs were needed, and occasional medium pace bowler. He was also an England rugby international.

H.E. (Tom) Dollery, born in Reading, Berkshire, on 14 October 1914, was a very good middle-order batsman, strong on the off-side, and slip fielder who had played for Berkshire at the age of 15, and Warwickshire at 19. After the war he was the county's first and very successful professional captain.

W.Eric Hollies, born in Old Hill, Staffordshire, on 5 June 1912, was nicknamed 'Spike'. He was chubby and fair-haired, an expert floater of accurate leg-breaks off a short, bouncy run-up, who usually took more wickets than he scored runs. He toured the West Indies in 1934-5 and played again for England after the war.

Mr Robert Elliott Storey (Bob) Wyatt, born in Milford, Surrey, on 2 May 1901 and moved to Coventry when he was 11. Wyatt was a heroic, steadfast and dedicated amateur, who was able and willing to give his all for county and country full-time. As far as the England selectors were concerned, he was always 'Mr Second Choice'. He was in and out of the Test side as a stop-gap captain from 1930 and toured Australia in 1932-3 as Jardine's loyal vice-captain. In 1934-5 he was England's captain for three full series but, alas, lost them all. As a late replacement he went again in 1936-7 but had been out of the side since. His batting was strong and orthodox, he bowled intelligently at fast-medium pace and captained with great skill and tactical insight. But in all departments he lacked that spark of genius and luck that is reserved for the great players. He was balding, rather dour-faced, thick-limbed and was unlucky in the way of breaking bones throughout his career. He once batted in a Test with a metal plate on a broken hand. Thinking that his chances of favour for 1938 were slim, he signed a contract to write on the Tests for the *Daily Mail.*

Wyatt would open the batting if required, but in 1938 the county used 42-year-old A.J.W.Croom, an experienced, steady and efficient player, and F.R.Santall, an attractive and popular cricketer who had been playing since 1919. After them came Jimmie Ord, a short, consistent batsman from Northumberland; and when available after playing for Cambridge University, Mr John R.Thompson, who could also open the innings.

The best opening bowler was J.H. (Danny) Mayer, from Kingsbury Colliery, aged 36, a lively fast-medium with late swing. He was partnered by Kilburn Wilmot, from Nuneaton. Complementing Hollies was shy Londoner, George Paine, a slow left-arm bowler and good slip field, now hampered by rheumatism. He played four Tests in the West Indies but was not quite good enough to displace Verity in the England side. Jack Buckingham was the Yorkshire-born wicketkeeper, small, unorthodox, an improving batsman.

Worcestershire

The team that played in sight of the lovely cathedral had some good players, but did not fulfil their potential. They were 15th in 1937 and had never exceeded tenth place since World War One.

Their colourful captain was the Hon Charles J.Lyttelton, born in London on 8 August 1909, later the tenth Viscount Cobham. He missed the XI at Eton and lacked natural skill but made himself into a strong hitter, helped by a powerful golf swing.

Harold H.I.Gibbons, born in Devonport, Devon, on 10 October 1904, was called 'Doc' because he carried his cricket attire in a black bag. He emerged, via the groundstaff at Lord's and the Birmingham League, as a small elegant opening bat, often on the verge of the England side.

R.T.D. (Reg) Perks, born on 4 October 1911, at Hereford where his father was groundsman at the racecourse, opened the bowling, a tall and hearty right-arm fast medium, also close to Test selection, and a six-hitting left-hand bat.

Gibbons' opening partner was Charles H.Bull, who had started with Kent, a stroke-playing right-hander and table-tennis player, who was killed in a road accident in May 1939. In the middle order were Eddie Cooper, from Bacup in the Lancashire League, tall with a high back swing; B.P. (Phil) King, resilient, if a little impetuous; Mr C.D.A. ('Plug') Pullan, an amateur boxer, on holiday from the Gold Coast; and, for a few games, the Nawab of Pataudi, class batsman of delicate health who played for England in 1932-3 and captained India in 1946. Mr Charles Palmer was a spectacled medium pace all-rounder who made his debut in 1938. Reg Perks shared the new ball with Sid Martin from Natal, who did the double in 1937. For 1938, though, that honour was to be conceded to Bob Crisp, the quick, accurate South African bowler who had taken 100 wickets on the tour of England in 1935. The spin bowling was strong: Dick Howorth, a tall, rugged-faced

Lancastrian slow left-armer and versatile bat; Percy Jackson, a Scottish-born medium-pace off-spinner and a great leg slip with distinctive cropped fair hair; and Roley Jenkins, a small leg-spinner and useful bat who, like Howorth, played for England after the war. The wicket-keeper was dignified and unfussy, J.S. (Syd) Buller, from the Yorkshire Council League. Buller was badly injured in the accident in 1939 which killed Bull. He became a well-respected Test umpire in later years.

Yorkshire

In all its glittering history, the White Rose county was perhaps in full bloom in 1938, a team of seasoned professionals and an outstanding captain, for whom Yorkshire cricket was life itself. Only a native-born Yorkshireman was allowed to play for the county and usually only after several years patient apprenticeship in the Second XI and Leagues. Never lower than fifth since World War One, winners five times in the previous seven seasons, winners in 1937, Yorkshire were the only side that began the season expecting to win the Championship. Notice how many of the players featured below had only one Christian name.

Mr Arthur *Brian* Sellers, born in Keighley on 5 March 1907, of St Peter's School, York, son of a county amateur, took over the captaincy in 1933 after a series of figurehead amateurs. This man was a bold, imaginative captain, a disciplinarian who demanded and deserved the total loyalty of what he called his 'crackerjack' team. He made everthing of his limited batting ability and scored 104 against the 1934 Australians. He batted at number-six or seven and tailoring his innings to the needs of the situation. He was also an aggressive fielder whether at cover or fearlessly crowding the bat. He was appointed an England selector in 1938 and was an outside possibility to lead the Test side.

Wilfred Barber, known as 'Tiddly-push', was born in Cleckheaton on 18 April 1901. He was a quiet accumulator of runs and a good outfielder who won a regular place only in 1932 and played twice for England in 1935.

William Eric (Bill) Bowes, born in Elland on 25 July 1908, was brought up in Leeds and was working as an estate agent's clerk when he got a trial at Lord's where his bowling for MCC soon caught the attention of his native county. He was 6ft 4in tall, bespectacled with slightly balding sandy-hair and an awkward mover. Apart from his height, Bowes looked more like a shy young church organist than one of England's leading fast bowlers. He had an ungainly action with very little follow-through and used his height to bang the ball down, getting pace and lift off the pitch, swinging the ball both ways. He was in and out of the England team and was one of the bodyline battery in 1932-3. He was a poor batsman and rather static fielder.

Yorkshire's Hedley Verity, the slow left-armer who took over the mantle from Wilfred Rhodes and became the greatest English bowler of the 1930s.

After the war, in which he was a PoW, he retired and became a shrewd journalist.

Mr Paul A.Gibb, born in Brandsby on 11 July 1913, was schooled at Oxford and went to Cambridge University where in 1938 he was playing most of his cricket, not yet being a regular for Yorkshire. He was balding, thin and bespectacled, a patient and effective defensive opening bat, a safe but not outstanding wicketkeeper and a keep-fit fanatic. The England selectors saw more promise in him than there actually was. He played as a professional for Essex after the war and ended his days as a bus driver in Surrey.

Leonard (Len) Hutton, born in Fulneck village, Pudsey, on 23 June 1916, was spotted early by Sutcliffe and George Hirst. He was so good an opening batsman that he made his county debut aged 17 and was a regular by 19. In 1934 he suffered a broken nose on a re-bound from the 'keeper's gloves when batting in the Roses Match. He was near to going to Australia in 1936-7, then made his Test debut in 1937, scoring 0 and 1. But he was clearly on the threshold of becoming one of the greatest of opening batsmen. His style was founded on a very orthodox, sound defence, a classic off-drive and leg-glance. In his young days he was also a useful leg-break bowler. After the war, despite shortening his left arm in a training accident, he was the rock of England's batting and her first professional captain.

Maurice Leyland, born in Harrogate on 27 July 1900 and christened 'Morris', was the leading middle-order batsman, a left-hander, and occasional purveyor of the 'Chinaman'. In his teens he played with his father for Moorside in the Lancashire League. He had been a stalwart of the Yorkshire team since 1923 and for England since 1928-9. He was short and stocky, wide in the beam with sloping shoulders. After a careful start he punched and shovelled the ball away fluently. He was a good deep fielder, despite a painful left shoulder. He was renowned for many sagacious observations, such as: "None of us likes fast bowlin' but some of us don't let on."

Arthur Mitchell, born in Baildon on 13 September 1902, was the archetypical Yorkshireman, a dour, cautious batsman, not pretty to watch but supremely dependable. A distinctive figure, over 6ft tall, he was lean, dark-haired and wore an angled cap. He was a brave close fielder and excellent anywhere. He played in six Tests in the mid-1930s. They called him 'Ticker' because of his non-stop chatter on the field.

Ellis P.Robinson, born in Denaby Main on 10 August 1911, bowled off-spin, batted left-handed as a tail-ender and was a great close-in catcher.

T.F. (Frank) Smailes, born in Ripley on 27 March 1910, won a regular place in 1934 after a spell in Forfarshire. He bowled medium

Len Hutton, clearly on the threshold of becoming one of the greatest of opening batsmen.

pace with a late swing, or on wet wickets slightly slower off-breaks, and batted left-handed at number-seven.

Herbert Sutcliffe, born in Harrogate on 24 November 1894, orphaned at six and brought up by his aunts in Pudsey, had been Yorkshire's permanent opening batsman since 1919, and England's between 1924 and 1935. A copperplate batsman with immaculately parted hair and high-waisted trousers, Sutcliffe was a professional of the highest standing who refused the Yorkshire captaincy in 1928. His stroke play was limited by his restricted swing of the bat, but he was a strong off-driver and hooker, played to his strengths and had a supreme temperament. He was still good enough to open for England but was now a little slow in the field.

In 1930 the torch of slow left-arm bowling for Yorkshire was passed from Wilfred Rhodes to Hedley Verity. Born in Headingley on 18 May 1905, he was brought up in Rawsdon and became the greatest English bowler of the 1930s. Before that he had played in the Lancashire League and had a trial for Warwickshire in 1928. Thoughtful and considerate, less forthright than his colleagues, he let his fingers do the talking. He was tall and had a high action at almost medium pace off a quick, straight run-up. His faster yorker was very speedy. Reducing his pace on turning wickets, Verity was deadly, as when he took 14 wickets in a day to beat Australia in the Lord's Test of 1934. He was also a solid defensive batsman and a good slip. In 1943, a captain in the Green Howards, he died of wounds in enemy custody in Sicily and the cricket world mourned the loss of a great man.

Yorkshire's wicketkeeper was the chubby-faced, effervescent and popular Arthur Wood, born in Fagley, Bradford, on 25 August 1898. The crowds loved his style and his cheeky batting. He came into the Second XI in 1924 and made the county side in 1928.

Mr Norman W.D.Yardley, born Royston, Barnsley, on 19 March 1915, of St Peter's School, York, was the Cambridge University captain in 1938. He was a good stroke player, especially strong on the on-side, and a deceptively useful medium-pace bowler. After the war, when he became a wine merchant, he succeeded Sellers and Hammond as Yorkshire and England captain. Later, his reassuring middle-class Yorkshire accent was heard for many years on Test Match radio commentaries.

The 11 players (that is all the above except Gibb and Yardley, who could not appear until July) were automatic members of the Yorkshire side. With so many likely Test calls and occasional injuries, the county had reserve strength in depth. The best of these was Cyril Turner, loyal and popular, a left-handed batsman, right-arm medium-pace bowler and short-leg fielder. There was also Frank Wilkinson, a swing bowler from Hull, and Mr George Wilson, a middle-order batsman.

The Universities

As still today, those who attended England's two greatest universities had the opportunity to play first-class cricket against the counties, at home in May, on tour in June, and in the traditional Varsity Match at Lord's in July. Neither side had great prospects for 1938.

Oxford University had had a poor time since 1921, although in 1937, A.P. (Sandy) Singleton (by now with Worcestershire) had led successfully and well. The new captain was John Grover, a right-hand bat, a Wykehamist, from Northumberland. Other batsmen were E.J.H.Dixon, a small figure, Yorkshire-born; John Eggar, another Wykehamist, who also played a little for Hampshire; John Lomas, a slight freshman of delicate health, up from Charterhouse; Micky Walford, a hockey and rugby player from Durham. All-rounders E.D.R. (Desmond) Eagar, slow left-arm, also of Gloucestershire and a post-war Hampshire captain; and P.M.Whitehouse of Kent. The pace bowlers were R.F.Darwell-Smith, in his fourth year; Etonian David Macindoe with a long run, who played for the Gentlemen at Lord's in his first year; and William Pershke. Douglas Young bowled leg-breaks. Roger Kimpton was a nimble wicketkeeper-batsman from Melbourne.

Cambridge University had also declined since the 1920s, except for a very good side in the mid-1930s. The captain was Norman Yardley of Yorkshire (*qv*). John Thompson (see *Warwickshire*) and Lancastrian Bertram Carris, a Harrovian who played for Middlesex, opened the batting. Paul Gibb (see *Yorkshire*) was a wicketkeeper-batsman. Then came J.D.A.Langley of Middlesex; George Mann of Middlesex, son of an England captain and a post-war England captain; Peter Studd, later Lord Mayor of London; and Sam Silkin, future Labour Attorney-General. Pace bowling came from William Rees-Davies, future Conservative MP, and M.A.C.P.Kaye. The spinners were Gethyn Hewan and John Wild.

Note: Career records of the Australian tourists and leading English cricketers of 1938 can be found on page 245.

The Thousand-run Race

THE Australians docked at Southampton on 20 April and took the train to Waterloo station where the police had erected barriers to control the large crowd. Amongst those present were Lord Hawke, Sir Pelham Warner, Sir Stanley Jackson, all former England captains, and G.O.Allen, captain of the last MCC tour to Australia, in his Homburg hat and City suit. There was a message of welcome from the Dominion Secretary, Mr Malcolm Macdonald.

Apart from Barnes' injured wrist, Bradman said that all his team were fit and McCabe had recovered from the 'flu. That evening, Bradman went with Dr Pope to visit Sir Douglas Shields, the doctor who had saved Bradman's life in 1934. Next day they practised under a watery sun at Lord's, and Bradman was bowled in the nets by a 17-year-old left-arm pace bowler, a member of the groundstaff, Paul Brooks. [Alas, the coming war deprived Brooks of a chance to establish himself in county cricket; he died in hospital in 1946, of injuries received in action, but is still remembered today for that one ball he bowled at the Lord's nets in 1938.]

A large crowd, paying a shilling each, came to watch the Australians go through their early paces. In the coming week the tourists stayed at their London base, the Victoria Hotel in Northumberland Avenue, just off Trafalgar Square and opposite the inn where Sir Henry Baskerville stayed in the famous Sherlock Holmes novel. Nets at Lord's alternated with official lunches and dinners: dinner at Lord's hosted by the retired Prime Minister, Lord Baldwin, with a speech by the Australian Attorney-General, Mr Robert Menzies; a reception at Australia House; lunch at the British Sportsmans' Club, where Bradman said that he hoped any dispute about the principles of the game would be settled man-to-man.

Because of Barnes' injury, a request was cabled to the Australian

Board of Control for an extra player but the Board refused on the ground that the injured man was not a key member of the Test team; a disappointment for Keith Rigg or Ross Gregory. Otherwise it was a pleasant week, not greatly distracted by the rumblings from Europe, where the *Anschluss* of Austria with the German Reich was now followed by demands of Henlein, leader of the Sudetenland Germans, for autonomy within the State of Czechoslakia.

April 30 to May 3: Hoarse Umpire, Deaf Bowler

On Friday, 29 April, the Australians were greeted by a huge crowd at Worcester station, and on a cold but sunny Saturday, Worcestershire's captain, the Hon Charles Lyttelton, son of Lord Cobham, put them in to bat on a perfect wicket — because that was what the big crowd (which grew to 11,500) wanted to see. When Bill Brown was lbw on the back foot to Crisp at 11.45am, Bradman was cheered to the wicket. On neither of his previous outings here (at Worcester) had he failed to reach 200 runs. Crisp, a lively South African fast-medium bowler, was working his outswinger well and he beat the cautious Bradman three times in one over. Fingleton was caught at cover for a useful 41 and at lunch Bradman was only 37 after 75 minutes.

Upon the resumption the spectators, now ringed around the ground five deep, saw McCabe punish some loose bowling until Perks bowled him at 139. From now on it was Bradman's show. He reached 50 in 135 minutes (very slow for him), 100 in 165, 150 in 200 and 200 in 240 minutes. Badcock made an impressive English debut in a partnership of 277 in 150 minutes. Lyttleton did not take the new ball until the score was 315 — as Neville Cardus wrote for Monday's *Manchester Guardian*:'Probably he was right; a new ball costs money and Worcestershire is not a wealthy club'.

At one time there were five men deep on the off-side but the Don still found the gaps. He gave no chance and never hit the ball in the air until past 200. Eventually he edged the slow left-armer, Howorth, to slip and departed. In all, Bradman hit one five (due to overthrows) and 33 4's in 258 made out of 419 in 290 minutes. Yet there were a few in the crowd who sagely opined that it was not the Bradman of 1930 and 1934.

If Saturday was a day of easy triumph, Monday caused serious worry, even embarrassment for the tourists. From a weekend score of 474-6, Hassett led a morning assault and they were all out for 541, made at a rate of 4.34 runs per over. McCormick, their fastest bowler since the 1920s, was expected to be a vital member of the attack. He marked out his 30-yard run and proceeded to bowl four no-balls in his first five deliveries. Off the third, Charles Bull tried to hook and deflected the ball for a thump on the forehead, just above the right eye, and had to retire. There were eight no-balls in that first over, nine in

Above: The Australians open the 1938 tour at Worcester where a record crowd of some 11,500 are seated five-deep around the boundary.

Left: The Hon Charles Lyttelton spins the coin and Bradman calls incorrectly. To the crowd's delight, however, the Worcestershire skipper asked the tourists to bat first.

Opposite page: Bill Brown plays a straight bat to Worcestershire's Reg Perks.

WORCESTERSHIRE v AUSTRALIA

Played at Worcester, on April 30, May 2, 3, 1938.
Australia won by an innings and 77 runs.

AUSTRALIA

J.H.Fingleton	c Crisp b Howorth	41
W.A.Brown	lbw b Crisp	2
*D.G.Bradman	c Martin b Howorth	258
S.J.McCabe	b Perks	34
C.L.Badcock	c Singleton b Perks	67
A.L.Hassett	c Howorth b Perks	43
†B.A.Barnett	b Crisp	16
E.S.White	b Crisp	26
W.J.O'Reilly	b Perks	11
E.L.McCormick	b Crisp	5
L.O'B.Fleetwood-Smith	not out	6
Extras	(B 13, LB 15, W 2, NB 2)	32
Total		**541**

Fall: 1st inns 1/9, 2/77, 3/139, 4/416, 5/428, 6/451, 7/513, 8/529, 9/531.

WORCESTERSHIRE

*Hon C.J.Lyttelton	b Fleetwood-Smith	50	c Badcock b White	35
C.H.Bull	not out	37	c McCormick b Fleetwood-Smith	69
E.Cooper	c Hassett b Fleetwood-Smith	61	lbw b White	16
H.H.Gibbons	b Fleetwood-Smith	29	c Brown b O'Reilly	9
S.H.Martin	b White	1	c Fingleton b O'Reilly	5
Mr R.H.C.Human	c Fingleton b Fleetwood-Smith	10	lbw b Fleetwood-Smith	26
R.Howorth	c Hassett b Fleetwood-Smith	12	c McCabe b O'Reilly	0
Mr A.P.Singleton	st Barnett b Fleetwood-Smith	5	run out	14
†J.S.Buller	lbw b O'Reilly	5	c Fleetwood-Smith b McCormick	10
R.T.D.Perks	c McCabe b Fleetwood-Smith	21	c McCabe b Fleetwood-Smith	4
Mr R.J.Crisp	c Hassett b Fleetwood-Smith	11	not out	0
Extras	(B 4, LB 5, W 1, NB 16)	26	(B 5, NB 3)	8
Total		**268**		**196**

Fall: 1st inns 1/103, 2/164, 3/165, 4/175, 5/183, 6/187, 7/197, 8/224, 9/252.
2nd inns 1/65, 2/87, 3/104, 4/123, 5/160, 6/161, 7/169, 8/190, 9/191.

WORCESTERSHIRE	O	M	R	W
Crisp	37.3	5	170	4
Perks	34	3	147	4
Martin	29	8	70	0
Howorth	21	1	85	2
Singleton	3	0	37	0

AUSTRALIA	O	M	R	W	O	M	R	W
McCormick	8	0	44	0	12	2	51	1
McCabe	4	0	16	0	5	1	13	0
O'Reilly	14	2	77	1	23	9	56	3
Fleetwood-Smith	29	8	98	8	13.1	0	38	3
White	11	7	7	1	10	1	30	2

Umpires: J.Smart and H.G.Baldwin.

the second, so that the first three overs of the innings took 26 minutes. Bradman asked umpire Baldwin if he was dragging over the line. "Dragging?" was the reply, "He's jumping two feet over it." There were two calls in McCormick's third over and Bradman took him off, as the crowd had already suggested. The bowler himself did not seem too annoyed by his troubles, but his captain's thoughts are best left to the imagination. O'Reilly came on at 49 and even he bowled a no-ball, to the amusement of the 4,000 present. Lyttelton took a swing at him and sent two 4's clean past his head. At lunch, Worcestershire were 99 for no wicket in an hour. The manager, Mr Jeanes, visited the specially erected Press box and said of McCormick: "I'm afraid this is going to upset him. Why, you could see from the ring that he was well over the crease. Unfortunately, McCormick has not properly tried out his full run in this country. Owing to the back net he shortened his run during practices at Lord's and it was only during his last outing there that he was able to bowl all out."

Fleetwood-Smith opened the bowling after lunch. Off his first ball, Lyttleton late cut for his 50; his second, he was late on and chopped on to his wicket. Although looking far from match fit, when he found his length the double-barrelled purveyor of chinamen and googlies bamboozled the county men and saved Australian blushes. McCormick improved in his second spell. In five overs he was called five times and had 'Doc' Gibbons dropped at first slip. Edwin Cooper hit seven 4's in a stylish 61. Bull returned at the fall of the sixth wicket and resisted stoutly.

Crisp tarried long enough to swing a big six over the trees and on to Leamington Road and then Worcestershire followed-on 273 behind and made 74-1 at the close. McCormick bowled five no-balls in five overs, called this time by umpire Smart. Commenting on the day's events, umpire Baldwin said, "He lost his run, I had to do my duty." McCormick said, "I wish he was hoarse." The matter gave rise to a standing joke in the Australian team. If a member of the public greeted McCormick in the street, he would walk straight on without a turn of the head. A colleague would explain to the bemused cricket lover that the shouts of no-ball had affected his hearing.

Tuesday was cold and damp. Two hours' play in four sessions lasting until 4.30 was needed to complete an innings victory. McCormick no-balled twice in four overs, changed his run-up and consulted with Bradman several times. In a short spell later, he bowled three more bringing the match total to 35. Despite the cold weather the tourists fielded smartly. Once Bradman chased a straight drive, threw back on the turn, White in the middle of the pitch received it, turned in a flash and hit the stumps to run out an unsuspecting Singleton. Charles Bull, forehead plastered, stayed two and a half hours for 69.

Stan McCabe, clean blowed by Perks for 34.

Don Bradman hits one of his 33 4s on his way to 258. The Worcestershire wicketkeeper is Syd Buller.

Jack Fingleton.

Don Bradman.

Stan McCabe.

Sid Barnes.

After the match an X-ray showed that he had batted with a broken finger and he was out of action for a month.

Before leaving Worcester, the Australians visited the Royal Worcester Porcelain Works. Bradman was presented with a vase specially painted with a view of the beautiful Worcester ground and him batting. Each member of the side was given a plate.

At Lord's, meanwhile, a blank third day spoiled the match between MCC and the county champions, Yorkshire. On Saturday, it had started inauspiciously when the Yorkshire captain, A.B.Sellers, objected to the validity of the toss, done in the dressing room, and it had to be repeated in front of the Pavilion. Of England's trio of hopeful young batsmen, Bill Edrich (104) and Denis Compton (77) batted well, but Len Hutton was unimpressive. Elsewhere, Herr Hitler arrived by train in Rome and was driven with the King of Italy through floodlit streets filled with cheering onlookers.

May 4 to 6: Crash Course for Students

The Australians moved on to Oxford by train and overwhelmed a scratch University side. Brown and Fingleton scored only 98 in two hours before lunch, thanks mainly to the steady medium pace of the Etonian, D.H.Macindoe (19-6-23-0). But the middle-order showed less respect and then they closed the day at 481-5 (Macindoe 48-10-129-2). Fingleton hit 124 in four hours. McCabe gave a superb display of pulling and driving for 110 in 105 minutes, although he was dropped twice before passing 11.

On Thursday, thanks to Hassett's fluent 146 with 24 4's they added a further 198 in two hours and Bradman declared at lunch. McCormick carefully marked out his run-up and six deliveries proved sufficient to complete his first over, but he was called four times in his next three overs by umpire Hendren (brother of 'Patsy') and looked innocuous. He did not bowl again in the match. J.D.Eggar held out for 95 minutes, although when he was 23, Bradman at mid-on dropped a catch that was so easy that it caused laughter among the 5,000 spectators. Fleetwood-Smith again tied up the batsmen, taking 5 for 28 in 24.5 overs.

In the follow-on, Eggar was promoted to open but he was caught at second slip for a duck. Having dismissed four for 29 by the close, the Australians needed only 45 minutes of the last day to finish the match. When Walker bruised a finger, Fingleton deputised for him behind the wicket and stumped Desmond Eagar and Murray-Wood. He eschewed an easy chance to run out the last man, Whetherly, and stumped him off the next ball. Fingleton kept the match ball and asked his three victims to sign it, which they did with exclamation marks appended. Afterwards, McCormick took the opportunity to practise bowling on the match wicket for half an hour, with Bill

OXFORD UNIVERSITY v AUSTRALIA

Played at Christ Church ground, Oxford, on May 4, 5, 6, 1938.
Australia won by an innings and 487 runs.

AUSTRALIA

J.H.Fingleton	c Whetherly b Evans	124
W.A.Brown	c Evans b Macindoe	72
*D.G.Bradman	lbw b Evans	58
S.J.McCabe	b Macindoe	110
A.G.Chipperfield	c Whetherly b Darwall-Smith	53
A.L.Hassett	b Darwall-Smith	146
M.G.Waite	c Kimpton b Evans	54
†C.W.Walker	not out	31
Extras	(B 21, LB 9, W 1)	31
Total	(7 wickets, declared)	**679**

Fall: 1st inns 1/140, 2/245, 3/310, 4/431, 5/433, 6/558, 7/679.
F.Ward, E.L.McCormick and L.O'B. Fleetwood-Smith did not bat.

OXFORD UNIVERSITY

Mr M.M.Walford	b Waite	17	(3) c Waite b McCabe	5
Mr E.J.H.Dixon	c Walker b Ward	17	c Fleetwood-Smith b Waite	2
Mr J.D.Eggar	not out	51	(1) c McCabe b Waite	0
†Mr R.C.M.Kimpton	b Fleetwood-Smith	2	c Walker b Fleetwood-Smith	15
*Mr J.N.Grover	b Fleetwood-Smith	2	c Chipperfield b Ward	10
Mr E.D.R.Eagar	st Walker b Ward	0	st Fingleton b Fleetwood-Smith	25
Mr W.Murray-Wood	run out	11	st Fingleton b Ward	0
Mr G.Evans	run out	0	hit wkt b Fleetwood-Smith	9
Mr D.H.Macindoe	b Fleetwood-Smith	2	b Fleetwood-Smith	0
Mr R.F.Darwall-Smith	b Fleetwood-Smith	0	not out	3
Mr R.E.Whetherly	b Fleetwood-Smith	0	st Fingleton b Ward	1
Extras	(B 3, LB 7, W 1, NB 4)	15	(B 4, LB 1)	5
Total		**117**		**75**

Fall: 1st inns 1/30, 2/64, 3/69, 4/73, 5/76, 6/102, 7/106, 8/115, 9/115.
2nd inns 1/0, 2/5, 3/15, 4/29, 5/45, 6/45, 7/71, 8/71, 9/72.

OXFORD UNIVERSITY	O	M	R	W
Darwall-Smith	39.4	4	162	2
Macindoe	68	11	207	2
Evans	47	9	171	3
Kimpton	13	1	53	0
Murray-Wood	9	1	55	0

AUSTRALIA	O	M	R	W	O	M	R	W
McCormick	4	0	10	0				
Waite	11	2	25	1	9	4	11	2
Ward	28	13	39	2	7.2	4	16	3
Fleetwood-Smith	24.5	11	28	5	10	3	31	4
McCabe					6	3	12	1

Umpires: D.Hendren and N.Harris.

Brown taking slow-motion cine film. He found it better when he reduced his run-up to 27 paces.

Whilst Oxford University went down by an innings and 487 runs, the county programme was dribbling into action. Many counties would not start until 7 May and the men of Glamorgan were not due to don their whites in anger until the 14th. A leading runner for the Test captaincy, Walter Hammond, scored 112 as Gloucestershire, set 383 at 85 an hour to beat Hampshire, failed by 30 runs off the penultimate ball. But it was interesting to note that R.W.V.Robins was appointed to lead MCC against the Australians. G.O.Allen would probably have been asked to captain the side but he declined to play because of lack of match practice. Edrich scored his second century of the season at Lord's and Compton made one as well, for MCC against Surrey.

May 7 to 10: The Spectre of Bodyline

McCabe took the side to Leicester. Bradman stayed in London, where on Saturday he went to Wembley to watch Salford beat Barrow 7-4 in the Rugby League Cup Final, not only watch but review the team line-up at the start and present the trophy to the winners. Leicestershire were a strong batting side, captained by the very gifted New Zealander, Stewart Dempster, with one of the most solid county opening batsmen, Les Berry, and two young all-rounders from Sydney, Walsh and Jackson.

In McCormick's first over the fifth ball — a no-ball — struck Berry above the left ear and he retired until lunch. In his third over, McCormick struck Dempster twice in the ribs and the crowd shouted, "Take him off!" Jackson scored freely off the spinners and greeted McCormick's return with three successive cuts to the boundary. Leicestershire, 150-6 at lunch, made 212. McCormick bowled ten no-balls. Australia started slowly on a perfect wicket against a weak attack, but in the last 110 minutes of the day, Badcock and Hassett added 183 and the Australians reached 243-2.

On Monday, untroubled by smoke from the nearby electricity works, Hassett hit strongly for 148 in 200 minutes, until Badcock's push for a single and Dempster's throw from square leg ran him out. Badcock was caught in the gully, two short of a double century. Both innings were chanceless. Chipperfield was dropped at 28 and 71 but was unbeaten at 104 in two and a half hours when McCabe declared at tea. The combined analysis of the two 'Sydney-siders' was 63-5-285-2.

In the county's second innings, McCormick sent back Berry and Armstrong with consecutive balls and when he pitched short, he struck Prentice and Dempster on the body. In his first over, O'Reilly got a fortuitous wicket when Prentice snicked a ball on to his pads and it popped up to short leg. [Fifty years later, modern spin bowlers

LEICESTERSHIRE v AUSTRALIA

Played at Leicester, on May 7, 9, 10, 1938.
Australia won by an innings and 163 runs.

LEICESTERSHIRE

L.G.Berry	c McCabe b Ward	10	c Waite b McCormick	12
F.T.Prentice	c White b McCormick	5	c Fingleton b O'Reilly	12
N.F.Armstrong	c Fingleton b O'Reilly	26	hit wkt b McCormick	0
*Mr C.S.Dempster	b McCormick	0	c Badcock b Ward	105
G.S.Watson	st Barnett b Ward	43	b Ward	8
Mr V.E.Jackson	c Waite b McCormick	47	c White b McCormick	6
Mr N.Dowen	st Barnett b Ward	44	lbw b O'Reilly	26
G.Geary	c Fingleton b Ward	1	st Barnett b Ward	3
Mr J.E.Walsh	lbw b Ward	5	c Badcock b Ward	0
†G.O.Dawkes	lbw b O'Reilly	24	b White	9
W.H.Flamson	not out	0	not out	8
Extras	(B 1, NB 6)	7	(B 17, LB 6, NB 3)	26
Total		**212**		**215**

Fall: 1st inns 1/12, 2/13, 3/56, 4/87, 5/139, 6/150, 7/170, 8/178, 9/212.
2nd inns 1/30, 2/30, 3/45, 4/72, 5/107, 6/145, 7/156, 8/156, 9/191.

AUSTRALIA

J.H.Fingleton	b Walsh	34
C.L.Badcock	c Dempster b Flamson	198
*S.J.McCabe	lbw b Walsh	0
A.L.Hassett	run out	148
A.G.Chipperfield	not out	104
M.G.Waite	c Flamson b Geary	49
†B.A.Barnett	not out	42
Extras	(B 7, LB 7, NB 1)	15
Total	(5 wickets, declared)	**590**

Fall: 1st inns 1/60, 2/60, 3/375, 4/410, 5/496.
E.S.White, F.Ward, W.J.O'Reilly and E.L.McCormick did not bat.

AUSTRALIA	O	M	R	W	O	M	R	W
McCormick	10	1	61	3	14	0	54	3
Waite	9	1	29	0	6	2	14	0
O'Reilly	15.1	4	46	2	21	10	33	2
Ward	16	3	69	5	21.1	1	73	4
White	-	-	-	-	8	4	15	1

LEICESTERSHIRE	O	M	R	W
Flamson	34	4	113	1
Jackson	30	4	134	0
Geary	37	7	80	1
Walsh	33	1	151	2
Prentice	18	1	72	0
Dowen	5	0	25	0

Umpires: F.Walden and E.Robinson.

seem to regard this as the only respectable way to get a batsman out.] At the close, Dempster was 50 not out in a total of 107-5.

On Tuesday morning he took half an hour to add to that score, playing five maidens to O'Reilly. He was 93 when last man Flamson came in. A straight-driven four off Ward and three singles made him, after three hours, the first centurion against the 1938 tourists. Leicestershire's total of 215 took 70.1 overs, exactly 20 more than the first innings of 212. There was a wholly unfounded report in a Sunday newspaper that Harold Larwood was in Leicester to help Ernie McCormick, but in any event McCormick had a much better match, taking 6-115, although he bowled 15 no-balls. Like previous touring teams, the Australians were entertained during their stay by Mr. J.H.Corah at Queeniborough Hall, near Syston, three miles north of Leicester.

Seven County Championship matches were played which produced some heavy scoring. Hammond treated the Saturday crowd at Bristol to 237 in five and a half hours. Eddie Paynter made a faultless 291 at Southampton, where Lancashire strode to their second easy victory in two matches. Surrey opener Bob Gregory hit 243, with 30 4's against Somerset on a hard, fast pitch at The Oval. But the place to be was Gravesend. Kent beat Essex in a match of 1,422 runs for 34 wickets, and five centuries, scored by Nichols and Peter Smith (both bowlers) and O'Connor for Essex, and Ames (170) and Valentine (151) for Kent, plus two delightful cameos by Frank Woolley.

Hitler left Rome proclaiming Axis solidarity but saying nothing new. The British and French Governments urged Czechoslovakia to go to 'the utmost possible limit' to settle the Sudeten problem, consistent with state security. At Markham Colliery in Derbyshire, 79 men died in a mine explosion.

May 11 to 13: 'Flannelled Fools' at Paddington Station

Cambridge University were a weak side apart from two Yorkshiremen, Norman Yardley and Paul Gibb, who were Test prospects. On an excellent Fenners pitch, Waite and O'Reilly bowled them out just after lunch. Yardley mastered O'Reilly for a time, hitting 11 4's in 110 minutes until he swung at O'Reilly's slower ball and Fingleton at long-on leant backwards and plucked the ball out of the skies. Brown was lbw to the second ball of the Australian innings; Fingleton scored 111 in 145 minutes, when on that score he ran three before it was discovered that a bail was dislodged and he was given out bowled.

Bradman made an assured, uneventful 137. Badcock and Hassett put on 275 in under three hours. Hassett's 220 not out — his first double century — took only 280 minutes, with 35 4's. At the tea-time declaration on the second day, on the tour so far the Australians

CAMBRIDGE UNIVERSITY v AUSTRALIA

Played at Cambridge, on May 11, 12, 13, 1938.
Australia won by an innings and 425 runs.

CAMBRIDGE UNIVERSITY

†Mr P.A.Gibb	b Waite	1	not out	80
Mr J.V.Wild	c White b Waite	0	b Ward	18
Mr J.D.A.Langley	b O'Reilly	18	c & b Ward	0
*Mr N.W.D.Yardley	c Fingleton b O'Reilly	67	b O'Reilly	29
Mr M.St.J.Packe	lbw b O'Reilly	2	c Fingleton b Ward	15
Mr F.G.Mann	lbw b O'Reilly	1	b White	1
Mr P.M.Studd	lbw b Waite	12	c Badcock b Ward	4
Mr M.A.C.P.Kaye	b Waite	13	c Bradman b White	0
Mr S.M.A.Banister	lbw b O'Reilly	0	c Brown b White	2
Mr H.G.Jameson	b Waite	0	b Ward	4
Mr W.R.Rees-Davies	not out	4	st Barnett b Ward	0
Extras	(LB 1, NB 1)	2	(LB 9, NB 1)	10
Total		**120**		**163**

Fall: 1st inns 1/1, 2/2, 3/55, 4/67, 5/69, 6/92, 7/116, 8/116, 9/116.
2nd inns 1/55, 2/55, 3/106, 4/134, 5/139, 6/144, 7/144, 8/150, 9/157.

AUSTRALIA

J.H.Fingleton	b Kaye	111
W.A.Brown	lbw b Rees-Davies	0
*D.G.Bradman	c Mann b Wild	137
C.L.Badcock	c Mann b Rees-Davies	186
A.L.Hassett	not out	220
A.G.Chipperfield	st Gibb b Banister	8
M.G.Waite	not out	30
Extras	(B 10, LB 5 W 1)	16
Total	(5 wickets, declared)	**708**

Fall: 1st inns 1/3, 2/218, 3/281, 4/556, 5/567.
†B.A.Barnett, W.J.O'Reilly, F.Ward and E.S.White did not bat.

AUSTRALIA	O	M	R	W	O	M	R	W
Waite	16.3	7	23	5	6	0	18	0
White	5	5	0	0	19	12	22	3
O'Reilly	21	6	55	5	22	8	49	1
Ward	10	3	40	0	35.4	13	64	6

CAMBRIDGE UNIVERSITY	O	M	R	W
Rees-Davies	43	2	214	2
Jameson	29	4	127	0
Kaye	17	0	100	1
Wild	45	12	143	1
Banister	22	2	91	1
Yardley	5	1	17	0

Umpires: W.Wainwright and J.J.Hills.

had scored 2,518 runs for 28 wickets. Cambridge were 73-2 at the close and surrendered quietly on Friday, though Gibb carried his bat and gave no chance, batting in a style that reminded Jack Fingleton of Herbert Sutcliffe.

Lancashire lost easily to Derbyshire, getting the worst of the Liverpool wicket. At Ilford, Yorkshire needed 257 at 80 an hour to beat Essex, and Sellers and Hutton ensured victory with 15 minutes to spare. Then they had to race to Paddington station to get the evening express to Gloucester. At Lord's, a Hammond century took him past 600 runs for the season; Gloucestershire made 478, but Middlesex, thanks to a stand of 304 by Edrich and Compton, tied on the first innings. Middlesex needed 244 in 145 minutes to win and did it by three wickets with 18 minutes to spare. The Gloucestershire team, some still in their flannels, rushed to Paddington to catch the same train as the Yorkshiremen.

On 11 May at Aldershot, keeping wicket for the Corps of Military Police, Lance-Corporal J.L.Richardson was struck on the chest by the ball and died in hospital, aged 44. The Sudeten leader, Konrad Henlein (secretly briefed by the German Foreign Ministry) made a surprise visit to London and lunched with Mr Winston Churchill. At this time Parliament was debating plans for the expansion of the RAF. The Czech government agreed to talks on its nationality laws.

By 13 May, public interest was aroused at the prospect of a batsman reaching 1,000 runs by the end of May. Hammond had 633, Edrich 592, Hassett 557 and Bradman 453. Surely at least one of these would do it.

May 14 to 17: No Joy for England Selectors

The first major match of the tour — and the first in London — was against MCC. They had a good pace attack but were not a strong side, containing only three professionals. Middlesex, who had no game, provided those three and Walter Robins, the captain. Essex provided three men (Farnes taking time off from school), although they were playing — and losing — to Yorkshire. There was no-one from Lancashire or Yorkshire.

On Saturday there were long queues at Lord's and the crowd built up to 32,000 when the gates were closed at 3pm. Bradman won the toss and Farnes, from the Pavilion End, soon beat Brown with late outswing. Out strode Bradman to face that great-hearted Essex pace bowler, Captain Stephenson. 'Steve's ' first ball was a full toss which Bradman missed. The second hit him hard on the left foot and he hobbled about painfully, while Fingleton, the non-striker, pointed up to a passing aeroplane which displayed an advertisement saying 'for sore feet, rub it in'. Another blow on the thigh from Farnes did

A packed Lord's on the first day of the Australians' match against MCC. There were 32,000 people in the ground when the gates were closed in mid-afternoon. This photograph shows the Tavern and beyond it the Mound Stand.

Ken Farnes sends Bill Brown's off stump flying and the Australians are 11 for one.

not stop Bradman from cruising to 50 out of 83, having cut three 4's in an over off Jim Smith.

Fingleton, dropped when 37, was bowled for 44 after two and a half hours. McCabe was beaten by a quick straight ball from Smith, and Badcock failed. Hassett drove strongly in a stand of 162 until he was bowled trying to cut. Bradman completely dominated, reaching 100 in 150 minutes, 200 in 270 minutes, and 257 at the close in a total of 428-5.

On Monday, Bradman made his first real mistake when he gave a low, skimming catch to Robins at cover and departed for 278 in six hours, with 35 4's and, unusually, one six. Stephenson got Barnett in his second over. Waite looked set but got out to a quicker ball which kept low. Smith took 4-39 in 65 balls that morning and finished with 6-139.

When MCC batted, Wilcox, another Essex schoolteacher, was beaten by Waite's late inswing. McCormick, from the Pavilion End off a shorter run, bowled only one no-ball and hit Edrich in the stomach. Edrich was caught at second slip, off the back of the bat when pulling at Fleetwood-Smith. After lunch, McCormick dismissed Human and Maxwell with successive balls and struck Wyatt on the elbow, but later retired with a strained tendon. Compton got tied down by O'Reilly and in trying to scatter the leg-trap he missed a straight ball. Wyatt resisted stubbornly for 135 minutes.

M.C.C. v AUSTRALIA

Played at Lord's, on May 14, 16, 17, 1938.
Match drawn.

AUSTRALIA

J.H.Fingleton	b Smith	44
W.A.Brown	b Farnes	5
*D.G.Bradman	c Robins b Smith	278
S.J.McCabe	b Smith	33
C.L.Badcock	b Stephenson	14
A.L.Hassett	c Maxwell b Compton	57
M.G.Waite	lbw b Smith	26
†B.A.Barnett	lbw b Stephenson	1
W.J.O'Reilly	c Compton b Smith	17
E.L.McCormick	c Maxwell b Smith	9
L.O'B Fleetwood-Smith	not out	3
Extras	(B 3, LB 11 NB 1)	15
Total		**502**

Fall: 1st inns 1/11, 2/149, 3/217, 4/248, 5/410, 6/454, 7/459, 8/481, 9/499.

M.C.C.

Mr D.R.Wilcox	b Waite	6	b McCabe	16
W.J.Edrich	c McCabe b Fleetwood-Smith	31	not out	53
D.C.S.Compton	lbw b O'Reilly	23	not out	12
Mr R.E.S.Wyatt	not out	84		
Mr F.G.H.Chalk	lbw b Fleetwood-Smith	15		
Mr J.H.Human	b McCormick	5		
†Mr C.R.Maxwell	b McCormick	0		
*Mr R.W.V.Robins	c McCabe b O'Reilly	12		
Capt J.W.A.Stephenson	c & b Fleetwood-Smith	1		
C.I.J.Smith	c Hassett b Fleetwood-Smith	17		
Mr K.Farnes	c Fingleton b O'Reilly	0		
Extras	(B 5, LB 15)	20	(B 5, LB 1)	6
Total		**214**	(1 wicket)	**87**

Fall: 1st inns 1/18, 2/50, 3/89, 4/141, 5/164, 6/164, 7/180, 8/182, 9/210.
2nd inns 1/43.

M.C.C.	O	M	R	W
Farnes	32	3	88	1
Smith	42.5	9	139	6
Stephenson	29	5	112	2
Robins	18	2	69	0
Wyatt	7	0	27	0
Compton	10	2	37	1
Edrich	2	0	15	0

AUSTRALIA	O	M	R	W	O	M	R	W
McCormick	13	1	55	2	3	1	8	0
Waite	11	2	28	1	9	3	18	0
O'Reilly	16.2	6	42	3	5	2	8	0
Fleetwood-Smith	20	2	69	4	5	0	25	0
McCabe	-	-	-	-	7	2	22	1

Umpires: J.Hardstaff and J.Newman.

Above: Bob Wyatt, whom the selectors considered for the First Test. Opposite (top): Bradman batting against MCC, on his way to another double century. Opposite (bottom): Fingleton hits a leg-side boundary off Jim Smith in his 44 against MCC.

MCC followed-on and Wilcox was bowled when he lost sight of a ball by McCabe in the gloomy weather. But Edrich seized on everything short of a length to hit 50 in an hour. On Tuesday, light but persistent rain prevented any play and the match was abandoned at 3.45pm.

The England selectors asked R.E.S.Wyatt if he was available for the First Test. He said he hoped that the *Daily Mail* would release him from his writing contract, but the selectors decided to take no action for the time being. For them it had been an unhelpful match.

The race to Paddington station the previous day was the most exciting feature of the Gloucestershire-Yorkshire match at Gloucester. The batting was dull and when rain stopped play after lunch on the third day, Yorkshire were 124 behind with ten second innings wickets standing. Hammond, although not at his best, made 124 and took his aggregate to 757. Derbyshire beat Surrey on a very low, flat wicket at Chesterfield. Lancashire and Sussex both won by an innings away from home. On Saturday, at the Berlin Olympic Stadium in great heat, Hess, Ribbentrop, Goebels and the British Ambassador, Sir Neville Henderson, and 115,000 others saw the England football team beat Germany 6-3. Before the kick-off, at Henderson's request, the England players gave the Nazi salute. In a Cabinet reshuffle, Lord

Swinton was replaced at the Air Ministry by Sir Kingsley Wood, a supporter of rearmament.

May 18 to 20: The Juggernaut Rolls On

At Northampton station the Australians were greeted by the Dagenham Girl Pipers, but only a few hundred people braved the cold to see Brown and Badcock score 126-0 at the County Ground before rain stopped play at 1.10pm. On Thursday, Bradman came in and stayed only 20 minutes, so that on his three tours to England he had scored only 149 runs in five innings at the Northampton ground.

Brown played himself into form and suffered some mild barracking, but speeded up during a partnership of 100 with Walker. When Bradman declared, the home captain, R.P.Nelson punished the Australian attack (which was minus McCormick and O'Reilly) mercilessly and was hard on Fleetwood-Smith. At 78, Nelson was dropped by Bradman at mid-off, but as they went for a single, Bradman recovered, threw back to the wicketkeeper and Greenwood was run out. Nelson was bowled by Waite after 105 minutes and Northants were 139-3 at the close.

On Friday morning the Australians fielded keenly in the wintry conditions and got back into the pavilion after 80 minutes. In that time, Ward took 5-35, getting some spin. White was off the field with a bad foot. O'Brien was given out caught and bowled by umpire Chester and was obviously not convinced that Chipperfield took it cleanly. He spoke to the square-leg umpire on the way out and some of the members shouted, "Was that fair?" Northants lasted only 160 minutes in the follow-on, McCabe taking 4-1 in five overs and soon after tea the weakest county in England had fallen under the Australian juggernaut.

Lancashire went to the top of the table, beating Middlesex at Lord's, although Denis Compton scored 134 and 60 and Jim Smith, in a quick 25, hit a six into the luncheon room in the Tavern. Yorkshire beat Essex at Bramall Lane, Sheffield, after a blank first day. On a soft wicket at Gillingham, Kent put Gloucestershire in and Douglas Wright took the third hat-trick of his career; Hammond declared at 3pm on the second day, leaving Kent only 298 to win but Sinfield was too good for them. This was A.P.F.Chapman's final appearance for Kent. Edrich now had 736 runs, Hammond 781 and Bradman 733.

The Home Office started to advertise for ARP (Air Raid Precaution) recruits, and Germany denied troop movements on the Czech border.

May 21 to 24: Boos for Bradman

For the Australians' first appearance at The Oval, 18,000 people came to watch and the tourists scored 432-5, although Surrey's Edward Watts bowled well. After 90 minutes, when Fingleton was bowled by a full

NORTHAMPTONSHIRE v AUSTRALIA

Played at Northampton, on May 18, 19, 20, 1938.
Australia won by an innings and 77 runs.

AUSTRALIA

W.A.Brown	not out	194
C.L.Badcock	c James b Partridge	72
*D.G.Bradman	c James b Partridge	2
S.J.McCabe	c Merritt b Partridge	13
A.G.Chipperfield	lbw b Timms	18
M.G.Waite	lbw b Timms	43
†B.A.Barnett	lbw b Timms	1
C.W.Walker	not out	29
Extras	(B 22, LB 12)	34
Total	(6 wickets, declared)	**406**

Fall: 1st inns 1/131, 2/143, 3/165, 4/214, 5/304, 6/306.
E.S.White, F.Ward and L.O'B.Fleetwood-Smith did not bat.

NORTHAMPTONSHIRE

*Mr R.P.Nelson	b Waite	74	b Fleetwood-Smith	10
H.W.Greenwood	run out	24	b McCabe	43
Mr A.W.Snowden	c Chipperfield b Ward	28	b Waite	13
J.E.Timms	lbw b Ward	5	b Waite	5
D.Brookes	b Ward	37	lbw b McCabe	15
Mr G.B.Cuthbertson	b Ward	4	b McCabe	0
F.P.O'Brien	c & b Chipperfield	5	c sub b Ward	3
†K.C.James	c Brown b Ward	2	b Fleetwood-Smith	21
W.E.Merritt	not out	5	lbw b McCabe	1
R.J.Partridge	st Barnett b Ward	0	not out	16
E.J.Herbert	b Fleetwood-Smith	1	lbw b Waite	1
Extras	(B 5, LB 4)	9	(B 4, LB 3)	7
Total		**194**		**135**

Fall: 1st inns 1/78, 2/132, 3/134, 4/139, 5/153, 6/174, 7/183, 8/189, 9/189.
2nd inns 1/22, 2/35, 3/55, 4/84, 5/88, 6/89, 7/91, 8/92, 9/131.

NORTHAMPTONSHIRE	O	M	R	W
Partridge	36	7	82	3
Herbert	30	6	75	0
Timms	20	4	68	3
Nelson	14	1	56	0
Merritt	16	0	81	0
O'Brien	3	0	10	0

AUSTRALIA	O	M	R	W	O	M	R	W
Waite	15	4	41	1	22	10	28	3
McCabe	13	4	22	0	18	8	28	4
Fleetwood-Smith	11.1	1	33	1	22	5	55	2
Ward	28	7	75	6	8	3	17	1
Chipperfield	13	6	14	1				

Umpires: F.Chester and A.Dolphin.

toss, Bradman came in and took control after lunch. Again it was noticed that he did not seem to be the 'Boy Bradman' of previous tours. His batting was not as spectacular and audacious, he took fewer risks, was more orthodox, but his unique ability to place the ball made it impossible to score slowly. His demeanour on the field was more relaxed and cheerful.

When he passed 50 in 70 minutes, the Surrey captain, Errol Holmes, overheard his response when Brown congratulated him: "Thanks Billy, it's nice to get a few now and again." Watts got Brown with the new ball at 210 and Bradman was caught behind. His 143 in 200 minutes had been almost faultless.

Hassett began slowly and in the mid-afternoon lull, the crowd showed impatience. Then he drove a no-ball by Gover for six, and twice in an over hit Watts straight back for 4's. On Monday, two short of a three-hour century, Hassett played too soon at a short ball from fast-medium Berry and spooned up a catch. A minor collapse enabled Ward to make his first walk to a crease in England, but he did not manage to make his first run.

After lunch, O'Reilly took the first five Surrey wickets for 58, although Gregory hit four 4's off him in two overs. Fishlock hit Ward for a six which landed on the road. Barling hit two sixes off O'Reilly and Surrey closed the day at 269-8. One over by O'Reilly was enough to finish the innings on Tuesday morning. Bradman declined to enforce the follow-on, and later the manager explained that several of the team were stiff.

Badcock and Barnett opened with a stand of 206 in 150 minutes. The captain did not bat. Eight bowlers were used and the small crowd barracked at the pointless play. Bradman declared at 4pm, with 75 minutes left, and boos greeted him as he came out to field. Fishlock hit 93 and was caught in the last over of the day. Earlier, Gregory had retired when hit on the head hooking at Waite.

Wednesday's newspapers criticised Bradman's decision and it was fortunate that he had not gone to the wicket himself, so no-one could accuse him of putting more importance on the pursuit of 1,000 runs in May than on playing a game of cricket. He issued a statement to the Press: "It was regrettable that spectators at The Oval disapproved of my action but I feel sure that they would have been more tolerant had they been aware of the true position. I consider it my primary duty to see that the team are at their fittest for the Test Matches." Fleetwood-Smith, McCormick, Waite and McCabe were injured, White recovering from a minor toe operation, O'Reilly had a tooth abscess. Having bowled on Monday, then gone to the Surrey CCC dinner, Bradman did not want his bowlers to have another day in the field and then the possibility of yet another day in the field at Southampton.

Lancashire beat Northants in two days and stayed at the top.

SURREY v AUSTRALIA

Played at The Oval, on May 21, 23, 24, 1938.
Match drawn.

AUSTRALIA

J.H.Fingleton	b Brown	47		
W.A.Brown	c Brooks b Watts	96		
*D.G.Bradman	c Brooks b Watts	143		
C.L.Badcock	c & b Brown	32	(1) c Watts b Gregory	95
A.L.Hassett	c Squires b Berry	98		
A.G.Chipperfield	b Gover	20	(3) c Brooks b Gregory	6
M.G.Waite	c Brooks b Watts	35		
†B.A.Barnett	not out	33	(2) not out	120
E.S.White	b Berry	7	(4) not out	5
F.Ward	b Brown	0		
W.J.O'Reilly	c Brooks b Brown	0		
Extras	(B 8, LB 8. NB 1)	17	(B 4, LB 1, NB 1)	6
Total		528	(2 wickets, declared)	**232**

Fall: 1st inns 1/90, 2/210, 3/290, 4/349, 5/383, 6/460, 7/501, 8/523, 9/528.
2nd inns 1/206, 2/214.

SURREY

R.J.Gregory	c Hassett b O'Reilly	60	retired hurt	5
L.B.Fishlock	st Barnett b O'Reilly	24	c White b Chipperfield	93
H.S.Squires	b O'Reilly	7	not out	4
T.H.Barling	lbw b Ward	67		
*Mr E.R.T.Holmes	c Brown b O'Reilly	10		
Mr H.M.Garland-Wells	c Brown b O'Reilly	2		
Mr F.R.Brown	b O'Reilly	15		
F.Berry	st Barnett b Ward	31		
E.A.Watts	b O'Reilly	22		
†E.W.Brooks	not out	16		
A.R.Gover	b O'Reilly	0		
Extras	(B 8, LB 9)	17	(LB 2)	2
Total		271	(1 wicket)	**104**

Fall: 1st inns 1/54, 2/66, 3/129, 4/140, 5/150, 6/188, 7/206, 8/251, 9/271.
2nd inns 1/104.

SURREY	O	M	R	W	O	M	R	W
Gover	20	4	100	1	6	0	20	0
Watts	23	4	69	3	10	1	47	0
Berry	33	6	92	2	6	3	12	0
Brown	35	0	147	4	5	0	23	0
Squires	20	2	68	0	8	2	29	0
Gregory	9	3	23	0	7	4	10	2
Garland-Wells	3	0	12	0	15	1	62	0
Holmes	-		-	-	4	0	23	0

AUSTRALIA	O	M	R	W	O	M	R	W
Waite	15	3	34	0	7	4	4	0
O'Reilly	36	9	104	8	4	2	12	0
Ward	30	6	96	2	8	1	50	0
White	17	8	20	0	7	1	16	0
Chipperfield	-	-	-	-	3.1	1	20	1

Umpires: E.J.Smith and A.Dolphin.

Bradman edges a ball from Surrey's Alf Gover between first and second slip.

Bradman is out, caught Brooks bowled Watts for an almost faultless 143.

Brooks catches Brown off Watts to make Australia 210 for two against Surrey.

Middlesex were second after beating Notts by an innings and 51 runs at Lord's. Before a 7,000 Saturday crowd, Bill Edrich made 228 not out by the close of play. As the Sunday and Monday newspapers trumpeted, Edrich needed 32 more for his 1,000 runs, but with 19 still needed, he hooked at a ball from Arthur Staples that kept low, and played on. G.O.Allen, making his first appearance of the season, scored 64 runs and took 5-90 in the match. Kent hit 602-7 against Worcestershire but showers helped to prevent a win. Yorkshire slipped further down the table at Leeds, where rain deprived them of a likely victory over Sussex, whose amateur left-hander Hugh Bartlett twice hit three sixes in an over by Verity. Bartlett got to 94 in 75 minutes, then the Yorkshire wicketkeeper, Arthur Wood, told him that it was easy to hit sixes off slow bowlers. Bartlett had a dip at medium-pace Smailes and was caught head-high at long-on. Bill Bowes made his first appearance for Yorkshire, taking 6-39 despite a strapped ankle.

The runners for 1,000 in May were still Edrich (981), Bradman (876) and Hammond (still 781 as Gloucestershire had no match). All had a maximum of four innings left in the month.

In Europe there seemed a slight easing of tension. German troop movements ceased and Henlein had talks with the Czech Prime Minister. There was a general hope that the crisis might pass without conceding Hitler's demands.

May 25 to 27: Bradman Contends Against the Weather

Persistent rain developing into a downpour at lunch time prevented any play at Southampton, where some 2,000 people came into the ground and hundreds more waited outside. The only event to talk about was Bradman's statement about the Surrey match. On Thursday, 2,000 spectators were there at the start but Bradman disappointed them by putting Hampshire in on a soft wicket. McCormick opened with three fast overs off 20 yards, although Arnold hooked him for six. Then O'Reilly effected his usual collapse. He produced a splendid ball for Paris which pitched leg and hit the top of the off, and then beat Crease with the slower ball. Pothecary edged a ball into his face and Walker went forward to take a simple catch. Hampshire lunched at 141-7 and did not tarry long afterwards.

Baring opened the bowling very fast but soon tired, as Brown and Fingleton nudged and glanced their way to 78. Boyes had Brown caught at mid-off (to the relief of all present) and Bradman, whose target was 124, scored one of them by tea. He played himself in, with 10,000 spectators sitting in hushed expectancy, then flashed three leg-side 4's and reached 71 by the close, the score then being 204-1.

Overnight rain made the turf soft but lifeless. Bradman reached his hundred two overs ahead of Fingleton. When he was 109, rain stopped play for half an hour until 12.55pm. Steele and Baring made Bradman fight for every run. Rain returned but the players stayed on. Then a four to leg off Baring and the suspense was over. Bradman declared at the lunch score of 320-1 and no more play took place. It was his second achievement of 1,000 runs before the end of May and the previous in 1930 was also completed in a rain-affected match at Southampton. It was all the more creditable for his having eschewed any contrivance to facilitate the feat. The manager said to the Press: "Bradman is very pleased but he does not talk about himself and has not said very much about it."

His main rivals were not so lucky. After Worcestershire had been bowled out for 83 at Lord's, Edrich faced the South African Test bowler, Crisp, in glorious weather. He drove his second ball hard and Crisp leapt to his left to catch him one-handed. Unfortunately, Middlesex won by an innings and Edrich remained on 981. Hammond was 79 not out at the close on the second day in Gloucestershire's first innings against Surrey, so it was unlikely that the match situation would allow him to score the necessary runs. In the event he was bowled for 113, playing no stroke to Gover, and stuck on 894. Lancashire

HAMPSHIRE v AUSTRALIA

Played at Southampton, on May 25, 26, 27, 1938.
Match drawn.

HAMPSHIRE

†N.T.McCorkell	c Chipperfield b O'Reilly	10
J.Arnold	b O'Reilly	23
*Mr C.G.A.Paris	b O'Reilly	18
W.L.Creese	b O'Reilly	22
Mr R.H.Moore	b Fleetwood-Smith	5
A.E.Pothecary	c Walker b O'Reilly	16
Revd J.W.J.Steele	run out	24
G.Hill	c Fingleton b White	11
G.S.Boyes	c Bradman b O'Reilly	11
Mr A.E.G.Baring	b White	0
G.E.M.Heath	not out	4
Extras	(B 9, LB 2, NB 2)	13
Total		**157**

Fall: 1st inns 1/27, 2/47, 3/66, 4/77, 5/85, 6/110, 7/141, 8/141, 9/144.

AUSTRALIA

J.H.Fingleton	not out	123
W.A.Brown	c Pothecary b Boyes	47
*D.G.Bradman	not out	145
Extras	(B 4, LB 1)	5
Total	(1 wicket, declared)	**320**

Fall: 1st inns 1/78.

A.L.Hassett, A.G.Chipperfield, E.S.White, W.J.O'Reilly, E.L.McCormick, S.J.McCabe, †C.W.Walker and L.O'B Fleetwood-Smith did not bat.

AUSTRALIA	O	M	R	W
McCormick	3	1	16	0
McCabe	3	0	9	0
O'Reilly	20.5	0	65	6
White	11	3	19	2
Fleetwood-Smith	9	0	35	1

HAMPSHIRE	O	M	R	W
Baring	20	2	97	0
Heath	16	1	54	0
Steele	15	2	60	0
Boyes	17	5	39	1
Hill	19	4	45	0
Creese	9	5	20	0

Umpires: W.Reeves and E.J.Smith.

consolidated their lead with a win by nine wickets over Derbyshire at Ilkeston, needing 107 to win. Paynter was hit on the chin by Copson but carried on.

May 28 to 31: Last Chance for Edrich

The next match, against Middlesex, was a matter for great anticipation. They were Championship runners-up in 1937 and currently second in the table, the strongest opposition that the Australians had faced so far and with two candidates for the England captaincy, Allen and Robins. Edrich was on the threshold of a great achievement. The England captain and team for the First Test team were to be selected within the week.

Unfortunately, Saturday was a wash-out; play was abandoned at 2pm without the teams being chosen. 'Gubby' Allen retired to bed with back trouble but hoped to be fit for Monday (which he wasn't). The teams for the England v The Rest trial match were announced: Hammond was made captain of the England XI. Allen was to skipper The Rest, and expressed himself surprised not to be captain of the England XI. The grievance seems hard to justify: he had not played regularly, nor in any Test since leading the tour to Australia in 1936-7; it was reasonable to give Hammond a trial as captain (he was not captain of his county) and England's premier batsman could hardly be picked to play for The Rest. The most surprising omission from the trial teams was Maurice Leyland and it was a pity not to see Gregory of Surrey or Fagg of Kent given a chance.

Back at Lord's there was continuous rain on Sunday, but play began promptly at 11.30am on Monday. The sun was shining as 'Big Jim' Smith ran in from the Pavilion End. His sixth ball came back to take the off-stump, Fingleton playing no stroke. The pitch was soft and made wetter by a 15-minute stoppage for rain. Bradman looked uneasy. He was dropped by Human at long leg, then skied a catch off Nevell, which Denis Compton ran back from first slip to take. Badcock holed out to long leg. More rain before lunch and the afternoon session was wiped out.

McCabe played on to his leg stump, and William Nevell, a 21-year-old fast-medium bowler who was not a regular first XI player, had 3-22. Hassett and Chipperfield made 54 in 35 minutes and McCormick lofted a full toss by Robins into the Mound Stand. Otherwise the Australian attempt to force the pace on a difficult wicket was a complete failure and they were all out for 132.

From the shadow of the Pavilion, McCormick ran in from 20 yards with six men behind the bat. He bowled three no-balls but got Price lbw with a half-volley and Webster went to a good wide off-side catch by Walker. Edrich was bowled through the gate by O'Reilly and was still ten runs adrift of the magic target. The day finished at 49-4.

MIDDLESEX v AUSTRALIA

Played at Lord's, on May 28, 30, 31, 1938.
Match drawn.

AUSTRALIA

J.H.Fingleton	b Smith	2	c Edrich b Smith	32
C.L.Badcock	c Human b Nevell	10	b Nevell	0
*D.G.Bradman	c Compton b Nevell	5	not out	30
S.J.McCabe	b Nevell	9	not out	48
A.L.Hassett	lbw b Sims	27		
A.G.Chipperfield	c Compton b Robins	36		
M.G.Waite	b Sims	8		
†C.W.Walker	not out	4		
W.J.O'Reilly	lbw b Robins	0		
E.L.McCormick	c Smith b Sims	12		
L.O'B.Fleetwood-Smith	st Price b Sims	10		
Extras	(B 2, LB 6, NB 1)	9	W	4
Total		**132**	(2 wickets, declared)	**114**

Fall: 1st inns 1/2, 2/16, 3/22, 4/34, 5/88, 6/106, 7/106, 8/106, 9/119.
2nd inns 1/0, 2/52.

MIDDLESEX

W.J.Edrich	b O'Reilly	9	not out	20
†W.F.Price	lbw b McCormick	1		
Mr W.H.Webster	c Walker b McCormick	0		
D.C.S.Compton	b O'Reilly	65	(2) not out	1
J.H.A.Hulme	b O'Reilly	4		
Mr J.H.Human	b O'Reilly	24		
*Mr R.W.V.Robins	b McCormick	43		
J.M.Sims	lbw b McCormick	0		
C.I.J.Smith	c Fingleton b McCormick	11		
W.Nevell	b McCormick	0		
J.A.Young	not out	4		
Extras	(B 20, LB 3, NB 4)	27		
Total		**188**	(No wicket)	**21**

Fall: 1st inns 1/16, 2/16, 3/16, 4/35, 5/92, 6/160, 7/161, 8/175, 9/175.

MIDDLESEX	O	M	R	W	O	M	R	W
Smith	15	5	23	1	12	4	26	1
Nevell	12	1	38	3	7	2	16	1
Young	4	1	10	0	5	2	7	0
Sims	7.3	0	25	4	5	0	23	0
Robins	6	1	27	2	4	0	10	0
Human	-	-	-	-	2	0	14	0
Compton	-	-	-	-	4	1	14	0

AUSTRALIA	O	M	R	W	O	M	R	W
McCormick	15	3	58	6				
O'Reilly	19.2	5	56	4				
McCabe	7	4	16	0	3	1	7	0
Waite	12	2	31	0	3	0	14	0

Umpires: F.Chester and F.Walden.

On Tuesday morning, Compton played patiently through the gloom and drizzle. Human lofted O'Reilly straight into the Pavilion and Robins swung him for two sixes into the Mound Stand, which set O'Reilly complaining about the wicket being pitched too far over to the south side of the ground. McCormick beat Robins for pace and got Sims lbw with a full toss on the toe. Smith hit two big drives, then another went sailing over Fingleton's head at wide long off; he stretched both hands up, stopped it and caught it as it dropped. McCormick yorked Nevell and, on his hat-trick, bowled — a no-ball. Compton was last out after two and a half hours. McCormick had his best performance of the tour, though he bowled seven no-balls, some called by umpire Chester for straddling the return crease.

Australia batted again at 2.45pm and with play due to finish at 5.30pm or 6pm, Bill Edrich could wave farewell to his chance of 1,000 runs and immortality. Nevell bowled Badcock, pulling, and twice beat Bradman in an over. Edrich made a memorable catch diving at second slip to his left to dismiss Fingleton.

Then, at 5.10pm. something odd happened. Bradman declared and the crowd booed him as they thought it was a device to finish the match early. In fact he did so solely in order to enable Edrich to have one final chance at the record. The youngster was amazed and felt scarcely worthy of the favour granted by such an illustrious man. It brought life to a match dying in the gathering gloom. As Edrich took guard, Bradman said to him: "We're not going to give them to you, Bill." However, Edrich hit three 4's and the object desired by all was achieved.

The County Championship programme had been destroyed by the weather. Six of the eight matches reached no decision and did not count. There was one result at Frome. Northamptonshire, without a point in the season and without a win since 1935, nearly stole victory. Somerset needed 61 to win, collapsed to 30 for 5, but Lyon pulled them through. At Bristol, a subdued Hammond made 57 on the first day against Warwickshire and rain prevented a second innings, so he fell short of 1,000 runs in May by 49. In that match, Tom Goddard, England's foremost off-spinner, fractured a thumb and was expected to be out for a month. Not a ball was bowled at Chesterfield. At Trent Bridge, Saturday 28 May was blank, and there were only 20 witnesses to the unfurling of a new flag by the High Sheriff of Nottingham, exactly 100 years after William Clarke had started the first cricket there.

The Sudetenland crisis seemed to be passing over, with talks continuing, Czech reservists discharged and little trouble at municipal elections. But there were grim reminders of war elsewhere: 200 killed in bombing of Catalonia as the Spanish Civil War raged on, Canton bombed by the Japanese, and a trial black-out in the Southend area.

The First Test

NOW that June had arrived in almost autumnal weather, thoughts were turned to the main business of the summer, and in particular, who would lead England into it.

June 1 to 3: Howling June

There was no play on Wednesday, Derby Day, at Bristol, where the wicket was very slippery. Bradman felt a twinge in his back and took a taxi to London for an examination, which gave him the opportunity to watch play in the Test Trial match at Lord's.

On Thursday at 12.15pm, play started on a saturated saw-dusted wicket and McCabe wisely allowed McCormick only four overs. The likely England opener, Charles Barnett, looked uncomfortable. Gloucestershire were 61-2 at lunch but were all out half an hour after it, all leaden feet against O'Reilly, who in that time took 3.5-1-3-5. Brown and Badcock opened with 47 in an hour, which caused some ironic cheering, then off-spinner Reg Sinfield broke through to make it 57-2 at tea. Rain delayed the restart and eased the wicket, but the Australians still showed their obvious dislike of such pitches, exploited by Sinfield and his leg-trap, and by Cranfield, also an off-spinner. Parker and Basil Allen held excellent catches.

The tourists were all out early on Friday for 164. In the Gloucestershire second innings only Allen showed any confidence against O'Reilly, hitting, in all, six 4's off him, until he was caught off the splice at mid-wicket. Sinfield edged a three through the slips to make Australia bat again, but Gloucestershire were 96-8 at lunch and the match was over by 3pm.

The Test Trial at Lord's was spoilt by the sort of weather that would not have graced the Shetland Islands. On the eve of the match, Gubby Allen dropped out with a strained back. Morris Nichols of Essex replaced him in The Rest team and D.R.Wilcox, the Essex schoolmaster, took over as captain. On the first day, The Rest scored 180-5 on a dead wicket before rain stopped play. Fishlock of Surrey

GLOUCESTERSHIRE v AUSTRALIA

Played at Bristol, on June 1, 2, 3, 1938.
Australia won by ten wickets.

GLOUCESTERSHIRE

*Mr B.O.Allen	lbw b O'Reilly	41	c McCabe b O'Reilly	42
C.J.Barnett	lbw b O'Reilly	15	c Fleetwood-Smith b McCormick	1
G.M.Emmett	b Fleetwood-Smith	0	lbw b Fleetwood-Smith	6
Mr B.H.Lyon	b O'Reilly	5	b Fleetwood-Smith	4
J.F.Crapp	c Fleetwood-Smith b O'Reilly	0	st Barnett b O'Reilly	4
W.L.Neale	b Fleetwood-Smith	0	c Hassett b O'Reilly	20
Mr G.W.Parker	c Waite b O'Reilly	0	b Fleetwood-Smith	0
R.A.Sinfield	lbw b Fleetwood-Smith	0	c Chipperfield b O'Reilly	8
†E.A.Wilson	not out	3	b Fleetwood-Smith	2
L.M.Cranfield	run out	3	not out	8
Mr C.Tyler	st Barnett b O'Reilly	0	b O'Reilly	2
Extras	(B 3, LB 8)	11	(B 6, LB 4)	10
Total		**78**		**107**

Fall: 1st inns 1/49, 2/49, 3/66, 4/66, 5/69, 6/69, 7/70, 8/70, 9/78.
2nd inns 1/2, 2/15, 3/19, 4/24, 5/79, 6/79, 7/79, 8/85, 9/103.

AUSTRALIA

W.A.Brown	c Crapp b Sinfield	18		
C.L.Badcock	c Parker b Sinfield	51		
*S.J.McCabe	b Sinfield	0		
A.L.Hassett	c Allen b Sinfield	29		
A.G.Chipperfield	hit wkt b Cranfield	9		
M.G.Waite	c Neale b Sinfield	6	(1) not out	18
†B.A.Barnett	c Emmett b Sinfield	8		
F.Ward	c Lyon b Sinfield	1	(2) not out	7
W.J.O'Reilly	c Barnett b Sinfield	23		
E.L.McCormick	not out	0		
L.O'B.Fleetwood-Smith	b Tyler	3		
Extras	(B 12, LB 4)	16		
Total		**164**	(No wicket)	**25**

Fall: 1st inns 1/47, 2/47, 3/100, 4/111, 5/123, 6/137, 7/151, 8/161, 9/161.

AUSTRALIA	O	M	R	W	O	M	R	W
McCormick	4	1	10	0	3	0	9	1
Waite	5	4	3	0	2	1	4	0
O'Reilly	12.5	4	22	6	15	2	45	5
Fleetwood-Smith	11	0	32	3	15	4	39	4

GLOUCESTERSHIRE	O	M	R	W	O	M	R	W
Barnett	7	4	9	0				
Lyon	3	2	4	0	5	2	6	0
Sinfield	30	8	65	8				
Tyler	8.2	3	20	1				
Cranfield	18	3	50	1				
Allen					4.4	1	19	0

Umpires: W.Reeves and E.Robinson.

ENGLAND v THE REST (Test Trial Match)

Played at Lord's, on June 1, 2, 3, 1938.
Match drawn.

THE REST

*Mr D.R.Wilcox	c Ames b Verity	20	b Farnes	0
L.B.Fishlock	c Hutton b Farnes	2	not out	109
E.Paynter	c Edrich b Verity	79	lbw b Smith	1
Mr N.W.D.Yardley	c Ames b Farnes	31	b Farnes	28
H.E.Dollery	c Hutton b Brown	25	not out	40
Jas.Langridge	c Compton b Hammond	14		
M.S.Nichols	lbw b Smith	32		
G.H.Pope	not out	47		
†W.Farrimond	b Verity	16		
D.V.P.Wright	b Verity	7		
R.Pollard	c Verity b Farnes	4		
Extras	(B 10, LB 10, NB 1)	21	(B 5, LB 5)	10
Total		**298**	(3 wickets)	**188**

Fall: 1st inns 1/11, 2/31, 3/100, 4/161, 5/174, 6/218, 7/222, 8/267, 9/289.
2nd inns 1/0, 2/1, 3/86.

ENGLAND

L.Hutton	c Wilcox b Wright	40
W.J.Edrich	c Wilcox b Wright	80
Mr R.E.S.Wyatt	c Pollard b Pope	24
*Mr W.R.Hammond	b Pollard	107
D.C.S.Compton	c Farrimond b Pope	14
J.Hardstaff	b Pollard	35
†L.E.G.Ames	b Pollard	0
Mr F.R.Brown	b Pollard	0
H.Verity	c Pope b Pollard	29
C.I.J.Smith	not out	21
Mr K.Farnes	c Paynter b Wright	4
Extras	(B 5, LB 11, W 1, NB 6)	23
Total		**377**

Fall: 1st inns 1/113, 2/140, 3/169, 4/190, 5/249, 6/249, 7/249, 8/352, 9/352.

ENGLAND	O	M	R	W	O	M	R	W
Farnes	23.3	7	51	3	9	2	19	2
Smith	22	5	58	1	14	7	14	1
Verity	34	14	71	4	9	2	39	0
Hammond	19	6	29	1	3	2	2	0
Brown	16	1	68	1	12	1	59	0
Compton	-	-	-	-	4	0	33	0
Hutton	-	-	-	-	6	1	12	0

THE REST	O	M	R	W
Nichols	35	9	89	0
Pollard	25	9	57	5
Pope	27	11	57	2
Wright	37.3	9	135	3
Langridge	3	0	16	0

Umpires: F.Chester and J.Newman

was soon caught at short leg off Farnes. Wilcox batted well until he cut at a wide ball. Hammond dropped Yardley, who seemed inhibited by the occasion, at slip. Smith dropped a sitter off Paynter. Paynter drove and pulled well for 160 minutes until he was caught at cover. Farnes bowled well but Brown and Verity made no great impact.

On Thursday, Verity bowled with three short legs and no slip, although the ball was turning. Nichols made one big hit to long on and the game was held up until the ball was found. George Pope hit one six in a patchy innings.

For the England XI, Hutton and Edrich made a successful opening pair, scoring 113, with Edrich playing the aggressive hand. Wilcox dropped Wyatt but took a good catch to dismiss Edrich. Compton fell to very good catch down the leg-side by Farrimond, the Lancashire wicketkeeper, and the England XI ended Thursday on 204-4. On Friday, the sun shone and Hammond celebrated some good news with a century, although it took four hours and he was dropped four times and gave a stumping chance. Pollard was rewarded for his worthy toil when he bowled Hardstaff, Ames and Brown with the first, second and fourth balls of an over. The Rest batted again at 3.15pm with no prospect of a result. Fishlock got some practice and reached 100 in two and a half hours. He was severe on his county colleague, Brown, who bowled too short, and on Compton and Hutton.

The trial match was of little help to the selectors, although Paynter and Edrich probably sealed their Test places. The chairman of the selectors, Sir Pelham Warner, was very impressed by the leg-spin of Wright, whose figures were not pretty to look at but who had four catches and a stumping missed off him. It was that sort of match.

There was snow in the Lake District and gales across southern England. An overnight storm blew over tents at Southend and tore up the wicket end covers, and the Essex and Worcestershire teams had to lunch in the town. Three days' play there produced receipts of £35. There was no decision between Lancashire and Sussex at Preston, where George Duckworth came in to replace Farrimond behind the stumps. Sure enough he made his presence felt. When John Langridge stepped out to drive the leg-spinner Wilkinson, then changed his stroke and played the ball a foot away, 'Duckie' came around and scooped up the ball, broke the wicket and ran Langridge out. Oxford University beat Middlesex by two wickets. Lancashire lead the county table an average of 10.28 points from seven matches, Middlesex were second with 9.60 from five, Yorkshire fifth with 6.40 from five.

The Selectors' Dilemma

The good news for Walter Hammond was the announcement on

Thursday, 2 June that he was to be England captain in the First Test. In the end it was no surprise. Walter Robins was in theory the captain in situ, but he was not of proven Test class as a player and he did not do enough for MCC against the Australians to advance his claims. Gubby Allen was out of practice and not fully fit. Bob Wyatt's selection would have required negotiation with the *Daily Mail* and he, too, was not an automatic selection as a player. Brian Sellers, a member of the selection committee, was an outstanding county captain but not a top-class player. Kenneth Farnes was just starting his season, had no captaincy experience and, as a fast bowler, would not commend himself for the role. Hammond was the best batsman in England, a good tactician in leading The Players in previous summers against The Gentlemen, and was now a genuine amateur. He was certainly the public's choice and probably that of the cricketers.

The following day, in consultation with the new captain, the selectors announced the 13 names for the Test. Wyatt was regarded as unavailable, but kept in mind for later Tests, Leyland was considered unfit (although playing for Yorkshire), and bowlers, G.O.Allen, Bowes, Voce and Goddard, were also adjudged unfit. Harold Gimblett, the aggressive Somerset opening bat, was not considered due to lack of form. The 13, in approximate batting order, were:

L.Hutton (Yorkshire)
C.J.Barnett (Gloucestershire)
W.J.Edrich (Middlesex)
Mr.W.R.Hammond
(Gloucestershire, capt).
E.Paynter (Lancashire)
D.C.S.Compton (Middlesex)
J.Hardstaff (Notts)
L.E.G.Ames (Kent, wicketkeeper)
Mr.J.C.Clay (Glamorgan)
G.H.Pope (Derbyshire)
H.Verity (Yorkshire)
D.V.P.Wright (Kent)
Mr.K.Farnes (Essex)

Hutton was an automatic choice, with 773 runs (av.77.30) so far in the season. Barnett was of proven class, although not in great form. Edrich had 1,090 runs (av.83.84), and Hammond had missed the 1,000 runs in May but now had 1,058 (av.81.38). Paynter, with 652 runs (av.54.33), was assured of selection because Hammond insisted on him as a counter to O'Reilly. Compton had scored 756 runs (av.58.15); Hardstaff 371 (av.53.00); Ames 288 (av.57.60). Clay was the surprise choice, coming from an unfashionable county, having taken 23 wickets (av.13.65). So also was George Pope, with 30 wickets (av.19.30). Verity was an automatic choice with 45 wickets (av.16.85). Wright, who had 27 wickets (av.22.48), had done well in the Test Trial. Farnes had been teaching at his school throughout May and the Test Trial was his first match, but he was now available for the rest of the season. It was a versatile 'squad', with eight batsmen, four pace bowlers, and three spinners.

Kent wicketkeeper Leslie Ames, named for the First Test at Trent Bridge.

June 4 to 7: Summer Arrives for Whitsun

On the advice of an Australian doctor, Bradman rested from the match against Essex, to ensure that his back recovered fully before the Test. At last the good weather returned to Southend and it was sunny with a fresh wind. Some 8,000 people saw the Australian batting machine falter again. At lunch they were 100-5, Farnes taking 3-19. Only Brown, who was dropped when seven, could stay. After lunch, Farnes got some unexpected bounce and Waite was hit above the left ear, but carried on after a brief stoppage. The leg-spinner, Peter Smith, finished the innings with two return catches, one low, one high. The Australian wrist-spinners saved them the indignity of a first-innings deficit, although Wilcox stayed for two hours. Ward took a wicket with his first ball and finished off the innings with three in three balls, not a hat-trick because the middle one was a run out.

Fingleton had pulled a muscle but recovered on Sunday and on Whit Monday 1938, a record Essex crowd of 12,500 packed into the Southend ground. The nightwatchmen, Ward and Walker, added 42 for the first wicket. Nichols, with the help of the sea breeze, swung the ball and bowled fast. The Australians collapsed again to 108-6 at lunch, only 139 ahead. But then Stan McCabe made a much-needed return to form on the dusty wicket, with 50 in 75 minutes. Essex went in again at 3.10pm, needing 185 to win in a day and a half. Eastman spooned a catch to square leg off his first ball and Tom Pearce was promoted to force the pace. Pearce took 11 off one over by Waite. Wilcox drove Ward almost for six, then was stumped. Pearce was lbw and Nichols was bowled: 56-4 at tea. After tea, O'Connor was caught at mid-on and Dennis edged a leg-break to first slip. The last four wickets fell for four runs and Essex were all out in 90 minutes. During the innings, Walker retired from the field and Fingleton took over the gloves.

The Whitsun holiday round of eight Championship matches took place in excellent weather, temperatures reaching 70°F in the south of England. On Saturday morning, 4,500 cars per hour were counted driving out of London on the Great Western Road. But 16,000 people were left to go to Lord's, where in wicketkeeper Fred Price's benefit match, Middlesex scored 572-8 in six hours against Sussex. Jack Robertson, on his Championship debut, made 81 and Robins scored 137 in only two hours. Jim Smith came in at 6.10pm; by the close 20 minutes later, he had 68 on the board, with six 6's and two 4's, all well-timed shots and no slogging. Middlesex went on to win by ten wickets and moved to the top of the table. Leicestershire beat Northants in two days and found themselves, amazingly, second. At Derby's County Ground, Warwickshire, needing 311 to win, were 39-5, with Wyatt bagging a 'pair', then Tom Dollery and John Buckingham put on 220 in 155 minutes to achieve an extraordinary four-wicket triumph.

ESSEX v AUSTRALIA

Played at Southend, on June 4, 6, 1938.
Australia won by 97 runs.

AUSTRALIA

J.H.Fingleton	b Farnes	7	(4) c Wade b Nichols	1
W.A.Brown	hit wkt b Smith	55	(3) lbw b Smith	15
*S.J.McCabe	c Wilcox b Stephenson	4	(7) c Wilcox b Nichols	50
C.L.Badcock	b Nichols	11	(5) lbw b Nichols	23
A.L.Hassett	b Farnes	26	(6) c Dennis b Farnes	4
A.G.Chipperfield	b Farnes	3	(8) b Nichols	3
M.G.Waite	c Pearce b Stephenson	5	(9) c Wade b Nichols	0
E.S.White	b Farnes	11	(10) not out	7
†C.W.Walker	c & b Smith	5	(1) b Nichols	18
F.Ward	not out	5	(2) b Smith	23
L.O'B.Fleetwood-Smith	c & b Smith	8	c Wade b Stephenson	0
Extras	(B 1, LB 4)	5	(B 4, LB 5)	9
Total		145		153

Fall: 1st inns 1/14, 2/25, 3/52, 4/92, 5/100, 6/105, 7/126, 8/128, 9/133.
2nd inns 1/42, 2/42, 3/46, 4/68, 5/75, 6/88, 7/114, 8/130, 9/151.

ESSEX

*Mr D.R.Wilcox	b Ward	38	st Walker b Ward	20
L.C.Eastman	lbw b Ward	21	c Brown b Waite	0
M.S.Nichols	b Ward	5	(5) b Ward	1
J.O'Connor	c Chipperfield b Fleetwood-Smith	6	c White b Ward	14
Mr T.N.Pearce	b Fleetwood-Smith	0	(3) lbw b Fleetwood-Smith	23
Mr C.T.Ashton	c & b Ward	8	c McCabe b Fleetwood-Smith	17
Mr J.N.Dennis	c & b Ward	18	c Chipperfield b Fleetwood-Smith	6
T.P.B.Smith	lbw b Ward	10	not out	1
†T.H.Wade	run out	3	b Ward	0
Capt J.W.A.Stephenson	not out	0	lbw b Fleetwood-Smith	1
Mr K.Farnes	c Waite b Ward	0	c sub b Fleetwood-Smith	0
Extras	(LB 5)	5	(B 2, LB 1, W 1)	4
Total		114		87

Fall: 1st inns 1/27, 2/33, 3/44, 4/44, 5/53, 6/98, 7/101, 8/114, 9/114.
2nd inns 1/0, 2/32, 3/52, 4/56, 5/67, 6/80, 7/83, 8/85, 9/86.

ESSEX	O	M	R	W	O	M	R	W
Farnes	21	7	43	4	13	5	24	1
Nichols	16	5	34	1	18	8	25	6
Stephenson	10	3	20	2	9.4	1	36	1
Eastman	5	1	18	0				
Smith	9.5	2	25	3	19	3	59	2

AUSTRALIA	O	M	R	W	O	M	R	W
Waite	6	1	17	0	6	1	21	1
McCabe	5	0	9	0	3	1	8	0
Ward	23.3	6	51	7	14	6	26	4
Fleetwood-Smith	13	8	17	2	11.4	5	28	5
White	10	3	15	0				

Umpires: G.M.Lee and E.Cooke.

At Trent Bridge, Surrey left Notts to score 275 to win. Joe Hardstaff had injured his left forearm with a spanner (thus dropping out of the Test team) and hoped not to bat. Notts were 194-4 at lunch but then collapsed and Hardstaff had to come in at No.11 with 17 needed. Alf Gover bowled him for 0.

The Roses Match at Park Avenue, Bradford, was a classic of its kind. On Saturday, Lancashire scored 232 in 122 overs. "I have seldom suffered tedium as dreadful as this," wrote Cardus. In the 13,000 crowd, the cloth-capped and scarved regulars, huddled under the stands to avoid the sun, no doubt reflected that they were not there to enjoy themselves. Nutter took two and a half hours for 45, Farrimond an hour over eight runs. The bowling got slower and slower. Some 20,000 people returned on Monday when Yorkshire busied themselves towards a first-innings lead of 41. At lunch on Tuesday, Lancashire were 79 ahead with six wickets left, the match drifting to stalemate. But 45 minutes later they were all out and Yorkshire won by eight wickets. For the Bradford crowd the suffering had been vindicated in ultimate triumph. Lancashire dropped to third place, Yorkshire moved up to fourth.

The local contest between Somerset and Gloucestershire at Taunton was something of a contrast. On the third morning Hammond reached 140 not out in 270 minutes and Somerset were left to get 284. Arthur Wellard entered the fray at 172-7, with 65 minutes left, and hit 68 in 40 minutes with six 6's. Now 30 were needed in 25 minutes. Sinfield started the last over at 276-9. Walter Luckes drove a four, then swung again. Jack Crapp ran in from long on to catch the ball but it dropped just in front of him and bounced on to the boundary. The Somerset supporters rushed on and shouldered Luckes to the pavilion.

June 8 to 10: Preparing for Battle

The build-up to the First Test favoured Australian hopes, first because injuries dogged the England ranks, second because the weather promised to be fine and dry. J.C.Clay dropped out on Monday, 6 June and R.A.Sinfield (Gloucestershire) replaced him. Sinfield had taken 8-65 with his off-breaks for the county against the tourists just a week before. On Tuesday, Joe Hardstaff had injured his forearm with a spanner whilst working on his car at home. Oddly, the year before a beam in his garage fell on him and hurt his nose but did not stop him playing in the Lord's Test against New Zealand. But this time, Mr.N.W.D.Yardley (Cambridge University & Yorkshire) became the 15th name to be called up for this Test. He had batted quite well for the University against the Australians and in the Test Trial. On arrival at Nottingham, Yardley was met by Sir Pelham Warner and taken to the Victoria Hotel. In his autobiography, Yardley recalled, "When I met the players they all looked disgustingly healthy and my hopes sank."

For Australia, the reserve wicketkeeper Walker was found to have fractured a finger on his left hand at Southend and would be out for some time. There was better news of Barnes, whose wrist was out of plaster. Bradman, Hassett, Badcock, Fingleton, Brown and Barnett had all scored heavily. McCabe was averaging only 33.44, but he came good at Southend. McCormick had 23 wickets, the spinners Fleetwood-Smith, O'Reilly and Ward all had over 40.

Lord Hawke, who had said at the Yorkshire annual meeting in 1924 that he prayed no professional would ever captain England, returned his tickets for the Test and had to issue a statement denying that it had anything to do with Hammond's appointment.

On Thursday, the Australians arrived early for practice and 500 people, paying 6d each, watched them. A few England players practised. Both teams were staying in the Victoria Hotel and Bradman and Hammond dined together and signed the menus for the staff. Compton and Edrich arrived after a four-hour train journey from London. Denis Compton later recalled walking into the dining room to be welcomed by Don Bradman and being taken aside for a couple of hours' chat with O'Reilly and Fleetwood-Smith about cricket in Australia, retiring to bed at 10pm. The Trent Bridge groundsman pronounced the wicket to be fast and the weather promised to be fair with the possibility of very localised showers.

The round of Championship matches which ended on the first day of the Test produced one vintage game at Manchester. It started with 78 in 95 minutes by Frank Woolley and ended with Lancashire, chasing 266 in 160 minutes, winning by two wickets with four minutes to spare. Middlesex beat Hampshire to stay at the top. Northamptonshire lost their fifth match out of five. Yorkshire obtained a first-innings lead of 374 on their way to beating Warwickshire. Meanwhile, the Sudeten Germans resumed their demands for autonomy and two British ships were sunk in Spanish ports by General Franco's fascist air force.

Friday 10 June: Youth and Enterprise Have Their Day

After a fried breakfast the England party went to the Trent Bridge ground by taxi. Crowds cheered their arrival and there were telegrams in the dressing-room. There was a sharp shower just before the wicket was uncovered at 10am and the England team was announced with Yardley made 12th man and Pope left out. Yardley spent the day answering letters for Walter Hammond and even sometimes forging his signature from a specimen provided. Doug Wright was so surprised when Mr Perrin told him he was in the England side that he had a nose bleed.

The Australian team was much as expected, the only surprise being

Crowds flock over the River Trent to see the First Test of the 1938 series at Nottingham.

that a third spinner, Ward, was preferred to Waite, who became 12th man. So each team had only one specialist pace bowler. Bradman's biographer, Michael Page, has revealed that Bradman did not want the third spinner and was overruled by the other selectors.

At 10.55am, Hammond and Bradman went out, Hammond spun a half-crown; Bradman called heads, the coin came down tails and Hammond had no hesitation in batting. At 11.25am, Howard Marshall came on the air for the first stint of what was to be 65 minutes of radio commentary during the day on BBC regional and national programmes.

At 11.30am, Hutton and Charlie Barnett emerged to resume their opening partnership begun a year before against New Zealand. It was a sunny day with the temperature in the low 60s, and the ground was beginning to fill up. McCormick bowled the first over and started well, as was his wont. With his sixth ball Barnett edged to the left hand of Brown at gully and the chance went down. O'Reilly (a leg-spinner!) shared the new ball.

In McCormick's second over, Hutton played dead bat to a shortish delivery and although the pace of the ball took it back on to the stumps, neither bail was disturbed. Umpire Chester inspected the wicket thoroughly because under the Laws of Cricket rules 20 and 21, the wicket was 'down' if either bail was disturbed from its original

With only one run to his name, Hutton turns to see the ball strike his wicket. But the bails were not dislodged and the England opener went on to make 100.

position on top of the stumps. McCabe bowled an over to allow the openers to change ends, and the tension eased as Barnett began to find his shots. He hit 11 off Fleetwood-Smith's first over, assisted by a full toss and a long hop. When he was 38, he gave that bowler a hot, high return chance which went on for four runs. Barnett reached 50 out of 69 in an hour then drove a full toss off O'Reilly which Bradman at mid-off ran to catch but could not hold.

Black clouds and distant thunder quietened the scoring now. Hutton had hardly been noticed so far, but he was putting a steady bat to all that was offered to him. At 1.10pm he reached his 50 with a square cut for four off Ward.

Barnett, meanwhile, strode masterfully into the 90s. He was 98 when O'Reilly began the last over before lunch to Hutton. Barnett told his young partner not to worry about the century, just play out the over, and Hutton hit a four but could not get a single to give Barnett the strike. England lunched at 169 for no wicket.

Off the first ball after lunch, Barnett cut Ward through the covers for his century. Clouds elbowed out the blue skies and a thundery shower stopped play for ten minutes. When play resumed, O'Reilly made another effort to rally the forces and beat both batsmen. But, with the new ball, it was McCormick who broke through, bowling Barnett with a good length ball. He thus left the wicket at 3.17pm, having scored 126 out of 219 in 172 minutes, with 18 4's. Barnett took risks, giving chances at 3, 38 and 51, but he had set the Australians back on their heels. Incredibly, it was England's first-ever home double century opening stand against Australia. Hutton then needed 17 for his century and half an hour later he moved from 96 with a drive for four off a Fleetwood-Smith full toss. He had made hardly an error in 200 minutes and hit 14 4's, a good effort in his first-ever sight of an Australian attack (which, to be honest, was not at its most accurate). Next ball he was out to a rather poor sweep shot.

Edrich had played confidently for half an hour, driving O'Reilly for four, until he unluckily glanced O'Reilly's faster ball on to his foot, whence it made its way to the stumps. So at 3.50pm in the high afternoon, the intiative seemed back with Australia. And there it stayed as Hammond and Paynter played carefully through to 4.30pm and tea, when the score was 274-3. England had thus scored 169-0 in 120 minutes before lunch; 125-3 in 125 minutes after it.

Hammond was just getting into the mood when, at 5pm, O'Reilly drew him forward and squeezed a flighted inswinger past his bat. At 281-4 England were not yet safe. Compton stepped nervously out to the middle and heard O'Reilly say, "Best of luck, Denis, but I'll be trying to send you back quickly." (Or words to that effect). His first ball pitched middle and turned away and Compton edged it just short of first slip. Ben Barnett behind the stumps declaimed, "My

Charlie Barnett reaches his century off the first ball after lunch. He and Hutton put on 219 for the first wicket, a record opening partnership for England against Australia in England.

Bill O'Reilly bowling in the First Test. He took the wickets of Edrich, Hammond and Sinfield.

heavens, that turned." But thereafter, young Denis brought a breath of fresh air to the England batting and touched Paynter with his bravado. In the last 90 minutes they added 141 runs, Compton scoring 69 with 11 4's. He constantly pierced O'Reilly's leg-side field with cheeky pushes, and drove Fleetwood-Smith through the off. Paynter slashed hard and often through the close-set off-side field and brought the spectators to their feet with a six into the pavilion off Ward. The last ball of the day gave England four overthrows.

To sum up that first day, England had triumphed with 422-4 (Paynter 75 not out, Compton 69 not out) in 345 minutes off 125 overs. O'Reilly never gave up and had the best figures: 38-8-106-2. McCormick was steady and not too expensive. Ward had the worst return: 24-2-108-0. Cardus said that 'his length was frequently so short that the ball appeared to reach the batsman under protest'. All in all, those old friends of the batsman, the full-toss and the long-hop, abided benevolently at Trent Bridge and the England players made them welcome. The Australian fielding flagged occasionally, but did not deteriorate during the day. The attendance was 18,100, of whom 10,100 paid on the day (£1,406 5s).

That evening some members of both teams went to the Palais de Danse where a clock was presented to the Australian manager to mark the fact that he had emigrated from Nottingham to Australia at the age of two.

Saturday 11 June: Young Denis Learns a Lesson

With a similar forecast for the weather, queues started before midnight. Before the England players went out to practice, greeted by a burst of sun, Hammond told Compton, "When you get a hundred, make sure that you get two hundred." Fleetwood-Smith bowled the first over, then McCabe and McCormick took the new ball at 425. A mixture of impudent singles and cuts and pulls through the field flustered the fielders. The Australian throwing was loose and once they had to thank umpire Chester for being in the way of a hard throw by Hassett. Paynter drove two 4's through the covers off McCabe and when 88 he charged down the wicket to him and missed, but Barnett fumbled the chance. Paynter reached 100 just after noon, by dint of taking 14 off an over by O'Reilly. Then Compton cut a loose ball from O'Reilly for his first Test century, but at once he swept at Fleetwood-Smith, middled it perhaps too well and Badcock, on the square-leg boundary, caught it. On his debut against Australia, Compton had scored a chanceless 102 in 138 minutes with 15 4's. With the great applause still ringing in his ears, he was greeted by his captain, who said, "You don't do that against Australia. I thought I told you to get 200." A more diplomatic skipper might have waited a few moments before imparting that salutary advice. In any event,

Eddie Paynter returns to the Trent Bridge pavilion after his unbeaten 216, then the highest Test score by an England player against Australia in England.

Compton was the youngest centurion for England against Australia, and the stand of 206 was a fifth-wicket record in Ashes Tests.

Ames started quietly, then began to cover-drive nicely, whilst Paynter carried on. In 55 minutes they added 90. The fielding faltered again. O'Reilly and Fleetwood-Smith were blunted by the unresponsive wicket. Ward came to be the nearest they had to a much-needed stock bowler. Ames missed a rank long-hop and was bowled off his pads. At lunch England were 589-6, Paynter 155 not out. Hammond did not declare, though, and on 163, Paynter gave a very hard chance to short leg, where Fleetwood-Smith got a hand to it. Verity and Sinfield took up little time, and when Wright came in, Paynter was 186.

The Kent spinner's batting was an unknown quantity up north and the crowd cheered his every defensive shot. He scored one in half an hour as Paynter made another 30. The total passed 636, England's highest-ever score against Australia. And Paynter became the highest scorer in a Test in England against Australia. When at last Hammond declared at 3.15pm, Paynter came in to a standing ovation, having scored 216 in 319 minutes with one six, one 5 and 26 4's. He gave chances at 88 and 163, was always dominant and never tired.

The England innings of 658-8 declared had lasted 525 minutes and 188 overs, a rate of 75.19 runs per hour, 3.50 runs per over, with 21.48 overs bowled per hour.

As O'Reilly trudged into the pavilion, Mr.R.G.Menzies, Australia's Attorney-General, said to him rather mischievously: "I always thought you were a spin bowler." O'Reilly responded with a few choice metaphors about the state of the wicket.

Farnes opened the England bowling from the Radcliffe Road End and six runs came from his first over. Then Hammond, from the Pavilion End, bowled a maiden to Brown. After 24 business-like runs in half an hour, Sinfield was on for Hammond, and at 29, Wright replaced Farnes. His first ball was wide and Brown drove it for four. He took a single off the third ball and the fourth was very short: Fingleton tried to force it and edged on to his stumps.

The crowd received Bradman like a gladiator and the sight of him inspired Wright. The Don started as uncertainly as he had ever done on a batsman's wicket. He nearly gave a chance to Farnes at short leg. Then Wright was millimetres away from immortality when he stuck out his right hand to a hard return chance which did not stick. And off the last ball before tea, Ames appealed for a stumping. After tea, Bradman continued to show anxiety against Wright and Sinfield, but he pierced the field a couple of times when Verity came on.

Farnes returned in gloomy light and Bradman, then 47, slashed to gully where Edrich dropped the catch. At 51, Bradman pushed forward defensively at Sinfield. The off-break nipped through to Ames,

Bradman falls to Sinfield, edging the ball into Ames' hands after scoring 51.

Above: Kent's D.V.P.Wright bowling in the First Test. He took five wickets in the match.

Left: Stan McCabe plunders another boundary in his brilliant innings of 232.

who whipped off the bails and appealed to the square-leg umpire who ruled not out; then Ames looked at umpire Chester, who said "Out, caught at the wicket." Sinfield had not appealed at all. Bradman later confirmed that he had got a very thin inside edge and congratulated Chester on his extraordinary perception. The Don had been in 89 minutes and hit five 4's.

So, at 5.55pm, McCabe joined the watchful Brown. The light was no better and Brown had hit three 4's in 150 minutes at the wicket when he snicked Farnes, bowling from the Pavilion End, to be caught by Ames. Nine men crouched around Ward, the night-watchman, but at the close, Australia were 138-3 (McCabe 19 not out, Ward 0 not out) off 61 overs in 165 minutes.

The gates had been closed after lunch on this second day and the attendance was 30,098 — 800 short of the Trent Bridge record set in 1934. Turnstile receipts were £2,698. For the customers it was a day to savour, both because England seemed half-way to victory, and because three new men — Compton, Sinfield and Wright — had done so well.

Sinfield's feat gave pride to one spectator, C.B.Fry, on whose training ship *Mercury* he had once been a crew member. Compton got a telegram from Arsenal FC: 'Well done Denis. Carry on the good work and tell all our Australian friends that you are on the retained list good and firm.' The news from Australia was of all-night radio parties in Sydney, which did nothing to help the fuel shortage caused by very cold weather in New South Wales.

On the Sunday, some of the players went golfing. Eddie Paynter spent the weekend at the home of his old friend from Bodyline days, Bill Voce. The not out batsman, Stan McCabe, out of form and troubled by a series of colds, stayed indoors all day. The forecast for Monday was fair but rather cool.

Monday 13 June: A Legendary Innings

There was another big crowd, although no early queues, and the spectators were entertained by music through a loudspeaker presented by local benefactor Sir Julien Cahn. Before play started, Sid Barnes had some one-handed batting practice, his wrist now out of plaster. The day turned out warm and fine, the temperature passing 70°F.

Farnes and Wright opened. McCabe drove Farnes effortlessly for four but in the Essex amateur's second over, Ward was bowled by a ball that cut away off the pitch and seemed wasted on him. Hassett drove at Wright's quicker leg-break and edged it into Hammond's midriff at first slip. Sinfield and Hammond had a try. McCabe cut wristily for three to reach 50 in 88 minutes. Badcock, never happy, tried to cut a ball too far up, a Wright googly that turned, and played on. At 12.40pm, Australia were 194-6, 464 runs behind.

Then McCabe imperiously hooked Farnes for six to raise the 200, but Hammond kept a spinner at one end and delayed taking the new ball. With left-hander Barnett in support, McCabe passed 100 out of 133 in 139 minutes. Lunch came at 261-7 (McCabe 105 not out.)

In the afternoon session, Farnes took the new ball at once and Barnett (22 in 55 minutes) drove at him and skied a catch to deep point. With another left-hander, O'Reilly, now in, McCabe (123) hooked Hammond through Edrich's right hand at short leg. He passed 150 in 200 minutes. Wright then mystified McCormick and at 3.06pm, with the score at 334-9, Fleetwood-Smith joined McCabe, who was now 160.

McCabe's innings, already brilliant, now passed into legend as he keel-hauled the England bowlers. He hit Wright for four 4's in an over and reached 200 in 223 minutes. He hooked and he drove and he never slogged. Finally, at 3.34pm, McCabe was caught at cover for 232 in 235 minutes, made out of 300, with one six and 34 4's. In the last-wicket stand of 77 in 28 minutes, Fleetwood-Smith faced 18 balls and scored five runs, McCabe faced 40 and scored 72 (56 in boundaries). He scored all of the last 66 runs. After lunch he made 127 in 79 minutes.

During McCabe's innings, Bradman called to those who were playing cards in the Australian dressing-room, telling them, "Come and look at this, you may never see its like again." And on McCabe's return he said, "If I could play an innings like that, I would be a proud man, Stan." It completed a trio of classic Test innings played by McCabe. Arthur Gilligan, S.F.Barnes and R.E.S.Wyatt all said it was the best innings they had ever seen. The innings closed for 411 in 364 minutes off 130.3 overs, which was 67.74 runs per hour, 3.15 runs per over and 21.51 overs per hour.

The follow-on had not been avoided but the psychological balance had shifted. Hammond's captaincy came under scrutiny, for not taking the new ball before lunch and for not using Verity to check McCabe's rampage. Verity bowled only 7.3 overs in the innings. Farnes and Wright looked the best bowlers, but the latter's figures were disfigured by three overs for 44 runs during the last-wicket stand.

A 15-minute interval was taken and Australia followed-on at 3.50pm and a five minute break for tea was taken at 5.05pm. The dead-bat policy of Fingleton and Brown was a strange contrast to what had gone before and the rest of the day produced little in the way of spectacular cricket, although there were two interesting incidents. In the middle of bowling an over, Edrich lost the heel of his left boot. He started to go off for repairs but the umpire required him to finish the over first, which he did off a short run. Barracking and slow handclapping built up and Bradman sent out a message, via Waite the 12th man, that Fingleton should pull away from the stumps if the noise continued during the bowler's run-up. As Verity came in, Fingleton moved away. Umpire Chester called down the pitch, asking the batsman what was he doing. Fingleton said, "Don sent out an order that I am to do this.' Hammond called out, "That's alright by me." The noise got worse. Fingleton pulled away again and this time sat down on the grass for a minute. Then the crowd quietened as he took guard again.

At ten past six, Fingleton was brilliantly caught left-handed by Hammond at first slip. He had scored 40 out of 89 in 135 minutes. Bradman played out the last 20 minutes in partnership with the tenacious Brown. At the close Australia were 102-1 (Brown 51 not out, Bradman 3 not out) in 155 minutes off 60 overs, still needing 145 to make England bat again. They could still save the game but, unless the McCabe lightning could strike again, all seemed to depend on one man. The attendance figure for the day was returned at 30,820, the gates were closed at noon and £2,948 was taken at the turnstiles. The weather forecast was good and a tense day in prospect on the morrow.

Tuesday 14 June: Who Wants a Fifth Day?

The crowd was much smaller and only 4,000 were in before the start of play, although that figure later grew to 11,000. It was to be an absorbing rather than an exciting day. In the first 13 overs 20 runs were scored and Bradman scored 16 in the first hour. At 12.50pm he hit his first four of the day.

Verity bowled over the wicket but the rough was not close enough to the leg stump and all six bowlers were tried before lunch. Brown reached 100 in 265 minutes just before the interval, which came at 199-1 (Brown 101 not out, Bradman 44 not out), with 97 scored in two hours under a cloudless blue sky. The new ball was taken at once. Bradman took 150 minutes to get one of his slowest-ever 50s. At 2.50pm his side went into credit but ten minutes later, Brown swept at Verity and gave an easy catch to fine leg.

Brown had hit 13 4's in 320 minutes and had done a superb job for his country, who were now 12 runs ahead with 195 minutes left. Verity was now getting some turn at the Pavilion End and McCabe was always vulnerable. He helped to add 72 in an hour until he edged Verity to slip: the lead was now 84 with 135 minutes left and seven wickets to fall.

Bradman reached his century in 253 minutes, a 100 which had only two 4's. Then Verity got a ball to kick, Hassett cocked it up and Compton flung himself forward to hold the catch at silly point: 90 ahead, six men to get out, 125 minutes remaining. Badcock survived until after tea, then Wright also found some spin and bowled Badcock with a googly. Bradman now shielded Barnett from Verity and all hope of England victory was shut out. The crowd, more frustrated than bored, started to cheer ironically. When Bradman asked Sinfield to stop landing his right foot on line with the wicket, they grew more voluble and Bradman stood away from his stumps until the noise subsided. Eventually, the Australian captain declared at 6.15pm, undefeated for 144 runs (five 4's) in 365 minutes in one of the few purely match-saving Test innings of his career. Playing on a dry but wearing wicket. Australia had scored 427-6 in 500 minutes off 184 overs, that is 51.24 runs per hour, 2.32 per over, 22.08 overs per hour. They finished 180 runs ahead with four wickets in hand and it is interesting to speculate as to which side would have most fancied a fifth day to be tacked on.

Australians turned off their radios and went happily to bed at 3.30am, having heard their commentators, M.A.Noble and Jack Gregory, praise the bowling of Verity. He and Wright extracted what life they could from the pitch. Sinfield could not turn his off-breaks on the last day. Farnes lost his fire as the match wore on and needed another fast bowler to support him.

The victor was the pitch produced by groundsman Arthur Widdowson. He denied that it had been doped. "Nottingham marl is the secret of this enduring wicket, nothing more," he said. The loser in the match was the cause of four-day limit Tests in England. History would call it 'McCabe's match'. But England got close enough to victory to take great encouragement for the rest of the series and there were no dissentients when Walter Hammond was reappointed skipper for the Second Test. Sir Home Gordon, in *The Cricketer* of 18 June, prophecied that the Trent Bridge Test would herald the dawn of an English cricket renaissance. The Australian batting was heavily criticised in the English newspapers and Mr Menzies, in a broadcast for home radio, spoke of 'the brilliant contributions to insular prejudice and Empire disunity made by most of the writers for the London evening papers.'

Jack Fingleton, a journalist himself, nearly got into trouble when some remarks he made about the barracking were quoted by William Pollock in the *Daily Express*,but the manager took no action as it was accepted that Fingleton had not knowingly given an interview.

In the County Championship, Lancashire returned on the top with a nine-wicket win over Glamorgan at Manchester. They scored 564-9 on the first day, the Welshmen made 163, but reached 397-3 in the follow-on before collapsing to the second new ball. Yorkshire beat Middlesex on a rain-affected game at Leeds in two days, despite the loss of half of the first day. At Tonbridge, where unlucky Kent lost in two days to Derbyshire, there was an unusual run out in Kent's second innings. 'Hopper' Levett drove a ball straight into the bowler's stumps, Captain (later Major-General) E.S.Cole was backing up and Tommy Mitchell ran in, ball in hand, and uprooted a stump. At Cambridge, the Free Forresters made 636-7 declared in 102 overs on Saturday, with eight 6's and 80 4's and the match produced 1,392 runs for 23 wickets.

Bill Edrich of Middlesex, scored only five runs on his Test debut but was nevertheless reckoned to be one of the men upon whom England would build for the future.

ENGLAND v AUSTRALIA

First Test at Trent Bridge, Nottingham.

Friday 10th, Saturday 11th, Monday 13th, Tuesday, 14th June 1938.
Umpires: F.Chester and E.Robinson.

ENGLAND First Innings (won toss)		mins	bls	4/6
L.Hutton lbw b Fleetwood-Smith	100	199	221	14
C.J.Barnett b McCormick	126	172	188	18
W.J.Edrich b O'Reilly	5	31	30	1
*Mr W.R.Hammond b O'Reilly	26	52	63	4
E.Paynter not out	216	319	333	26/1‡
D.C.S.Compton c Badcock (deep square leg) b Fleetwood-Smith	102	138	173	15
†L.E.G.Ames b Fleetwood-Smith	46	54	70	6
H.Verity b Fleetwood-Smith	3	23	22	0
R.A.Sinfield lbw b O'Reilly	6	20	20	0
D.V.P.Wright not out	1	30	19	0
Extras (B 1, LB 22, NB 4)	27			
Total (8 wickets, declared — 188 overs)	**658**	525	1138	

Mr K.Farnes did not bat.

New ball at 204, 427 and 641. Ten no-balls were bowled.

‡Paynter hit one five (4 overthrows); one of his fours was due to overthrows.

Timetable Of The Innings

Time	Score	Mins	Overs	
11.30 Friday start				
12.15	50	45	14	
12.56	103	86	30.1	
1.17	150	107	37.5	
1.30 to 2.15 lunch	169	120	42	Barnett 98 Hutton 61
2.40 to 2.50 rain	200	145	52.2	
3.17 Barnett out	1-219	172	62.2	Hutton 83
3.44 Hutton out	2-240	199	71.4	Edrich 1
3.50 Edrich out	3-244	205	72.5	Hammond 0
3.57	251	212	74.4	
4.30 to 4.50 Tea	274	245	87	Hammond 20 Paynter 7
4.58 Hammond Out	4-281	253	90.2	Paynter 8
5.23	300	278	100	
5.50	350	305	110.4	
6.23	400	338	122.3	
6.30 Close	422	345	125	Paynter 75 Compton 69 extras 21
11.30 Saturday start				
11.54	450	369	133	
12.18 Compton out	5-487	393	141.4	Paynter 107
12.28	500	403	144.4	
12.57	550	432	155.3	
1.13 Ames out	6-577	448	161.5	Paynter 146
1.30 to 2.15 lunch	589	465	166	Paynter 155 Verity 3
2.23 Verity out	7-597	473	169.2	Paynter 163
2.30	602	480	171.1	
2.43 Sinfield out	8-626	493	176.4	Paynter 186
3.11	650	521	186.3	
3.15 Innings closed	658	525	188	

Bowling

	O	M	R	W
McCormick (NB 7)				
lunch	10	0	40	0
tea	20	4	65	1
close	23	4	73	1
lunch	30	4	98	1
end	32	4	108	1
O'Reilly (NB 3)				
lunch	13	1	39	0
tea	26	4	68	1
close	38	8	106	2
lunch	47	10	142	2
end	56	11	164	3
McCabe				
lunch	1	1	0	0
tea	6	4	7	0
close	10	4	24	0
lunch	19	5	58	0
end	21	5	64	0
Fleetwood-Smith				
lunch	10	1	41	0
tea	21	7	55	1
close	30	8	90	1
lunch	40	8	123	3
end	49	9	153	4
Ward				
lunch	8	1	39	0
tea	14	1	63	0
close	24	2	108	0
lunch	30	2	142	0
end	-	-	-	-

Individual Targets

Barnett	51	59m	63b
	102	120m	135b
Hutton	53	102m	105b
	100	199m	220b
Paynter	50	96m	112b
	100	172m	171b
	150	253m	241b
	200	306m	309b
Compton	52	80m	97b
	102	135m	171b

AUSTRALIA First Innings		mins	bls	4/6
J.H.Fingleton b Wright	9	37	36	0
W.A.Brown c Ames(wkt) b Farnes	48	152	192	3
*D.G.Bradman c Ames(wkt) b Sinfield	51	89	96	5
S.J.McCabe c Compton (cover) b Verity	232	235	277	34/1
F.A.Ward b Farnes	2	15	16	0
A.L.Hassett c Hammond (slip) b Wright	1	9	10	0
C.L.Badcock b Wright	9	47	54	0
†B.A.Barnett c Wright (cover) b Farnes	22	55	56	2
W.J.O'Reilly c Paynter (short leg) b Farnes	9	35	25	1
E.L.McCormick b Wright	2	11	6	0
L.O'B.Fleetwood-Smith not out	5	28	18	1
Extras (B 10, LB 10, W 1)	21			
Total (All out — 130.3 overs)	**411**	364	787	

New ball at 263-6. Four no-balls and one wide were bowled.

Timetable Of The Innings

Time		Score	Mins	Overs	
3.30	Saturday start				
4.07	Fingleton out	1-34	37	14.4	Brown 19
4.30	to 4.46 Tea	46	60	23	Brown 20 Bradman 7
4.54		51	68	25.2	
5.39		101	113	44	
5.54	Bradman out	2-111	128	49.3	Brown 40
6.18	Brown out	3-134	152	57.5	McCabe 15
6.30	Close	138	164	61	McCabe 19 Ward 0
11.30	Monday start				extras 11
11.35	Ward out	4-144	169	63.3	McCabe 23
11.44		150	178	65.4	
11.46	Hassett out	5-151	180	66.3	McCabe 29
12.35	Badcock out	6-194	229	87.2	McCabe 62
12.40		202	234	88.1	
1.18		250	272	101.2	
1.30	to 2.14 lunch	261	284	105	McCabe 105 Barnett 20
2.16	Barnett out	7-263	286	105.4	McCabe 105
2.42		302	312	115	
2.52	O'Reilly out	8-319	322	117.4	McCabe 147
3.05	McCormick out	9-334	335	120.5	McCabe 160
3.13		353	343	122.4	
3.30		402	360	129.2	
3.34	McCabe out	10-411	364	130.3	

Bowling

	O	M	R	W
Farnes				
tea	9	4	15	0
close	18	7	31	1
lunch	27	8	61	2
end	37	11	106	4
Hammond				
tea	5	3	6	0
close	-	-	-	-
lunch	12	6	18	0
end	19	7	44	0
Sinfield				
tea	4	3	3	0
close	15	6	23	1
lunch	28	8	51	1
end	-	-	-	-
Wright (NB 4, W 1)				
tea	5	1	12	1
close	19	4	47	1
lunch	32	6	88	3
end	39	6	153	4
Verity				
tea	-	-	-	-
close	4	0	20	0
lunch	6	0	27	0
end	7.3	0	36	1

Individual Targets

Bradman	50	85m	94b
McCabe	52	88m	100b
	100	139m	161b
	150	199m	229b
	202	223m	259b

AUSTRALIA Second Innings(follow on: 247 behind)

		mins	bls	4/6
J.H.Fingleton c Hammond (slip) b Edrich	40	133	152	3
W.A.Brown c Paynter (fine leg) b Verity	133	320	378	13
*D.G.Bradman not out	144	365	379	5
S.J.McCabe c Hammond (slip) b Verity	39	59	73	6
A.L.Hassett c Compton (silly point) b Verity	2	8	9	0
C.L.Badcock b Wright	5	35	26	0
†B.A.Barnett lbw b Sinfield	31	55	70	5
F.A.Ward not out	7	14	22	1
Extras (B 5, LB 16, NB 5)	26			
Total (6 wickets — 184 overs)	**427**	500	1110	

New ball at 201. Six no-balls were bowled.

Timetable Of The Innings

Time	Score	Mins	Overs	
3.50 Monday start				
5.03	50	73	29	
5.05- 5.10 (tea on pitch)	50	75	30	
6.08 Fingleton out	1-89	133	52.2	Brown 42
6.22	101	147	57	
6.30 Close	102	155	60	Brown 51 Bradman 3
11.30 Tuesday start				extras 8
12.29	152	214	83.3	
1.30 to 2.15 lunch	199	275	106	Brown 101 Bradman 44
2.18	200	278	107.1	
2.52 Eng score equalled	247	312	118.4	
2.54	250	314	119.5	
3.00 Brown out	2-259	320	121.4	Bradman 70
3.40	303	360	137.5	
4.01 McCabe out	3-331	381	143.3	Bradman 96
4.11 Hassett out	4-337	391	146	Bradman 100
4.19	350	399	148.2	
4.30 to 4.45 Tea	361	410	152	Bradman 118 Badcock 5
5.03 Badcock out	5-369	428	158.3	Bradman 126
5.41	401	466	172.2	
6.00 Barnett out	6-417	485	178.3	Bradman 141
6.15 Innings declared	427	500	184	

Match abandoned as a draw.

Bowling

	O	M	R	W
Farnes				
tea	6	0	14	0
close	8	0	26	0
lunch	17	1	54	0
tea	24	2	78	0
end	-	-	-	-
Hammond				
tea	4	3	1	0
close	-	-	-	-
lunch	9	5	7	0
tea	-	-	-	-
end	12	6	15	0
Wright (NB 5)				
tea	6	1	13	0
close	12	2	24	0
lunch	20	3	45	0
tea	30	4	76	0
end	37	8	85	1
Sinfield				
tea	7	4	6	0
close	10	4	9	0
lunch	18	6	24	0
tea	26	6	57	0
end	35	8	72	1
Verity				
tea	7	2	13	0
close	19	11	20	0
lunch	33	19	38	0
tea	49	23	70	3
end	62	27	102	3
Edrich (NB 1)				
tea	-	-	-	-
close	7	1	14	1
lunch	9	2	17	1
tea	13	2	39	1
end	-	-	-	-
Barnett				
Tuesday				
tea	1	0	10	0
end	-	-	-	-

Individual Targets

Brown	50	147m	180b
	100	265m	318b
Bradman	50	150m	166b
	100	253m	269b

The Second Test

June 15 to 17: From Lord's to The Commons

THE day after the First Test ended, the tourists were at Lord's again to play the Gentlemen, captained by Walter Hammond, who drove there from Nottingham in his 3½ litre Jaguar with Norman Yardley as his passenger. The Australians won the toss and batted. Brown and Fingleton started with 64 and, oddly, both were caught down the leg-side by Paul Gibb, who kept wicket splendidly.

The sun shone after lunch and the crowd swelled to 8,000. McCabe made a fluent 79 in 105 minutes with one huge on-drive for six off Macindoe. The unobtrusive Chipperfield got 100 minutes' practice and Bradman made his seventh century of the season, 104 in two hours before being caught at long leg. White helped him add 68 for the eighth wicket.

The Gentlemen lost two wickets in 35 minutes before the close and on Thursday they collapsed to 109 for 6 against Ward's leg-spin. But the last four wickets added 192 in two hours and Yardley and Valentine added 84. Meyer, a part-time Somerset all-rounder, was bemused by Ward but stayed to avoid the follow-on, whilst Brown of Surrey took charge. In a last-wicket stand of 46 with Macindoe, Brown scored all but two extras and ended with 88 out of 108 in an hour. Bradman did not appear on the field because dust at Trent Bridge had affected his eyes.

In the second Australian innings, Fingleton bestirred himself to make 121 in two and a half hours and the tourists extended their first-innings credit of 96 by another 189 runs, losing two wickets in the process. That evening they dined at the House of Commons and were toasted by Sir John Simon, the Chancellor of the Exchequer.

On the final morning the tourists put the Gentlemen in an invidious position by adding 146 more in two hours before Bradman declared. Set to score 432 in three hours, a victory for the Gentlemen was impossible, yet there seemed no great point in playing for a draw in a match of this kind. Apart from Gibb, who hit a good 67 in 100 minutes, the batting lacked any sense of purpose and the last five wickets fell

GENTLEMEN OF ENGLAND v AUSTRALIA

Played at Lord's, on June 15, 16, 17, 1938.
Australia won by 282 runs.

AUSTRALIA

Batsman	1st innings	Runs	2nd innings	Runs
J.H.Fingleton	c Gibb b Meyer	38	c Stephenson b Macindoe	121
W.A.Brown	c Gibb b Meyer	30	c Valentine b Hammond	30
C.L.Badcock	b Brown	31	not out	112
S.J.McCabe	c Wilcox b Stephenson	79	(5) c Meyer b Brown	5
A.G.Chipperfield	b Stephenson	51	(6) not out	20
*D.G.Bradman	c Valentine b Meyer	104		
M.G.Waite	b Brown	6	(4) run out	32
†B.A.Barnett	c Gibb b Brown	0		
E.S.White	not out	42		
F.Ward	b Meyer	1		
L.O'B.Fleetwood-Smith	c Stephenson b Meyer	1		
Extras	(B 8, LB 6)	14	(B 7, LB 6, NB 2	15
Total		**397**	(4 wickets, declared)	**335**

Fall: 1st inns 1/64, 2/71, 3/137, 4/212, 5/286, 6/321, 7/321, 8/389, 9/395.
2nd inns 1/112, 2/187, 3/272, 4/284.

GENTLEMEN OF ENGLAND

Batsman	1st innings	Runs	2nd innings	Runs
Mr D.R.Wilcox	b Ward	50	b McCabe	1
†Mr P.A.Gibb	c Bradman b McCabe	6	b Fleetwood-Smith	67
Capt J.W.A.Stephenson	c Waite b McCabe	0	(10) c White b Fleetwood-Smith	10
Mr R.E.S.Wyatt	c White b Ward	37	(3) c Fingleton b McCabe	2
Mr F.G.H.Chalk	st Barnett b Ward	3	(4) b Fleetwood-Smith	11
*Mr W.R.Hammond	c White b Waite	7	(5) c White b Fleetwood-Smith	12
Mr N.W.D.Yardley	c Badcock b Fleetwood-Smith	49	(6) lbw b Ward	22
Mr B.H.Valentine	c Chipperfield b Ward	49	(7) b Fleetwood-Smith	10
Mr F.R.Brown	c Waite b Ward	88	(8) c Waite b Fleetwood-Smith	4
Mr R.J.O.Meyer	b Waite	1	(9) not out	0
Mr D.H.Macindoe	not out	0	b Fleetwood-Smith	0
Extras	(B 6, LB 5)	11	(B 6, LB 4)	10
Total		**301**		**149**

Fall: 1st inns 1/18, 2/18, 3/95, 4/100, 5/109, 6/109, 7/193, 8/240, 9/255.
2nd inns 1/1, 2/3, 3/33, 4/67, 5/125, 6/129, 7/138, 8/139, 9/149.

GENTLEMEN OF ENGLAND	O	M	R	W	O	M	R	W
Stephenson	25	5	94	2	22	2	69	0
Macindoe	22	7	57	0	17	3	53	1
Hammond	5	1	14	0	11	1	27	1
Brown	29	1	107	3	20	0	97	1
Meyer	26.2	4	66	5	22	3	57	0
Wyatt	10	0	45	0	8	1	17	0

AUSTRALIA	O	M	R	W	O	M	R	W
Waite	25	7	73	2	8	1	17	0
McCabe	6	3	6	2	7	2	14	2
White	30	8	62	0	7	1	23	0
Ward	30.1	5	108	5	7	0	41	1
Fleetwood-Smith	7	0	41	1	14.4	1	44	7

Umpires: F.Walden and W.Reeves.

for 24 runs, giving the Australians an extra hour to prepare for their journey up north to Manchester. Hammond failed in both innings, but Yardley did his prospects no harm with 49 and 22.

Elsewhere the number of batsmen past 1,000 runs increased to four. Paynter did it for Lancashire at Oxford; Hutton at Cardiff, where Yorkshire beat Glamorgan. At Bristol the Middlesex innings of 573 had a perfect coda when Big Jim Smith came in on the second afternoon. He passed 50 in 11 minutes, the fastest ever half-century in first-class cricket (it was beaten in rather false circumstances in 1965) and was out for 66 in 18 minutes, with two 4's and eight 6's, three in succession off Sinfield. Smith had been nearly caught off his first ball.

Kent achieved a rare victory, at Tonbridge over Worcestershire. On the first day, Woolley scored 100 before lunch, and for those there to see it, high summer had arrived. Hampshire, playing Derbyshire at Portsmouth, had to find three substitutes on the second day, the captain Paris arriving late because of a motor breakdown; one of the three stand-in fielders was the Derbyshire masseur, another was PC John Arlott. Despite or perhaps because of that, Hampshire won by 37 runs in extra time.

June 18 to 21: A Rest Home for Pigeons

On Saturday, the England 13 for the Second Test was announced. It comprised the team which played in the First Test, plus J.Hardstaff (Notts) and A.W.Wellard (Somerset). The latter, a hearty opening bowler, had 67 wickets in the season so far (av.18.68) and was preferred over Bowes and Jim Smith.

The last Australian game before the Test was against Lancashire at Manchester. On a green pitch and in a heavy atmosphere, the visitors were 35-3 after 50 minutes, Brown and Bradman both getting edges to Eddie Phillipson's away-swing. But Badcock, who changed his bat twice, found Wilkinson's leg-spin very acceptable. He and Hassett added 182 in 150 minutes, interrupted by two hours lost to rain and bad light. Badcock reached 1,000 runs before falling to the new ball. At the close the score was 262-5 (Hassett 118 not out). On Sunday, Fleetwood-Smith had a tooth out and with his mouth bruised and swollen he did not set foot on the field at all during the match.

On Monday, Hassett did not add to his score for half an hour, then was bowled by an in-swinger from Nutter. Lancashire found themselves batting by 12.50pm. Waite got some movement and claimed both the distinguished openers, Washbrook and Paynter, before lunch. Then there was, for the sixth time so far this season, a three-figure stand for Lancashire's third wicket. Norman Oldfield was a participant in all of them, this time with Iddon. McCormick broke through with a fiery spell of 3-15 in five overs. Oldfield's delicate 69 was the best

LANCASHIRE v AUSTRALIA

Played at Old Trafford, Manchester, on June 18, 20, 21, 1938.
Match drawn.

AUSTRALIA

J.H.Fingleton	b Nutter	10	c Wilkinson b Phillipson	96
W.A.Brown	c Farrimond b Phillipson	8	b Nutter	70
*D.G.Bradman	c Pollard b Phillipson	12	not out	101
C.L.Badcock	c Pollard b Phillipson	96	not out	14
A.L.Hassett	b Nutter	118		
A.G.Chipperfield	c Farrimond b Phillipson	5		
†B.A.Barnett	c Pollard b Phillipson	9		
M.G.Waite	lbw b Wilkinson	20		
E.S.White	not out	12		
E.L.McCormick	b Pollard	1		
L.O'B.Fleetwood-Smith	absent ill	0		
Extras	(B 2, LB 7, NB 3)	12	(B 3)	3
Total		**303**	(2 wickets, declared)	**284**

Fall: 1st inns 1/14, 2/35, 3/35, 4/217, 5/253, 6/269, 7/279, 8/298, 9/303.
2nd inns 1/153, 2/210.

LANCASHIRE

C.Washbrook	b Waite	7	b Chipperfield	11
E.Paynter	lbw b Waite	9	b Chipperfield	20
J.Iddon	c Badcock b McCormick	44	c Waite b White	1
N.Oldfield	c Badcock b McCormick	69	not out	30
J.L.Hopwood	run out	13	not out	17
A.E.Nutter	c & b McCormick	4		
*Mr W.H.L.Lister	c & b Chipperfield	7		
W.E.Phillipson	b Chipperfield	52		
†W.Farrimond	c Bradman b McCormick	49		
R.Pollard	not out	18		
L.L.Wilkinson	b White	1		
Extras	(B 6, LB 6, W 1, NB 3)	16	(LB 1)	1
Total		**289**	(3 wickets)	**80**

Fall: 1st inns 1/8, 2/19, 3/126, 4/147, 5/153, 6/157, 7/169, 8/240, 9/276.
2nd inns 1/32, 2/33, 3/33.

LANCASHIRE	O	M	R	W	O	M	R	W
Phillipson	35	11	93	5	17	2	71	1
Pollard	30.5	5	82	1	13	4	27	0
Nutter	23	7	61	2	20	2	81	1
Wilkinson	16	0	55	1	22	4	63	0
Iddon					7	0	20	0
Hopwood					4	0	19	0

AUSTRALIA	O	M	R	W	O	M	R	W
McCormick	26	4	84	4	3	0	20	0
Waite	21	7	64	2	3	1	7	0
White	21	3	67	1	9	2	30	1
Chipperfield	23	9	58	2	6	2	12	2
Badcock					2	0	10	0

Umpires: A.Dolphin and G.M.Lee.

of the innings and half of his ten 4s came from late cuts. Farrimond opened his shoulders but Lancashire were all out by the close, 14 runs behind. A collection for John Hopwood's benefit raised £79.

Next morning, Brown and Fingleton made no friends when they indulged in aimless batting practice. For most of the first hour, a pigeon stood undisturbed at mid-wicket, 40 yards from the bat, and moved away only when the sightscreen was shifted. Brown spent 40 minutes advancing his score by two and had 32 out of 90-0 at lunch. "Even a section of the long-suffering Old Trafford crowd barracked; the wonder is that they did not tear the railings down," wrote Neville Cardus. When he saw Bradman during the lunch interval, he said, "Poor stuff this morning," and Bradman responded, "Yes, something's got to be done about it." Something was done about it. The captain conveyed his views to the incumbent batsmen and 29 were scored in the first three overs after the interval. Brown scored another 38 in half an hour with six 4's. Now Bradman, who had never played a big innings at Old Trafford, put the bowling to sword with shots in every direction, especially the flashing drive off the back foot. He made 50 in 38 minutes, 100 in 73 minutes, the fastest century of the season so far. Lancashire batted out the last 70 minutes and stumps were pulled at 5.30.

Despite unsettled weather, the Championship yielded five results in seven matches. Yorkshire skittled out Surrey twice on Monday at Sheffield, Bowes and Smailes bowling unchanged in the first innings of 52. Middlesex, needing 241 to beat Essex, were steered to victory by Denis Compton, 87 not out. His only mistake was to run out Hulme, wrongly refusing a second run. When last man Arthur Baxter, a Scotsman, came in, Middlesex needed 24, and Compton scored all but one of them. Leg-spinner Peter Smith took 8-99 for Essex, having already scored 101. At Burton-on-Trent, against Derbyshire, Hammond scored two 100s in a match for the sixth time. The draw between Leicestershire and Hampshire produced 1,108 runs for 20 wickets and two odd incidents. Leicestershire wicket-keeper, 17-year-old George Dawkes, was hit on the face by a bail when Arnold was bowled; and when Lloyd Budd was given out caught behind, the Leicestershire captain Stewart Dempster spoke to the umpire and had him recalled. At Edgbaston, Northants bowled out the home team for 184, collapsed to 37-5, recovered to gain a first innings lead and their first points of the season, but lost comfortably in the end. Lancashire and Middlesex now shared the lead with an average of 9.60, with Yorkshire breathing down their necks on 9.20.

Monday saw the opening of the All England Lawn Tennis Championships at Wimbledon and Tuesday was the sunniest June day in Southern England since 1914.

June 22 to 24: Preparing for the Televised Test

For the Second Test at Lord's, the Australian camp had some anxious moments. Several players were suffering from eye trouble which was probably caused by hay fever. Meanwhile, after studying a film of his action, Ernie McCormick used the two free days to practise swinging his arms during his run-up. Sid Barnes, wrist plaster now off, practised in the nets against groundstaff bowlers. On Thursday, the Australians went to Wimbledon. The wicket, which was prepared only ten days before, was covered for 24 hours before start of play because of fears of overnight rain. MCC advised spectators to bring raincoats for sitting on the grass, but the weather forecast for Friday was fair and warm.

This Test was to make history, for it was the first cricket match to be televised, albeit broadcast only to the few thousand wealthy people in the London area who owned television sets. It was planned to show play from 11.30am to 12.30am, 2.30pm to 3.30pm and 3.50pm to 5.00pm. The cameras were positioned on a fire escape at the eastern corner of the ground, at fine leg when the bowling was from the Pavilion End.

Back in the Championship, Lancashire enforced the follow-on against Worcestershire at Dudley, but could not go on to win and dropped to third place. Eddie Phillipson and Percy Jackson collided in the field and both retired for the rest of the game. Yorkshire moved to second place, thanks to the bold captaincy of Sellers. His declaration set Glamorgan 163 to win in 170 minutes on a sticky wicket. The challenge was taken up and Yorkshire won by 12 runs. Middlesex, without a game, stayed at the top. A weak Sussex side lost to Oxford University by 112 runs at Worthing. Czech government talks with the Sudeten German leaders started in Prague.

Friday 24 June: An Innings for the King

As 11.30am approached, the sun got hotter and newspaper hats and handkerchiefs appeared on spectators' heads. The captains consulted with the groundsman and asked for the heavy roller. England left out Hardstaff and Sinfield, so that they fielded two specialist pace bowlers. Australia dropped the spinner, Ward, from their previous Test team, and Chipperfield came in. As the ground filled rapidly a loud laugh from Hammond betrayed that he had won the toss again. As Hutton and Barnett walked out to the middle, the televisual eye was trained on them and the voice of Captain H.T.B.(Teddy) Wakelam was heard. Howard Marshall, on the radio as usual, had a rather larger audience.

McCormick opened and was rather erratic. His third ball, a no-ball, was struck for two by Barnett, then he on-drove a three. However, it looked as if moisture had come to the surface, for McCormick was getting the ball to rise waist high and Bradman put in two short legs. McCabe opened with a wide and although in McCormick's second over, Hutton glanced a no-ball for four, the next ball jumped chest high and Hutton prodded it gently to Brown's hands at backward short leg.

Tension eased when McCabe was bowling and Barnett drove him nicely. In McCormick's third over, Edrich, hiding his nerves with exuberance, hooked blindly at him twice and the second attempt resulted in him pulling the ball on to his stumps. At 11.50am, Hammond was cheered all the way to the wicket. By noon the gates were closed with 32,000 in and they saw McCormick's fifth over produce a ball which kicked sharply from a length to have Barnett caught off his thigh by Brown. So, after 32 minutes at the crease, England were 31-3.

The new batsman, Paynter, had to contend with some short-pitched bowling, to the crowd's annoyance. Then McCormick came off with figures of 6-0-18-3. He had been wild and erratic, yet fast and lively.

Someone noticed that a ladder supporting the television apparatus was red, and it was repainted grey.

Hammond nursed Paynter and led the counter-attack. The mantel of England's cricket commander-in-chief was almost visible on his shoulders as he drove easily against O'Reilly and Fleetwood-Smith. Paynter was the unflappable sergeant-major. He played his part in blunting O'Reilly and pulled a full-toss from Fleetwood-Smith for six. McCormick returned at 1pm but his pace was now dulled. England went to lunch at 134-3 (Hammond 70 not out), the equilibrium restored.

The teams were presented to the King after lunch and the resumption was delayed to 2.20pm. Fleetwood-Smith and then O'Reilly were tried from the Nursery End. McCormick came on again and got some lift but was much too loose. Paynter was able to hit him dismissively through the slips for four. He reached 50 in 113 minutes and Hammond got to his 100 in 146 minutes. McCabe was given a go, then Chipperfield, and a merciless square cut by Paynter off Fleetwood-Smith put up the 200.

The Australian bowling wilted, although the fielding did not. McCormick took the new ball at 223 and his third delivery was a no-ball which Hammond drove for four. In humid heat, Paynter took over the reins. Then, one short of his century, he stepped back to glance a good-length ball from O'Reilly and, pinned back on his stumps, was lbw. He had scored 99 in 182 minutes out of a partnership of 222, with 13 4's and a six, and after lunch he had outscored Hammond.

Compton was next. Before the start of play, umpire E.J. ('Tiger') Smith, a former England wicketkeeper, had warned him about sweeping O'Reilly off the leg stump. Compton stayed for 15 minutes, then swung wildly across the line and was lbw to O'Reilly. Up went

McCormick extracts a great deal of life from the Lord's pitch in the first hour's play of the Second Test.

Above: Paynter, on 99, is lbw to O'Reilly.

Right: Edrich tries to hook McCormick early in his innings and this is the result, played-on for a duck.

Smith's finger. "You are a silly little chap," he said as Compton passed him. England were now 271-5, a quarter of an hour before tea, and Hammond must have been glad to see the level-headed Leslie Ames. Tea came at 283-5 (Hammond 139 not out).

It was a good but not great score. More had to be done. And more was done. In the last 105 minutes the two senior men in the team added 126 and O'Reilly had to bowl negatively to a leg-side field. Fleetwood-Smith set a defensive field, with five men on the ropes, but his length let him down. The fielding held up until late in the day and, as usual, Fingleton and Brown drew repeated applause for their efforts. While bowling, Chipperfield rashly put out his hand to stop a Hammond drive, and had to retire hurt. Hammond passed 200 in 314 minutes but just before the close, Ames called him for a short single and Hammond pulled a leg muscle, although he stayed on to end the day at 210. According to *The Cricketer* correspondent, Hammond was never once beaten during the day. Ames was on 50 and England handsomely placed at 409-5, made in 355 minutes off 115 overs. McCormick bowled 11 no-balls, O'Reilly sent down four.

It had been a historic day — a royal visit, a regal innings, a packed ground, a lovely June day. The BBC extended its television coverage, putting out an extra transmission from 6.15pm to the close, for the City businessmen coming home from work. The verdict of *The Times* on Saturday morning was: 'Cameras followed bowlers' run-up then instantly switched to the batsman'; and in Monday's paper: 'Test cricket was the delight of television viewers . . .and long periods of play were visible . . .It is a happy thing to be one with the Test crowd in your own home and to see the batsman sending the ball to the boundary and to hear the roar of the crowd. The transmissions were indeed excellent and at times the viewer must have felt himself almost on the pitch.'

Saturday 25 June: Crowds Envelop Lord's

Queues had begun to form outside Lord's at 10pm on Friday and before midnight there were 12 people sitting on camping stools. In the morning, another bright sunny day, there were thousands outside and ticket 'touts' were getting up to £5 for a single ticket. MCC allowed as many people as possible — 13,375 — through the turnstiles and the gates were closed at 10.45am. Thousands were left outside, perhaps as many as 20,000. When play was due to start, the crowd had spilled on to the playing area and the captains and umpires talked to the police and decided to bring the boundary rope in five yards. Play eventually began at 11.35am.

When the fielders came out, Waite reappeared as substitute for Chipperfield who had gone to hospital for an X-ray. McCormick and McCabe opened the bowling and Hammond lost no time in breaking

Wally Hammond during his record-breaking innings at Lord's

Paynter's two-week old record for an innings in a Test against Australia in England. He passed his own record for an innings for England in any home Test ((217 versus India at The Oval in 1936).

McCormick took the new ball at 426 and gave Hammond a blow on the left elbow that hurt. Nevertheless, that happy morning he added 30 runs — 24 in 4's — in 32 minutes, then played outside an inswinger. He left to a huge ovation: 240 out of 437 in 367 minutes with 32 4's and no chance except one which put Chipperfield's hand under the X-ray machine. It was his greatest Test innings in England. He had delighted two capacity Lord's crowds, a King and several thousand television watchers. As the members rose to him he must have wondered if he would ever enjoy such a moment of triumph again.

Ames, who had scored 68 out of the stand of 186 in 152 minutes, found no-one to support him. Verity stood there strokeless until, in O'Reilly's first over from the Pavilion End, he appeared to be bowled off his pads. Wellard pulled his second ball for four to square leg, but then skied his third for a towering catch to McCormick at deep mid-on. Ames edged Fleetwood-Smith to McCormick at slip after an excellent 83 with ten 4's in 190 minutes. Bradman juggled and dropped a catch off Wright. Then Farnes put up a no-ball into the sky and Fingleton dropped it, pretended to be thoroughly disgusted with himself, and his ham act fooled most of the crowd. Barnett conceded the first bye of the innings, which closed with Wright's dismissal at 12.50pm for 494 in 434 minutes off 137.3 overs. A rate of 68.29 runs per hour, 3.59 runs per over, 18.98 overs per hour. There were 19 no-balls in the innings. It seemed from the way the tail batted that Hammond did not want as big a score as he sought at Trent Bridge.

Farnes opened from the Pavilion End, the wind behind him, with three slips, a gully and two short legs. Wellard from the Nursery End, had a more orthodox field. Fingleton and Brown survived untroubled until lunch at 26-0. Wright came on at the Nursery End and was inclined to feed the batsmen on the leg-side, but he turned the ball slowly and Hammond brought up a second slip. Soon, Fingleton edged Wright into Hammond's hands at first slip. For Bradman's sake, Farnes replaced Wellard, and the Australian captain responded by thumping a memorable four to square leg.

The Don looked in ominous form and Verity came on for Wright to subdue him. Out of the blue, Bradman tried to late cut a wide ball and played it on to his stumps. McCabe was the next problem and he soon unleashed his hooks and cuts. Meanwhile, Brown passed 50 quietly and almost gave a slip catch off Farnes. McCabe hooked Verity for four and pulled Wellard over Hutton's head into the Mound Stand, rising to the challenge of a deep-set field. He took successive 4's off Wright when the Kent man reappeared, but it was too

Wellard sweeps his second ball, from O'Reilly, for 4. Off the next ball, however, Wellard skied a towering catch to McCormick at deep mid on.

Bradman, trying to late-cut a wide delivery from Verity, plays the ball on to his stumps and is out for 18.

presumptuous to last. After making 38 out of 51 in 30 minutes, with one six and five 4's, he square cut Farnes ferociously through the gully. Verity gripped the ball to his stomach and fell over, and for most people McCabe's walk away from the wicket was the first evidence that he was out.

Hassett stayed with Brown during a stand of 124 in 100 minutes. Brown had a tense time in the 90s and on 99 had his off-stump grazed by Wellard before reaching his priceless 100 in 193 minutes. Hammond kept the bowlers changed. Wright was given a spell from the Nursery End but was inclined to pitch short. At 272, Wellard was put on from the Pavilion End and in his first over claimed Hassett lbw, then bowled Badcock with a straight half-volley. Barnett stayed with the obdurate Brown for the last half hour to take the score to 299-5 (Brown 140 not out, Barnett 6 not out) in 263 minutes off 88 overs. The official attendance figure was 33,800.

Monday 27 June: Rain Returns

The weekend brought good news for Australia: Chipperfield's finger was intact and he would be able to participate. Despite unpromising weather, the crowds streamed in and the gates were again shut well before the start. Australia needed 46 to avoid the follow on as Farnes strode in from the Pavilion End with four slips and a gully. Verity partnered him and got two wickets in his first eight balls. Barnett drove rather casually and Compton ran back from cover to take the catch. Then Chipperfield, who received a special cheer, played no palpable shot and was lbw.

O'Reilly clubbed Verity to leg and drove him first bounce into the crowd. Another drive off Verity would have ended his sport but Paynter moved in too far and had to jump for it. O'Reilly fetched successive balls from Verity into the Mound Stand for six, taking 16 off the over. Wellard replaced Farnes and Brown bestirred himself with two off-side 4's of the utmost ease. Wright took Verity's end and had O'Reilly caught at cover off a no-ball, then bowled him next ball — off another no-ball.

O'Reilly had reached 42 in 44 minutes when Farnes bowled him at 393. McCormick gave an easy catch to short leg, first ball. On a hat-trick, Farnes saw Fleetwood-Smith edge to second slip where Compton grassed it. The clouds shed tears for Farnes' ill-luck at 12.30pm and there was no more play till 4.15pm. History was made again: the first televised rain at a cricket match — and no highlights of the 1986 Benson & Hedges Cup Final to fall back on!

Without adding to his score, Brown was badly dropped at mid-on, Paynter again misjudging the flight. Brown then turned a ball to fine leg for his 200, a shot typical of his innings. Fleetwood-Smith hung around for a frustrating 45 minutes, but when he was caught at square leg, Brown had become the sixth man to carry his bat through a Test innings, and, curiously, the third Australian to do so in a Lord's Test. He was undefeated for 206 in 369 minutes with one five, 22 4's and one chance; it was a masterpiece of concentration and strategy. In that time, Australia had scored 422 all out off 121.4 overs, at 68.62 runs per hour, 3.46 runs per over, 19.81 overs per hour. England's attack was disappointing apart from Verity and Farnes, and the fielding below par.

England openers Barnett and Hutton ventured forth at five o'clock but rain drove them back before play could start. Half an hour later, they came out again. McCormick bowled two balls and a wide and another shower caused a brief stoppage. The rain made the wicket soft on top and from 5.40pm to 6.30pm the batsmen faced a difficult time. About half of the 30,000 crowd had gone home. McCormick dug the ball in with eight man close to the bat, and O'Reilly also got lift. At 6.10pm a good length ball from McCormick reared up and Barnett edged it to McCabe in the gully. Verity came in as nightwatchman. Then Hutton edged a turning leg-break to first slip. Edrich avoided a 'pair' and he and Verity survived nervously until the close, at 39-2 (Verity 5 not out, Edrich 6 not out, McCormick

Left: Wright on the second day, bowling to Brown (out of picture); Right: Somerset's Arthur Wellard, who took two valuable Australian wickets on the second day.

7-1-16-1, O'Reilly 6-2-12-1). England were only 111 runs ahead and any of three results seemed possible on the morrow.

Tuesday 28 June: Vacancy for a Wicketkeeper

In the second over of the day, Edrich hooked McCormick for four, tried again and was caught at square leg. Whilst Paynter dealt efficiently with O'Reilly, Verity flashed several times outside the off-stump against McCormick, and once edged a four over slips' head. The Yorkshireman did better when he remembered his defence and the day was 40 minutes old when he lost his off-stump to McCormick. Verity stayed out in the middle because the next man Hammond needed a runner and with his leg strapped, the England captain played virtually one-legged and took 18 minutes to get off the mark. McCormick came off after nine overs this morning and a memorable spell of 2-18.

Hammond was never comfortable and sometimes he looked 'like a man moving on a cork leg' (Cardus). McCabe's third ball was down the leg side, Hammond scooped at it with his left hand only on the bat and Waite, substituting for Chipperfield, ran well from square leg to catch him. England were only 148 ahead with five wickets in hand and five hours left. Paynter was dropped at first slip off McCabe and Compton nearly played on when he was 12 to Fleetwood-Smith, on whom Bradman now gambled. Otherwise, Compton batted with all the aplomb of a wise yet innocent youth. O'Reilly had to come back on for the chinaman bowler. and when the stand had put on 52 in 35 minutes, Paynter pulled O'Reilly to long leg. Fleetwood-Smith fumbled, Paynter went for a second run, but back came the ball to the wicketkeeper, who whipped off the bails before the Lancastrian could get home. As he walked off, the man from Oswaldtwistle said, justly, to Compton, "It's not your fault, Denis." England were 128-6, 200 ahead, 260 minutes left, on a wicket which was now playing easily. The stalwart Ames was soon struck on a finger of his left hand by McCormick, but survived to lunch at 142-6.

Second ball after lunch, Ames was well caught at second slip. Wellard, a famous six-hitter, was a stranger to the middle of his bat for his first quarter-hour but then he settled down. Compton dealt expertly with the short-pitched bowling of McCormick. He simply waited for it and cut or pulled. Wellard took three 4's in an over by Fleetwood-Smith and pulled McCabe on to the Grandstand balcony for six. When he succumbed to the new ball, he had made 38 out of 74 in 45 minutes and done the same job as O'Reilly had done for Australia the day before. Compton carried on with the punishment until Hammond felt able to declare at 3.20pm, England having scored 242-8 in 235 minutes off 72 overs (61.78 runs per hour, 3.36 runs per over, 18.38 overs per hour). Compton was undefeated on 76 after two hours, with 56 of his runs in 4's. It was his most valuable innings to date for England, and Hammond could have no complaints. With Chipperfield unable to bowl and Fleetwood-Smith not at his best, Australia could not capitalise on the excellent morning spell of McCormick, who celebrated his 100th no-ball of the tour during the innings.

Australia needed 315 to win in 165 minutes, which meant a probable 50-55 overs. England's problem was to find a wicketkeeper, for Leslie Ames had fractured a finger. None of the team had experience behind the timbers, although Hammond might have done it but for his bad leg. It was a difficult decision, for fielding, even at first slip, is an entirely different skill from keeping wicket. Thoughts must have turned to the Oval Test of 1934, when Frank Woolley deputized for Ames and conceded 37 byes. Eddie Paynter piped up, "I used to keep wicket when I was a lad in short pants. I'll try skipper, if you like." "Get your pads on then", said Hammond. A few minutes later, Eddie was crouching with his back to the Pavilion, watching Fingleton touch a fast outswinger by Wellard. Paynter dived to his right, deflected the ball with his glove (how heavy the hands feel when you are not used to gloves) and Hammond nonchalantly took the catch. Farnes then welcomed Bradman with a ball that nearly decapitated him and those close to the wicket could see Bradman's face turn white. He got close to touching a Wellard outswinger but then hit him for three successive 4's. With an off-drive off Farnes, he passed Jack Hobbs' record Test aggregate and the Australian dressing-room applauded. Tea came at 59-1, Bradman 38 not out. With 105 minutes to go, the contest was effectively over.

After tea, Bradman played one extraordinary cross-batted shot, like a forehand drive in tennis, to the Pavilion rails. Having made 10 in 70 minutes, Brown was bowled round his legs by Verity and stayed there a full 30 seconds, thinking that the wind had removed the bails. Perhaps he could not bring himself to believe that the match could continue without his presence, for he had been on the field for every ball so far. The main interest now was whether Bradman would get a century. He passed 50 on the stroke of 5pm, with 90 minutes to go. McCabe took two 4's in an over twice off Verity, gave a chance in the slips, and at 5.30pm was caught at second slip, the ball having again taken the diversionary route via Paynter's glove. Hassett took advantage as the bowling faltered, sweeping a no-ball by Wright for six and then giving a possible stumping chance off him. He had hit 42 in 35 minutes before Wright produced a good ball to bowl him. Badcock fell to the first ball he received, well caught at slip off Edrich and thus out for a 'pair'. When he got back to the dressing-room, no-one could think of words to say to him; he broke the silence himself by putting down his bat and bursting into laughter.

In the sunlit evening, Barnett was not to be moved. Bradman used his feet, found the gaps as usual and reached his 100 with five minutes to spare. On the stroke of time, Barnett gave Paynter a well-deserved catch and the players left the field. The Australian captain was 102 not out, with 15 4's in 147 minutes and no chances. His century had probably saved the Test as it had at Nottingham. Australia finished on 204-6 in 160 minutes off 48.2 overs, 110 behind. That was a rate of 76.5 runs per hour, 4.22 runs per over, 18.12 overs per hour. Taking the gloves off his swollen hands and returning them to Les Ames, Eddie Paynter said, "If you made me a present of them, I wouldn't take on your job."

The crowd on the last day was 20,000, and for the whole match about 120,000 people watched, of whom 100,933 paid, a record for Lord's, It had been another good match for England but the bowling was a comparative failure. Farnes bowled too much at Brown's and Bradman's pads and Wright, although he spun the ball, was too loose and bowled too many no-balls. Wellard was keen and useful but not quite top-drawer. Verity was the best. In the batting, Hammond and Compton stood out like meteors. On the evidence of the two Tests, Australia seemed to be a four-man team: Brown, Bradman, McCabe and O'Reilly. The second draw of the series gave rise to a loud clamour in Australia against the futility of four-day Tests and the Board of Control looked for the end of time limit Tests in England. For some time *The Cricketer* had advocated five days. Bookmakers were offering odds of only 3-1 against a draw in the next Test.

On Wednesday 29 June, Hammond was reappointed England captain for the Third Test — a mere formality — after a specialist gave him fitness clearance.

June 25 to 28: Yorkshire Go Top

With Arthur Wellard playing in the Test, Bill Andrews had a chance to bowl with the wind for Somerset against Middlesex at Bath. The result: Middlesex 84 all out (Andrews 7-58). Somerset captain, B.H.Lyon, suggested that he might be too tired to make Middlesex follow-on. Andrews replied, "I've waited for years to see these buggers from Lord's follow-on." Follow-on they did and Andrews took 6-83 as Somerset won by nine wickets. With cold, wet weather in the north, Lancashire (v Surrey at Manchester) and Yorkshire (v Notts at Bradford) could take only first-innings points. Frank Woolley stroked 162 in 220 minutes against Sussex at Tunbridge Wells. Yorkshire changed places with Middlesex and went to the top of the Championship table for the first time that season.

News from Europe: the Spanish Government threatened to bomb territory of powers aiding the Fascists; Germany and Czechoslovakia signed a trade agreement.

ENGLAND v AUSTRALIA

Second Test at Lord's.

Friday 24th, Saturday 25th, Monday 27th, Tuesday, 28th June 1938.
Umpires: E.J.Smith and F.Walden.

ENGLAND First Innings (won toss)		mins	bls	4/6
C.J.Barnett c Brown (short leg) b McCormick	18	32	21	1
L.Hutton c Brown (short leg) b McCormick	4	11	9	1
W.J.Edrich b McCormick	0	7	5	0
*Mr W.R.Hammond b McCormick	240	367	394	32
E.Paynter lbw b O'Reilly	99	182	188	13/1
D.C.S.Compton lbw b O'Reilly	6	17	21	1
†L.E.G.Ames c McCormick (slip) b Fleetwood-Smith	83	190	154	10
H.Verity b O'Reilly	5	19	20	0
A.W.Wellard c McCormick (mid on) b O'Reilly	4	2	3	1
D.V.P.Wright b Fleetwood-Smith	6	20	23	1
Mr K Farnes not out	5	7	6	0
Extras (B 1, LB 12, W 1, NB 10)	24			
Total (All out — 137.5 overs, minus 2 balls)	**494**	434	844	

The 104th over is incomplete, as Chipperfield retired hurt after bowling four balls.
New ball at 223 and 426. 19 no-balls and one wide were bowled.

Timetable Of The Innings

Time		Score	Mins	Overs	
11.30	Friday Start				
11.41	Hutton out	1-12	11	2.4	Barnett 7
11.49	Edrich out	2-20	19	4.3	Barnett 13
12.02	Barnett out	3-31	32	8.1	Hammond 6
12.28		52	58	16.3	
1.07		103	97	29.5	
1.30	to 2.20 Lunch & King	134	120	37	Hammond 70 Paynter 33
2.34		153	134	40.5	
3.12		200	172	54.2	
3.52		250	212	67	
3.56	Paynter out	4-253	216	68.2	Hammond 121
4.14	Compton out	5-271	234	74.3	Hammond 132
4.30	to 4.47 Tea	283	250	80	Hammond 139 Ames 4
5.00		302	263	84.1	
5.45		350	308	99.3	
6.00	Chipperfield off	368	323	103.4	Waite substitute
6.21		400	344	111.1	
6.32	Close	409	355	115	Hammond 210 Ames 50 extras 22
11.35	Saturday start (delay for crowd)				
12.05		452	385	123.3	
12.07	Hammond out	6-457	387	124.5	Ames 68
12.27	Verity out	7-472	407	130.3	Ames 77
12.32	Wellard out	8-476	412	130.6	Ames 77
12.45	Ames out	9-483	425	135.2	Wright 1
12.54	Wright out	10-494	434	137.5	

Bowling

	O	M	R	W
McCormick (NB 13*)				
lunch	10	1	31	3
tea	17	1	59	3
close	21	1	76	3
end	27	1	101	4

*one no-ball cost four extras

McCabe (NB 1, W 1)				
lunch	5	0	14	0
tea	20	4	40	0
close	25	4	57	0
end	31	4	86	0

Fleetwood-Smith (NB 1)				
lunch	12	1	52	0
tea	15	1	73	0
close	28	1	127	0
end	33.5	2	139	2

O'Reilly (NB 4)				
lunch	9	2	23	0
tea	22	3	62	2
close	32	3	76	2
end	37	3	93	4

Chipperfield				
lunch	1	0	5	0
tea	6	0	36	0
close	8.4*	0	51	0
end	-	-	-	-

*incomplete 9th over

Individual Targets

Hammond	51	68m	86b
	100	146m	154b
	150	248m	251b
	200	311m	332b
Paynter	52	115m	109b
Ames	50	116m	95b

AUSTRALIA First Innings		mins	bls	4/6
J.H.Fingleton c Hammond (slip) b Wright	31	60	69	2
W.A.Brown not out	206	369	370	22§
*D.A.Bradman b Verity	18	26	26	2
S.J.McCabe c Verity (slip) b Farnes	38	32	32	5/1
A.L.Hassett lbw b Wellard	56	103	99	6
C.L.Badcock b Wellard	0	1	2	0
†B.A.Barnett c Compton (cover) b Verity	8	37	45	1
A.G.Chipperfield lbw b Verity	1	5	3	0
W.J.O'Reilly b Farnes	42	44	45	5/2
E.L.McCormick c Barnett (short leg) b Farnes	0	½	1	0
L.O'B.Fleetwood-Smith c Barnett (square leg) b Verity	7	43	44	0
Extras (B 1, LB 8, NB 6)	15			
Total (All out — 121.4 overs)	422	369	737	

New ball at 207. Seven no-balls were bowled.
§Brown hit one five. ‡One no-ball by Wright cost two extras.

Timetable Of The Innings

Time	Score	Mins	Overs	
1.06 Saturday start				
1.30 to 2.15 Lunch	26	24	8	Fingleton 10 Brown 15
2.32	50	41	13.3	
2.51 Fingleton out	1-69	60	20	Brown 35
3.14	100	83	27.4	
3.19 Bradman out	2-101	88	29.3	Brown 48
3.50	150	119	39.3	
3.53 McCabe out	3-152	122	40.2	Brown 60
4.30 to 4.46 Tea	194	159	54	Brown 78 Hassett 22
5.00	200	173	59.3	
5.38	250	211	71.5	
5.53 Hassett out	4-276	226	76.4	Brown 124
5.56 Badcock out	5-276	229	77	Brown 124
6.30 Close	299	263	88	Brown 140 Barnett 6
11.30 Monday start				extras 10
11.31	301	264	88.2	
11.35 Barnett out	6-307	268	89.5	Brown 145
11.42 Chipperfield out	7-308	275	91.2	Brown 145
12.11	350	304	101.1	
12.28 O'Reilly out	8-393	321	106.3	Brown 184
12.30 McCormick out	9-393	323	106.4	Brown 184
12.34 to 4.16 Rain	393	327	107	Brown 184 Fltd-Smith 0
4.30	401	341	111.2	
4.58 Fleetwood-Smith out	10-422	369	121.4	

Bowling	O	M	R	W
Farnes (NB 1)				
lunch	4	0	18	0
tea	18	2	73	1
close	28	3	99	1
rain	36	3	127	3
end	43	6	135	3
Wellard (NB 1)				
lunch	3	0	3	0
tea	10	1	32	0
close	17	1	67	2
rain	19	1	83	2
end	23	2	96	2
Wright (NB 5‡)				
lunch	1	0	4	0
tea	12	2	48	1
close	14	2	59	1
rain	16	2	68	1
end	-	-	-	-
Verity				
lunch	-	-	-	-
tea	12	2	33	1
close	25	8	59	1
rain	32	9	95	3
end	35.4	9	103	4
Edrich				
lunch	-	-	-	-
tea	2	1	1	0
close	4	2	5	0
end	-	-	-	-

Individual Targets

Brown	51	98m	92b
	100	193m	198b
	150	288m	295b
	200	354m	418b
Hassett	50	95m	93b

ENGLAND Second Innings

		mins	bls	4/6
C.J.Barnett c McCabe (slip) b McCormick	12	30	38	1
L.Hutton c McCormick (slip) b O'Reilly	5	35	16	0
H.Verity b McCormick	11	57	47	1
W.J.Edrich c McCabe (square leg) b McCormick	10	20	24	1
E.Paynter run out (Fleetwood-Smith-Barnett)	43	92	103	7
*Mr W.R.Hammond c sub (Waite) (square leg) b McCabe	2	24	16	0
D.C.S.Compton not out	76	119	137	14
†L.E.G.Ames c McCabe (slip) b O'Reilly	6	19	11	1
A.W.Wellard b McCabe	38	44	37	6/1
D.V.P.Wright not out	10	18	13	2
Extras (B 12, LB 12, W 1, NB 4)	29			
Total (8 wickets, declared — 72 overs)	**242**	235	442	

New ball at 216. Ten no-balls and one wide were bowled.

Bowling

	O	M	R	W
McCormick (NB 8, W1)				
close	7	1	16	1
lunch	19	4	43	3
end	24	5	72	3
O'Reilly (NB 1)				
close	6	2	12	1
lunch	21	9	36	1
end	29	10	53	2
McCabe (NB 1)				
close	-	-	-	-
lunch	7	1	28	1
end	12	1	58	2
Fleetwood-Smith				
close	-	-	-	-
lunch	4	1	11	0
end	7	1	30	0

Timetable Of The Innings

Time		Score	Mins	Overs	
5.10	Monday (Players appeared, rain, ball not bowled)				
5.37	Monday start				
5.40	to 5.43 rain	1	3	0.2	
6.10	Barnett out	1-25	30	8.4	Hutton 5
6.15	Hutton out	2-28	35	9.1	Verity 2
6.30	Close	39	50	13	Verity 5 Edrich 6
11.30	Tuesday start				extras 11
11.36	Edrich out	3-43	56	15	Verity 5
11.50		52	70	19.1	
12.09	Verity out	4-64	89	25	Paynter 15
12.34	Hammond out	5-76	114	32.3	Paynter 24
12.53		102	133	38.5	
1.10	Paynter out	6-128	150	46	Compton 21
1.30	to 2.15 lunch	142	170	51	Compton 29 Ames 6
2.16	Ames out	7-142	171	51.2	Compton 29
2.21		150	176	52.4	
2.55		202	210	63.4	
3.01	Wellard out	8-216	216	65.5	Compton 61
3.20	Innings declared	242	235	72	

(Hammond batted with Verity as a runner)

Individual Targets

Compton 53 80m 91b

AUSTRALIA Second Innings (set 315 in 160 mins)		mins	bls	4/6
J.H.Fingleton c Hammond (slip) b Wellard	4	11	14	1
W.A.Brown b Verity	10	70	59	1
*D.G.Bradman not out	102	147	135	15
S.J.McCabe c Hutton (slip) b Verity	21	25	22	4
A.L.Hassett b Wright	42	38	45	7/1
C.L.Badcock c Wright (slip) b Edrich	0	3	1	0
†B.A.Barnett c Paynter (wkt) b Edrich	14	17	17	2
Extras (B 5, LB 3, W 2, NB 1)	11			
Total (6 wickets — 48.2 overs)	**204**	160	293	

Three no-balls and two wides were bowled.
J.Hardstaff fielded substitute for Ames (injured) and Paynter kept wicket.

Bowling	O	M	R	W
Farnes (W 1)				
tea	8	3	19	0
end	13	3	51	0
Wellard (NB 1, W 1)				
tea	6	1	24	1
end	9	1	30	1
Verity				
tea	3	2	5	0
end	13	5	29	2
Wright (NB 2)				
tea	1	0	4	0
end	8	0	56	1
Edrich				
tea	-	-	-	-
end	5.2	0	27	2

Individual Targets

Bradman	51	62m	57b
	102	142m	133b

Timetable Of The Innings

Time	Score	Mins	Overs	
3.35 Tuesday start				
3.46 Fingleton out	1-8	11	4	Brown 1
4.20	51	45	14.3	
4.30 to 4.45 Tea	59	55	18	Brown 10 Bradman 38
5.00 Brown out	2-71	70	21.2	Bradman 49
5.14	101	84	25.1	
5.27 McCabe out	3-111	97	29.3	Bradman 66
5.59	150	129	39.3	
6.07 Hassett out	4-175	137	42	Bradman 87
6.11 Badcock out	5-180	141	42.4	Bradman 92
6.25	201	155	46.5	
6.30 Barnett out	6-204	160	48.2	

Match drawn

Bill O'Reilly (above) and Eddie McCormick (left).

June 29 to July 1: Day Off in the Peaks

THE Australians got back to their steamroller ways against Derbyshire at Chesterfield, where Barnes played his first game of the tour. The county batted first on a wet, lifeless wicket and left-hander Denis Smith was yorked by a good ball from Waite, but the rest fell mostly to poor shots. Worthington scored 67 in 135 minutes and was caught at cover off his first false stroke. George Pope drove O'Reilly straight for six and wicketkeeper Elliott stayed with him a while. Waite and Ward kept a good length.

Australia made a slow start but their batsmen found it easier when Copson switched to leg-stump attack. Brown, dropped at 7 and 50, was joined by Badcock at 50 and they took the score to 191-1 at the close. Badcock was lbw to George Pope's inswinger for 86. At 248-3, Barnes came in and grinned broadly when he glanced a single for his first run of the tour. Yet again, Brown played the permanent fixture in an Australian innings. He was 265 not out when McCabe declared at 3.30pm and apologised to him for depriving him of 300. Brown batted nearly six hours, hit 30 4's and gave three chances. Only once did he deliberately hit the ball in the air, a straight-driven six. He pulled a muscle during his innings and thereafter abandoned all caution, scoring his last 96 in 75 minutes. Derbyshire folded abjectly on the blameless wicket. They were 20-5, and Waite had taken 5-16 in 9 overs. He took two wickets in an over twice. O'Reilly did not have to bowl a ball and the total of 56 was the lowest so far against the tourists. Tommy Mitchell, the leg-spinner, did not field or bat on the second day due to injury. The Australians, nicely settled in their hotel in the Grindleford Hills in the rugged beauty of the Peak District, had a free Friday under a cloudless sky for an impromptu ramble around the countryside, lunching on cold chicken and strawberries in an old inn in the village of Froggatt.

Yorkshire beat Worcestershire by an innings and 18 runs, a good all-round team effort. Lancashire batted well on a soft wicket and beat Hampshire by ten wickets. Leicestershire beat Kent at Tunbridge Wells, captain Dempster hitting 142 in 165 minutes after retiring hurt. Gloucestershire, without Hammond, lost in two days in Essex. Somerset, needing 224 to beat Notts, were 89 short at tea with five wickets left and 90 minutes to go; 38 short with two wickets and half an hour left. Their last man, the burly Horace Hazell, came in with six needed in five minutes. He cut Voce for four and hit the next ball to leg to become the county hero.

On Friday, in the men's singles final at Wimbledon, Donald Budge (USA) beat H.W.('Bunny') Austin (GB) 6-1, 6-0, 6-3 in just over an hour, and caused a renewed clamour for the tournament to go 'open' so that Fred Perry could compete.

At the half way stage of the season, the County Championship table was as follows:

	P	W	L	Pts	Ave
Yorkshire	13	9	0	120	9.23
Lancashire	13	9	2	116	8.92
Middlesex	11	8	3	96	8.72
Leicestershire	7	4	0	56	8.00
Somerset	13	7	4	92	7.07
Derbyshire	12	5	5	76	6.33
Surrey	11	5	3	68	6.18
Warwickshire	10	5	3	60	6.00
Nottinghamshire	11	4	5	56	5.09
Sussex	13	4	5	60	4.61
Essex	11	3	8	48	4.36
Worcestershire	16	5	6	68	4.25
Kent	12	3	6	48	4.00
Hampshire	14	4	7	52	3.71
Glamorgan	9	1	5	24	2.66
Gloucestershire	13	2	8	34	2.61
Northamptonshire	9	0	8	4	0.44

At the start of the season, few would have bet that Leicestershire would have been fourth and Gloucestershire 16th.

The first-class averages were (minimum 800 runs), (minimum 40 wickets)

	Runs	Avge		Wkts	Avge
D.G.Bradman	1588	144.36	Bowes	48	11.91
W.R.Hammond	1742	82.09	Mayer	49	16.61
W.A.Brown	1304	81.50	L.O'B.Fl'-Smith	56	16.69
A.L.Hassett	1020	72.85	Verity	77	17.10
Edrich	1367	68.35	Pollard	91	17.38
C.S.Dempster	912	65.14	W.J.O'Reilly	56	17.73
Paynter	1329	63.28	F.A.Ward	54	17.77
Hutton	1091	60.61	Copson	49	19.10
P.A.Gibb	1090	60.55	Nichols	81	19.35
C.L.Badcock	1112	58.52	Wellard	78	19.55
Compton	1135	56.75	Cornford, J.H.	47	20.37
			Smith C.I.J.	82	20.36

DERBYSHIRE v AUSTRALIA

Played at Chesterfield, on June 29, 30, 1938.
Australia won by an innings and 124 runs.

DERBYSHIRE

D.Smith	b Waite	6	c McCabe b Waite	3
A.E.Alderman	lbw b Waite	8	lbw b Waite	3
T.S.Worthington	c Waite b Ward	67	c White b Waite	0
L.F.Townsend	c & b Ward	0	b Waite	4
G.H.Pope	b O'Reilly	14	b Waite	4
A.E.G.Rhodes	c & b Waite	10	lbw b White	8
A.V.Pope	c Barnett b White	4	not out	19
†H.Elliott	c Hassett b Ward	9	b Ward	2
*Mr R.H.R.Buckston	st Barnett b Ward	0	st Barnett b Ward	11
T.B.Mitchell	b Ward	10	absent hurt	0
W.H.Copson	not out	0	c Fingleton b Ward	0
Extras	(B 18, LB 5)	23	(B 1, LB 1)	2
Total		**151**		**56**

Fall: 1st inns 1/16, 2/23, 3/24, 4/71, 5/91, 6/102, 7/126, 8/132, 9/141.
2nd inns 1/6, 2/6, 3/9, 4/13, 5/20, 6/24, 7/32, 8/56, 9/56.

AUSTRALIA

J.H.Fingleton	b Mitchell	23
W.A.Brown	not out	265
C.L.Badcock	lbw b G.H.Pope	86
*S.J.McCabe	c Elliott b A.V.Pope	6
S.Barnes	b A.V.Pope	42
A.L.Hassett	not out	3
Extras	(B 1, LB 14, W 1)	16
Total	(4 wickets, declared)	**441**

Fall: 1st inns 1/50, 2/239, 3/248, 4/424.

M.G.Waite, †B.A.Barnett, E.S.White, W.J.O'Reilly and F.Ward did not bat.

AUSTRALIA	O	M	R	W	O	M	R	W
Waite	26	8	50	3	15	2	40	5
McCabe	5	0	11	0	5	3	2	0
O'Reilly	6	3	13	1				
Ward	20.2	6	45	5	4.2	0	8	3
White	6	1	9	1	5	4	4	1

DERBYSHIRE	O	M	R	W
Copson	31	2	115	0
A.V.Pope	32	6	79	2
G.H.Pope	22	2	71	1
Mitchell	12	0	45	1
Townsend	15	0	66	0
Rhodes	11	1	49	0

Umpires: T.Oates and F.Walden.

The Third Test and Gentlemen v Players

July 2 to 5: "Get on wi' Cracking"

THE Australians' charabanc drove the four or five miles from Grindleford down the slopes to Sheffield and entered a different world of red brick terrace houses, smoking chimneys and factories in the city of steel, to the cricket ground at Bramall Lane, which shared its field of grass with Sheffield United FC. For the 'Sixth Test' against Yorkshire, 15,000 people congregated on the terraces and saw Brian Sellers win the toss. On a wet pitch — play started at noon — he inserted the tourists.

There was a dropped catch and a rejected lbw appeal in the first five minutes, then Smailes bowled Fingleton round his legs and Bowes had McCabe caught at second slip. Badcock scored 11 in an hour, then turned Robinson to short leg. Bradman played a careful, fighting innings. After lunch he was troubled by Smailes and uncharacteristically charged down the track and Wood devoured the bails. Leyland came on and got Barnes with his second ball, but Hassett took charge of the rest of the innings, using his feet and waiting for the bad ball, but with no support from the other end. The machinations of Sellers, however, could not keep him away from the strike. Two 4's in an over off Robinson took him past 50, then down the wicket to drive two 6's into the Members' Stand off Smailes, then two 6's in an over off Robinson. Eventually Verity replaced the latter and got Hassett lbw for 94 in two hours, with those 6's and 12 4's. Smailes took 6-92, bowling off-breaks round the wicket to a leg-trap, and Australia had made a humble 222.

When Yorkshire batted, the wicket was easier. Waite bowled in emulation of Smailes from the Pavilion End and had Hutton caught at leg slip off a ball that got up. Then he sent back Barber and Leyland. When on 12, Sutcliffe retired hurt with a damaged finger

YORKSHIRE v AUSTRALIA

Played at Bramall Lane, Sheffield, on July 2, 4, 5, 1938.
Match drawn.

AUSTRALIA

J.H.Fingleton	b Smailes	2	lbw b Bowes	2
S.J.McCabe	c Smailes b Bowes	13	(4) lbw b Bowes	15
*D.G.Bradman	st Wood b Smailes	59	c Barber b Smailes	42
C.L.Badcock	c Turner b Robinson	11	(2) lbw b Verity	22
A.L.Hassett	lbw b Verity	94	lbw b Verity	17
S.Barnes	c Wood b Leyland	10	c Sellers b Smailes	19
M.G.Waite	lbw b Smailes	2	run out	0
†B.A.Barnett	c Robinson b Smailes	12	c & b Smailes	1
E.S.White	c Sutcliffe b Smailes	1	c Hutton b Smailes	2
E.L.McCormick	c Leyland b Smailes	9	b Verity	0
L.O'B.Fleetwood-Smith	not out	4	not out	7
Extras	(B 3, LB 1, NB 1)	5	(LB 5)	5
Total		**222**		**132**

Fall: 1st inns 1/6, 2/20, 3/58, 4/101, 5/122, 6/125, 7/155, 8/167, 9/210.
2nd inns 1/10, 2/34, 3/59, 4/100, 5/108, 6/108, 7/110, 8/116, 9/120.

YORKSHIRE

H.Sutcliffe	c Fingleton b Waite	24	(3) not out	36
L.Hutton	c McCormick b Waite	7	(4) c Fingleton b Waite	18
W.Barber	b Waite	2	(5) not out	15
M.Leyland	lbw b Waite	13		
C.Turner	b White	34		
T.F.Smailes	c Hassett b White	8		
*Mr A.B.Sellers	lbw b Waite	11		
†A.Wood	c Fingleton b White	41	(1) b McCormick	4
E.P.Robinson	b Waite	32		
H.Verity	c Hassett b Waite	5	(2) run out	9
W.E.Bowes	not out	0		
Extras	(B 11, LB 16, W 1)	28	(B 1)	1
Total		**205**	(3 wickets)	**83**

Fall: 1st inns 1/12, 2/20, 3/50, 4/81, 5/108, 6/115, 7/137, 8/179, 9/205.
2nd inns 1/13, 2/18, 3/58.

YORKSHIRE	O	M	R	W	O	M	R	W
Bowes	12	4	15	1	18	8	28	2
Smailes	29	7	92	6	19.2	4	45	4
Robinson	12	5	39	1	2	0	8	0
Verity	17	1	69	1	21	8	46	3
Leyland	3	1	2	1				

AUSTRALIA	O	M	R	W	O	M	R	W
McCormick	11	3	31	0	9	2	34	1
Waite	48	21	101	7	23	11	34	1
White	28.3	15	26	3	14	6	14	0
Fleetwood-Smith	10	2	19	0				

Umpires: W.Reeves and A.Skelding.

and at the close Yorkshire had made 74-3 in two hours. It was almost like a classic Roses Match. The paying attendance was 25,320.

There was more rain on Sunday, which kept the wicket interesting. Sutcliffe resumed his innings when Smailes was out, hooking two 4's off McCormick before skying a catch on the leg side. Turner lasted 110 minutes for 34 and Sellers played a few 'air' shots. At 137-7, Wood was joined by Ellis Robinson, who drove heartily, hit six 4's, all off Waite, scored 32 in 30 minutes, then played all around a ball from Waite. There was more rain during the lunch interval and then Verity stayed whilst Wood, cutting cheekily, brought up the 200 with three 4's. He was last out, caught at long on, and the champions were only 17 behind. Waite bowled unchanged through the innings. Now came the drama.

Bowes, steaming in from the Pavilion End, saw Badcock dropped at slip by Hutton, had Fingleton trapped lbw at ten and then saw Bradman dropped first ball, a hard chance, again to Hutton. Indeed, Bradman was beaten several times by Bowes and his bewilderment visibly amused the close fielders and non-striker Badcock. Bowes rested with figures of 11-6-14-1. After rain stopped play for 20 minutes at 4pm, Bowes came back and again troubled the mighty Don, who once put his hand over his mouth, shook his head and walked over towards Sellers. Sellers told him to "get on wi' cracking".

McCabe was lbw to a ball that kept low but Hassett, dropped off successive balls from Verity, helped add 41 with Bradman before he, too, was lbw and Australia were 100-4. Bradman stuck at it for another eight overs, then was caught at short leg via his pad off Smailes, who took 4-26 in his last spell. Fleetwood-Smith hit Verity for six but Australia collapsed and Yorkshire needed only 150 to win. The Tykes, though, had an awkward ten minutes to bat that night and Sellers sent in Verity and Wood, who were perhaps relieved when rain sent them back without a ball bowled. A memorable day had been watched by 20,000 people.

On Tuesday morning, play began on time after more overnight rain which left the pitch more docile. Verity and Wood came out again. It is interesting to speculate whether Sellers could have reverted to the normal batting order. In his third over from the Pavilion End, McCormick bowled Wood. Then Sutcliffe pushed a full toss past cover, Bradman and Hassett chased it and Bradman flicked the ball back for Hassett's throw to beat Verity on the third run. Now the regular Yorkshire openers were together at 18-2. Sutcliffe hooked whenever McCormick dropped short but White replaced him at 45 and checked the scoring. At 58, Hutton turned the ever-persistent Waite into the leg trap. Barber snicked his first ball just past the stumps but Sutcliffe remained in total command and Yorkshire were 83-3 at lunch. The Australians ate their roast beef facing the first defeat of the tour. Then the rain returned and there was an agonizing wait. Eventually, at 4pm, the captains agreed to abandon the match. Sellers magnanimously accepted that the pitch was not fit, so that Bradman did not have to call in the umpires. The Yorkshire supporters were not so charitable and some of the crowd expressed their views by throwing cushions on to the field.

During this match the Australians continued to lodge in Grindleford and one night Lindsay Hassett went out for a walk and brought back a goat to the hotel for the rest of the team to see. Next night, he returned with a hedgehog but all the players had locked their bedroom doors, so he produced it at breakfast instead.

On Sunday, 3 July, the England 13 for the Third Test at Manchester was announced. From the XI which played at Lord's, all the batsmen were retained. Ames (injured) was missing; Wellard and, surprisingly, Farnes were dropped. The newcomers were J.Hardstaff (Notts); Mr.P.A.Gibb (Cambridge University and Yorkshire); M.S.Nichols (Essex); T.F.Smailes (Yorkshire); and T.W.J.Goddard (Gloucestershire). Gibb's selection as wicketkeeper was a major surprise, for he had played only for the University so far in the season and had made a poor impression on the Saturday in the 'Varsity Match. Nichols had 81 wickets so far in the season, Smailes had 55. Goddard was just back after injury. It was asking a lot of Nichols to spearhead the bowling. His opening partner would have to be Hammond or Smailes, who was on the slow side of medium pace. The selectors announced that they considered Bowes to be not yet fully fit, despite his being top of the bowling averages!

The University Match at Lord's , as usual, concluded the students' season. This year, unusually, the game started on a Saturday in an effort to draw a bigger crowd. However, only 6,372 spectators turned up to see Oxford open with 317 (E.J.H.Dixon 73, J.M.Lomas 94 in three hours, G.E.Hewan 6-91, bowling off-breaks around the wicket to a leg trap). Gibb, as we have noted, was unimpressive behind the stumps. Cambridge were 18-1 over the weekend and on Monday, Gibb celebrated his Test selection with 122 in four hours, J.R.Thompson scored a more adventurous 79 in two and a half hours, N.W.D.Yardley hit a six and nine 4's in his 61, and M.A.C.P.Kaye drove hard for 55 not out. Cambridge made 425 (D.H.Macindoe 5-132). In one over on Monday evening, Oxford lost M.M.Walford to a magnificent short-leg catch by B.D.Carris. Rain on Tuesday prevented play till 4pm, when Oxford faced three and a half hours to survive on a drying wicket. J.N.Grover (35) and P.M.Whitehouse (26 not out and dropped twice), defended until stumps were drawn at 7.15pm.

A quirk of the Championship scoring system was demonstrated at Manchester, where Lancashire made 441-7 declared. With rain on the second and third days, Nottingamshire dragged out their first innings (Hardstaff 61 in 3 hours). Then fast-medium Cyril Edge broke through with three wickets in nine balls and Notts were all out for 209 with an hour left. Lancashire gained four points but that reduced their average — a 'no decision' would have suited them better. However, they stayed in second place because the weather allowed Middlesex only four points at Worcester. Hampshire beat Essex by 227 runs at Portsmouth, partly because Essex were caught on a nasty wicket on the third day. Surrey scored 547 at The Oval, where Errol Holmes' 103 with 17 4's out of 137 in 65 minutes was now the fastest century of the season. Alas for Surrey, rain ruined the match and the home side also had the misfortune to bowl out Sussex once just before the end. In fact, rain affected all eight county matches and on Tuesday lightning damaged houses and stopped electric trains in the South East.

At Wimbledon on Saturday, Donald Budge achieved the clean sweep, adding the men's doubles (with G.Mako) and the mixed doubles (with Alice Marple) to his singles title. Helen Wills-Moody beat Helen Jacobs 6-4, 6-0 in the women's final; they were 4-4 in the first set when Miss Jacobs wrenched an ankle. The unemployment figures for June were 1.8 million, an increase of 500,000 since June 1937.

July 6 to 8: 'Encouraging an Immoral Code of Life'

Preparations for the Test were overshadowed by controversy in the Australian camp. Early in the tour, the team had cabled a request to the Australian Board of Control to allow Don Bradman's wife, Jessie, to join him in England at the end of the tour (at his expense) as Mrs Woodfull had done in 1934. On Tuesday, 5 July, the Board's cable was received, refusing the request. The news broke next day and Bradman was quoted in the Press as saying: "I am very disappointed at the Australian Board of Control's decision but I cannot say at the moment whether I shall do anything further in the matter."

Because he was contracted not to talk to the Press, Bradman referred further inquiries to journalist A.G.Moyes and then drafted a letter of resignation from Test cricket. The team doctor, Roland Pope, persuaded him not to send it. Moyes drafted a statement saying that Bradman would not play again in any match under the authority of the Australian Board; a copy of it was shown to the manager, Mr Jeanes, who asked for it to be held back.

The rest of the team held a meeting in Bradman's absence — but with his knowledge — in their Manchester hotel and forced Mr Jeanes to send a cable of protest to the Board, which was sent on Friday. The relevant terms of the players' contract were clause 7, by which each covenanted 'that he will not be acompanied on the said tour or any part thereof by his wife or any member of his family or relative', and clause 8, by which he covenanted 'that during the period of the said tour of the team, neither his wife nor any of his children under his legal control will be in England or elsewhere outside Australia where the team from time to time may be touring'.

Such terms were habitually imposed on touring teams, both English and Australian, until recent years and it is amazing that such draconian restriction on freedom was tolerated for so long. What purpose it served is a mystery. It was never thought necessary to separate a player from his family when playing cricket in his home country and no-one has ever suggested that home players performed any the worse on the field for it. If such contractual clauses had been challenged in the courts, it is quite likely that they would have been declared void as being contrary to public policy. A contract in restraint of marriage (*ie* whereby a person promises not to marry), is void: see the case of Lowe v Peers (1770) reported in *English Reports, Vol.98, p.760.* It is but a short step to say that a contract which compels a man not to see his wife and family for a period of over six months is incompatible with the mutual obligation of cohabitation assumed on marriage and is liable to harm the stability of marriage, especially since the clauses in question do not prevent the player from forming attachments with other persons, male or female.

It is stated in the standard English text book *The Law of Contract* by Cheshire, Fifoot and Furmston (Butterworths 1986, 11th ed, p.378) that: 'The general view of English law is that any contract is void . . .which after marriage tends to encourage in one or both of the parties an immoral code of life incompatible with their mutual obligations.' The clauses, even if valid, were not binding on the wife, child, relative etc as they were not party to the contract, but if the wife persuaded her husband to bring her to England or if she tried to accompany him in England, she might be liable to an action by the Board of Control for inducing a breach of contract by the husband.

As for the Test itself, there had been a lot of rain in the Manchester area and the groundsman had prepared three pitches for possible use. It had been widely predicted that the Test would not produce a result in four days. The 1934 Test at Old Trafford had been a heatwave stalemate and the last result between England and Australia at Manchester was in 1902. It rained on Wednesday; on Thursday there was a lot more and the wicket was covered at 11.30am as permitted by the rules. The players could not even practise. Paul Gibb did a four-lap run round the ground and came back soaked but smiling. All the England squad were fit, and all the Australians except Walker. All reserved seats for the first three days had been sold.

In the county matches, which ended on the first day of the Test, five out of seven had no decision, including Yorkshire's and Middlesex's matches. Despite losing Thursday's play at Cardiff, Glamorgan beat Kent. In a low-scoring match at Northampton, Lancashire conceded first-innings points but won by seven wickets. In a spell of 5-13 in 11.1 overs, Dick Pollard became the first bowler to 100 wickets that season. By the end of the match he had 104 (av.16.50) — should he not have been at Manchester instead of Smailes? Nichols, who was at Manchester, was next wicket-taker with 92 wickets.

In Palestine, an outbreak of terrorism killed 33 people and British troop reinforcements were sent out. On Friday, the first day of the Test, there were gales in the English Channel and the passenger steamer *Rouen* went aground at Newhaven.

Third Test at Manchester: Frustration and Strawberries

Friday 8 July: There was a deluge before breakfast and only a few hundred ticket holders came in to Old Trafford. Most of the players went off to the pictures, but not O'Reilly; he had a boil on his leg lanced. There was no rain after 3pm and the wicket dried out.

Saturday 9 July: There was more early morning rain and the groundstaff worked between the showers. The clouds cleared but the umpires abandoned play at 4.10pm. Then several hundred ticket holders invaded the playing area and the Lancashire coach, Harry Makepeace, went over and appealed to them to stay off the middle, and told them that the turf near the wicket was too slippery to play.

Monday 11 July: After a dull and rainy Sunday, the wicket was dry on Monday morning but a deposit of rain at 11.30am put paid to the day, although there was no more wet weather. Lancashire officials suggested that the Test could be rearranged for 4, 5, 6, 8 August, but Scotland and Durham protested. MCC secretary, R.S.Rait Kerr, said that there were no plans to play an extra Test.

Tuesday 12 July: The Third Test of 1938 was laid to rest at 10.30am with 100 mourners in attendance. The teams were never selected. It was particularly galling for Morris Nichols, who had been 12th man three times in the 1934 Ashes series and who was certain of his place now. No doubt he could feel it in his bones that he would be dropped for the next Test. At least he and the other ten England professionals were paid the full £50 match fee.

It was confirmed that no new Test would be played. This was only the second time in history that a Test anywhere had been abandoned without a ball bowled; the first was Manchester 1890. The Australians travelled to Birmingham with their only memories being the wife controversy, the rain, the endless waiting and the strawberries every day for lunch. It looked likely that the Ashes would hinge on the Final Test at The Oval, which would now be timeless whatever happened at Leeds. It was just as well that the Old Trafford match was not timeless!

Ironically, of the eight county matches played on 9 to 12 July, seven were finished. Thirty miles away over the Peaks, at Chesterfield, the

Above and below: Depressing scenes at Old Trafford where the Third Test was abandoned without a ball being bowled.

pitch was soft but play was uninterrupted: bold captaincy by Sellers and pawky batting by Derbyshire gave Yorkshire an easy victory and they stayed at the top with an average of 9.42 from 14 matches. The Tykes were now the only unbeaten county, for Leicestershire went down by an innings to Lancashire; the dull weather kept down the attendance, which was particularly unfortunate as it was Les Berry's benefit match — and he had agreed to postpone his benefit year from 1937 because of Leicestershire's financial problems.

Lancashire stayed at second place with an average of 9.00 points. Leicestershire dropped to sixth. At Nottingham, Middlesex took the new ball and won just before the rain came, staying third with an average of 8.61. Surrey beat Kent at Blackheath in two days and rose to fourth. Somerset lost to Hampshire at Yeovil, Stuart Boyes taking 9-57 in Somerset's first innings. At Hove, where Sussex beat Essex by five wickets, Hugh Bartlett continued a run of fast scoring with 91 not out in 80 minutes.

A British White Paper was published with proposals for withdrawing foreign combatants from Spain; 200 were killed in air raids in China. Eccentric millionaire Howard Hughes flew from New York to Paris in a record 16½ hours on the start of a round-the-world flight.

Gentlemen v Players at Lord's: Bartlett and Farnes

The traditional fixture at Lord's, second only to Tests in repute, was a memorable encounter in 1938. The Players were as selected. The Gentlemen had to bring in R.H.Moore (Hants) and R.J.O.Meyer (Somerset) to replace B.H.Valentine and R.W.V.Robins. Walter Hammond, who had captained the Players several times, was now leading the amateurs; and in his farewell season, Frank Woolley was given the honour of leading the Players.

Wednesday 13 July: At 11.30am, before a large crowd, Nichols opened the Players' bowling from the Nursery End but rather wasted the new ball. Leg-spinner Peter Smith opened with two maidens then trapped Gibb, lbw to a top-spinner, and Wyatt. In between Pollard ran one down the hill to have B.O.Allen caught behind. From 35-3, Yardley led the scoring whilst Hammond seemed ill at ease. Lunch came at 100-3.

At 155, Hammond was caught at forward short leg by Compton off a shot from the meat of the bat. The partnership had added 120 in 105 minutes, whilst in the dressing-room, Hugh Bartlett fidgeted, smoked, changed his gloves. A left-hander, renowned as a nervous starter, he was nearly bowled by his first three balls but cracked the last delivery of the over past cover's left hand and never looked back. Woolley brought up another slip for him but it was too late.

Yardley was caught behind off a bad stroke. Moore timed the ball well, then was bowled offering no stroke. Brown smote two offside

Action from the Gentlemen versus Players match at Lord's. Above: Bartlett hits a 6 off Smith during his 175 for the Gentlemen.

Denis Compton is bowled by Farnes.

4's and was then caught and bowled one-handed by Smith. Meanwhile, Bartlett hit Smailes from the Pavilion End crease into the Mound Stand, a carry of 125 yards. Nichols turned to umpire Frank Chester and said, "He won't hit me like that." Later, when Nichols bowled from the Pavilion End, Bartlett on-drove him up to the roof guttering below Father Time. In one other over by Nichols he hit 4,4,0,4,4,4. In an over from Smith he struck 4,4,0,6,6,2, the first of those 6's reaching the 15th row of the Mound Stand and the second landing on the Grandstand roof. Bartlett was tall and free swinging. He put everything into his drives — arms, shoulders and wrists — but was ever elegant. When Meyer was eighth out, lbw second ball, Stephenson came in and batted soundly, although he tended to get too much of the strike, and Farnes played two elegant off-drives. With the help of these two Essex amateurs, Bartlett scored 108 of the 126 put on for the last two wickets, his last 75 coming out of 82 in only 46 minutes.

Woolley's captaincy was rather unimaginative. He used the three pace man for too long and ignored Edrich and Compton. As E.W.Swanton was to recall later, "He seemed almost unconcerned with the tactical situation in the enjoyment of watching . . .Bartlett." Perhaps Woolley saw an embodiment of himself at the crease. The Gentleman were all out when Farnes was caught by Price (who took four catches and conceded only two byes). Bartlett came off to a standing ovation; he had made 175 not out in 165 minutes with four 6's and 24 4's. He gave one hard chance to third slip off Smailes when 52.

Spectacle of another sort was to come just as the exhilarated spectators were gathering up to leave. The Players went in at 6.15pm and Edrich conceded to Hutton the right to choose ends. Hutton chose the non-striker's as Farnes marked his run-up in the shadow of the Pavilion. Angered by his omission from the abortive Manchester Test, Farnes ran up and bowled his first delivery wide of the off-stump. The ball reared from just short of a length and flew head high past Edrich. Interesting.

The second ball was similar but on the right line. Edrich put up a defensive bat but as the ball hurtled towards his eyes, he instinctively turned his head. It glanced off his glove and smacked him on to his forehead. He fell as if shot. Edrich remembered nothing of the blow nor of the catch made by Stephenson in the gully. The next thing he knew was someone saying, 'Have some more water, no hurry', and Hammond asking if he was alright. He was dazed, had a dull pain in the head and his teeth jarred against the glass. He pulled himself together and went back to his station. Then Stephenson said, "How'zat." Edrich thought he was joking until umpire Chester slowly raised the finger. Edrich walked off still confused. Bob Wyatt at deep cover explained to the crowd what had happened in mime.

In the Players' dressing-room Frank Woolley told Edrich why he

In the Gentlemen's second innings, Hammond is caught by Price, who also whips off the bails.

was out and solicited a nightwatchman. He lit upon Fred Price and asked him if he would like to oblige. "No, I bloody well wouldn't," replied the Middlesex wicketkeeper but somebody had to go. Price survived one fierce delivery then touched the next to Hammond at first slip. All heads turned to the Pavilion to see who would come next. Out stalked Eddie Paynter. He weaved out of the way of the last two balls and there was not time for an over from the other end. This one had lasted 15 minutes. The most spectacular day of the season, watched by a crowd of 10,000, ended with the Players 411 behind and two wickets down.

Thursday 14 July: Edrich spent the day in bed. When the innings resumed at 11.30am, Paynter took some measure of control. He punished Brown's irregular length with four 4's in an over. Once he tried to hit Stephenson to leg and sent the ball off the bottom of his bat over point. Then he stretched to a wide ball and got an edge. Hardstaff played a breakback from Farnes on to his wicket. Woolley strolled in to applause so great that he raised his cap. Neville Cardus wrote, "Hammond, who always does the right and courteous thing, came forward and welcomed him.". He saw the two young sparks out, Hutton lbw to a straight ball before lunch, and an ill-at-ease Compton bowled after it. Woolley made a classic 41 in an hour, leaning into the ball, then was caught behind cutting at round-the-wicket Meyer: 168-7. Nichols and Smailes quietly progressed to

GENTLEMEN v PLAYERS

Played at Lord's, on July 13, 14, 15, 1938.
Gentlemen won by 133 runs.

GENTLEMEN

			Mins	4/6			Mins	4/6
Mr B.O.Allen	c Price b Pollard	10	49	0	b Pollard	5	18	0
†Mr P.A.Gibb	lbw b Smith	18	42	1	c & b Smith	24	55	2
Mr R.E.S.Wyatt	lbw b Smith	4	13	0	c Smith b Smailes	30	77	2
*Mr W.R.Hammond	c Compton b Pollard	46	116	2	c Price b Smith	37	81	2
Mr N.W.D.Yardley	c Price b Smailes	88	137	11	(7) b Smith	34	54	5
Mr H.T.Bartlett	not out	175	170	24/4	c Compton b Smith	1	3	0
Mr R.H.Moore	b Nichols	24	41	4	(9) b Smith	4	6	0
Mr F.R.Brown	c & b Smith	23	19	5	(5)b Smailes	6	4	1
Mr R.J.O.Meyer	lbw b Smith	0	1	0	(10) not out	14	24	0
Capt J.W.A.Stephenson	c Price b Nichols	6	30	0				
Mr K.Farnes	c Price b Pollard	10	42	2	(8) not out	16	58	1
Extras	(B 2, LB 3, NB 2)	7			(LB 1)	1		
Total		**411**	339		(8 wickets, declared)	**172**	198	

Fall: 1st inns 1/27, 2/31, 3/35, 4/155, 5/193, 6/250, 7/285, 8/285, 9/329, 10/411.
2nd inns 1/14, 2/36, 3/86, 4//96, 5/99, 6/119, 7/140, 8/146.

PLAYERS

			Mins	4/6			Mins	4/6
W.J.Edrich	c Stephenson b Farnes	0	5	0	c Gibb b Meyer	78	161	7
L.Hutton	lbw b Farnes	52	129	4	lbw b Brown	6	29	0
†W.F.Price	c Hammond b Farnes	0	3	0	(9) c Gibb b Farnes	5	10	0
E.Paynter	c Gibb b Stephenson	36	49	5	(3) lbw b Stephenson	12	48	2
J.Hardstaff	b Farnes	25	60	2	(4) b Brown	0	1	0
*F.E.Woolley	c Gibb b Meyer	41	54	4	(5) c Moore b Brown	8	11	1
D.C.S.Compton	b Farnes	6	11	1	(6) lbw b Farnes	45	77	7
M.S.Nichols	b Farnes	23	65	1	(7) not out	31	73	4
T.F.Smailes	b Farnes	19	38	2	(8) b Stephenson	20	23	3
T.P.B.Smith	not out	9	12	2	c & b Farnes	9	12	1
R.Pollard	b Farnes	5	4	1	c Farnes b Stephenson	13	7	2
Extras	(LB 2)	2			(B 4, W 1)	5		
Total		**218**	222			**232**	234	

Fall: 1st inns 1/0, 2/0, 3/58, 4/114, 5/119, 6/139, 7/168, 8/203, 9/212, 10/218.
2nd inns 1/18, 2/53, 3/54, 4/64, 5/143, 6/152, 7/182, 8/200, 9/216, 10/232.
(Smailes hit one 5 in the first innings)

PLAYERS	O	M	R	W	O	M	R	W
Nichols	29	2	117	2	7	1	17	0
Pollard	27.5	4	60	3	22	4	53	1
Smith	38	6	140	4	27	6	68	5
Smailes	21	2	87	1	11	0	33	2

GENTLEMEN	O	M	R	W	O	M	R	W
Farnes	21.3	6	43	8	24	6	60	3
Stephenson	21	4	46	1	21.4	6	63	3
Brown	24	3	82	0	18	3	75	3
Meyer	9	0	34	1	16	4	29	1
Wyatt	5	1	11	0				

Umpires: F.Chester and J.Hardstaff.

203 then Farnes bowled both with the new ball. Pollard played the best shot of the day, a cover-drive for four off Stephenson before the Players conceded a lead of 193. Gibb kept efficiently and conceded no byes. Farnes had 8-43 and hit the stumps five times.

Hammond did not enforce the follow-on and the Gentlemen went in again at 4.05pm. Allen was late on a straight ball, Gibb caught and bowled. Hammond and Wyatt added 50 sensibly — Wyatt gently barracked — then Wyatt popped a catch to short leg. Brown, promoted, swung cross-batted. Bartlett was caught at long off — 99-5 — which prompted a general exodus to the gates among the crowd of 8,955. Hammond was out at 6.20pm. The day closed with the Gentleman 120-6, their efforts to force the pace having failed.

Friday 15 July: Only 2,500 turned up. Yardley added 18 in 15 minutes. Farnes played a static straight bat and then Hammond declared at 12.15pm. Light rain postponed the start of the Players' innings until 12.55pm, when they had four and half hours to score 366. Edrich, undaunted, opened. Hutton was lbw again, then rain over lunch delayed the resumption till 2.15pm. Paynter was lbw to Stephenson's low faster ball. Hardstaff faced two balls. The first brought an lbw appeal from Farnes; the second, a googly by Brown, bowled him. Woolley was caught at cover: 64-4. Edrich and Compton added 79, Edrich taking advantage of anything short by Brown. But he was caught at the wicket off the last ball before tea. Then Compton was lbw; Smailes played too late; Smith skied a catch; Pollard perished at mid-off. At 5.45pm, with 45 minutes to spare, the Gentlemen achieved only their second victory at Lord's since the Great War.

July 13 to 15: The Board Backs Down

There had been no rain in Birmingham for two days but the wicket at Edgbaston was soft. Barnett took a well-earned rest and Sid Barnes put on the gloves when Bradman won the toss and put Warwickshire in. He performed well enough, except for a weakness in taking the slow bowlers down the leg-side. When Santall took a swipe at Waite's off-break, Fingleton, at short leg, took the ball on the peak of his cap and it grazed his head. He retired for 15 minutes.

Warwickshire fell to 48-3, but Ord and Dollery added 69 before Dollery was deceived by Waite's slower ball. Ord batted faultlessly for two hours until he skied a sweep to fine leg. As so often, Ward mopped up the tail. Fingleton decided not to open the innings and McCabe, his replacement, played on at 17. Then it was the usual story: Brown at one end, Bradman starting slowly then accelerating by slide rule, 50 in 100 minutes, 100 in 135 minutes, 116 at the close in a score of 202-1. Hollies was accurate but caused no difficulties.

On Thursday their stand progressed to 206 in 165 minutes — Brown taking no risks, Bradman taking plenty in his 135 in 165 minutes.

WARWICKSHIRE v AUSTRALIA

Played at Edgbaston, Birmingham, on July 13, 14, 1938.
Australia won by an innings and 93 runs.

WARWICKSHIRE

A.J.Croom	c McCabe b Waite	2	b Waite	5
Mr J.R.Thompson	b McCormick	11	(3) b O'Reilly	9
F.R.Santall	c sub b O'Reilly	21	(2) b McCormick	2
H.E.Dollery	c sub b Waite	31	c Barnes b Waite	2
J.S.Ord	c Bradman b O'Reilly	61	c Barnes b O'Reilly	30
†J.Buckingham	b Ward	15	b O'Reilly	19
*Mr P.Cranmer	st Barnes b Ward	15	b White	37
G.A.E.Paine	b O'Reilly	1	b O'Reilly	0
K.Wilmot	lbw b Ward	1	run out	0
J.H.Mayer	st Barnes b Ward	1	not out	5
W.E.Hollies	not out	2	c O'Reilly b Waite	4
Extras	(B 10, LB 7, NB 1)	18	(LB 4, NB 1)	5
Total		**179**		**118**

Fall: 1st inns 1/11, 2/25, 3/48, 4/117, 5/153, 6/169, 7/169, 8/171, 9/171.
2nd inns 1/5, 2/13, 3/16, 4/28, 5/56, 6/101, 7/107, 8/107, 9/107.

AUSTRALIA

S.J.McCabe	b Wilmot	14
W.A.Brown	b Hollies	101
*D.G.Bradman	c Wilmot b Mayer	135
†S.Barnes	c Cranmer b Hollies	24
A.G.Chipperfield	c Buckingham b Hollies	46
J.H.Fingleton	hit wkt b Hollies	9
M.G.Waite	not out	35
E.S.White	c Wilmot b Hollies	2
W.J.O'Reilly	b Paine	0
F.Ward	not out	13
Extras	(B 4, LB 4, W 1, NB 2)	11
Total	(8 wickets, declared)	**390**

Fall: 1st inns 1/17, 2/223, 3/274, 4/291, 5/315, 6/352, 7/362, 8/366.
E.L.McCormick did not bat.

AUSTRALIA	O	M	R	W	O	M	R	W
McCormick	9	3	14	1	5	2	10	1
Waite	17	3	38	2	11.3	2	33	3
O'Reilly	27	9	69	3	18	8	33	4
White	10	4	14	0	7	3	19	1
Ward	8.2	2	26	4	4	1	18	0

WARWICKSHIRE	O	M	R	W
Mayer	16	2	49	1
Wilmot	27	4	90	1
Hollies	42	8	130	5
Paine	30	7	65	1
Santall	3	0	28	0
Croom	3	0	17	0

Umpires: G.Beet and C.V.Tarbox.

After that only Chipperfield batted well; the rest were tied down by Hollies and were out trying to hit him. Then Warwickshire collapsed quietly for 118, interrupted twice by showers. Ord again showed his mettle and Cranmer hit vigorously. The last five wickets fell for 17 runs as the rain held off.

Having earned a rest day on Friday, the team woke to excellent tidings from Australia. The Board of Control had relented and decided that not only Bradman but all the tourists could bring their wives to England at the end of the tour. Bradman said, "I am delighted, both for my own sake and for the other members of the team."

On Thursday, in a speech in his native Birmingham, the Prime Minister said, "The Government of which I am at present the head, intends to hold on its course, which is set for the appeasement of the world". Next day the Air Minister, Sir Kingsley Wood, on a visit to Lord Nuffield's factory, placed an order for 1,000 Spitfires. Howard Hughes and his four companions completed their round the world flight in New York in three days, 19 hours.

In the Championship the first six places remained unchanged. Yorkshire won easily at Peterborough. Lancashire had no decision at Nelson, where Somerset had bowled them out for 79. Surrey took a home county game outside the metropolis for the first time ever, playing Hampshire at Guildford. The new cathedral city did them proud with 10,000 spectators on the first two days. Surrey won by an innings and 71.

At Colchester, Kent scored 429 on the first day, Arthur Fagg scoring 244 out of 386 in five hours without a chance. Essex replied with 350, Tom Pearce and Ray Smith adding 131 for the ninth wicket. By Thursday night Kent were 142-0, Fagg 104 in 70 minutes to become the seventh player to score 200 and 100 in one first-class match. On Friday he and Sunnucks took their first-wicket stand to 283, when Sunnocks was out for 82. Watt was sent in for quick runs. Chalk held off the declaration until Fagg reached 202 not out (27 4's in 170 minutes, out of 313-1 declared, and became the first man ever to hit two double hundreds in one match. It was a tremendous achievement, although Essex were without four main bowlers, all playing at Lord's. Their wicketkeeper, Wade, did not concede a bye until 626 runs were scored. Essex were 8-2 at lunch but rain prevented a Kent win.

The Fourth Test

July 16 to 19: Old Battles Stilled

THE murky conditions at Nottingham brought only a few spectators to watch the Australians meet Nottinghamshire. On a green pitch, they saw Arthur Jepson and Bill Voce get a lot of movement and the tourists were all out in five hours.

Voce had bowled over the wicket with three short legs. In the corresponding fixture in 1934 he bowled around the wicket to the same field and dropped the ball short, so much so that the Australians threatened to abandon the match. But this time he kept the ball well up and there was no controversy. The lunch score was 107-5 and thereafter the grim struggle continued in poor light and drizzle. Barnes hit a brave 58, scoring mostly on the off-side. The bowling flagged as Ward and O'Reilly put on 61 and a run out was missed when both men were at the same end. Even Fleetwood-Smith played a classic cover-drive before being caught in front of the pavilion.

Rain allowed Notts only ten minutes to bat, in which time they lost Keeton, bowled playing no stroke. A better day on Monday attracted 6,000 people and on a blameless pitch, Notts lost six wickets in 75 minutes. Hardstaff lasted only two balls. Gunn, who drove without compunction, found a partner in Voce, and they added 80 in 75 minutes. The innings ended half an hour after lunch.

Voce and Jepson did not bowl as well in the Australian second innings and Brown and Badcock opened with 121. Bradman and Hassett joined in a partnership which took them into a cloudless Tuesday — 216 in 140 minutes. Hassett dominated. When 114 he pulled Harris for a six which was caught by a spectator, despite having the sun in his eyes. Bradman was subdued until he passed his 2,000 runs for the tour, then he hit four 4's in an over from Gunn, pulled Marshall for six, then skied a ball to cover and was on his way back to the pavilion when cover dropped it. After some practice for Barnes, the declaration came at lunch, leaving Notts 210 minutes to last to save the game.

NOTTINGHAMSHIRE v AUSTRALIA

Played at Trent Bridge, Nottingham, on July 16, 18, 19, 1938.
Australia won by 412 runs.

AUSTRALIA

W.A.Brown	c Marshall b Voce	4	c Harris b Heane	63
C.L.Badcock	c Wheat b Jepson	6	c Jepson b Voce	54
*D.G.Bradman	lbw b Jepson	56	c Jepson b Marshall	144
A.L.Hassett	lbw b Voce	2	c Wheat b Heane	124
S.Barnes	lbw b Harris	58	not out	34
A.G.Chipperfield	b Jepson	4	not out	27
M.G.Waite	c Wheat b Harris	25		
†B.A.Barnett	b Harris	3		
F.Ward	not out	29		
W.J.O'Reilly	lbw b Voce	33		
L.O'B.Fleetwood-Smith	c Jepson b Harris	8		
Extras	(B 8, LB 5, NB 2)	15	(B 4, LB 1, NB 2)	7
Total		**243**	(4 wickets, declared)	**453**

Fall: 1st inns 1/8, 2/18, 3/25, 4/99, 5/103, 6/156, 7/164, 8/167, 9/228.
2nd inns 1/121, 2/125, 3/341, 4/404.

NOTTINGHAMSHIRE

W.W.Keeton	b Waite	3	c Fleetwood-Smith b Hassett	1
C.B.Harris	c Hassett b O'Reilly	8	lbw b Fleetwood-Smith	21
J.Knowles	lbw b Fleetwood-Smith	16	lbw b O'Reilly	8
J.Hardstaff	b O'Reilly	1	not out	67
G.V.Gunn	c Bradman b Ward	75	st Barnes b Ward	15
*Mr G.F.H.Heane	c Barnett b Fleetwood-Smith	0	c Hassett b Fleetwood-Smith	1
G.Yates	c Barnett b Fleetwood-Smith	5	c Hassett b Ward	2
Mr E.A.Marshall	b O'Reilly	0	st Barnes b Fleetwood-Smith	2
W.Voce	b O'Reilly	32	b Fleetwood-Smith	4
†A.B.Wheat	not out	2	b Fleetwood-Smith	0
A.Jepson	b O'Reilly	0	c Barnes b O'Reilly	8
Extras	(B 5)	5	(B 1, LB 5, W 1, NB 1)	8
Total		**147**		**137**

Fall: 1st inns 1/4, 2/16, 3/22, 4/32, 5/34, 6/64, 7/65, 8/145, 9/147.
2nd inns 1/1, 2/21, 3/45, 4/72, 5/77, 6/86, 7/104, 8/114, 9/114.

NOTTINGHAMSHIRE	O	M	R	W	O	M	R	W
Voce	30	3	72	3	21	2	80	1
Jepson	23	6	38	3	19	2	81	0
Harris	24.5	5	60	4	28	5	106	0
Gunn	11	0	38	0	9	0	44	0
Marshall	5	0	20	0	7	1	34	1
Heane	-	-	-	-	31	7	85	2
Hardstaff	-	-	-	-	3	0	16	0

AUSTRALIA	O	M	R	W	O	M	R	W
Waite	14	3	38	1	7	0	15	0
O'Reilly	25.5	8	39	5	5.2	1	7	2
Fleetwood-Smith	12	1	35	3	20	4	39	5
Ward	8	0	30	1	15	0	64	2
Hassett	-	-	-	-	7	4	4	1

Umpires: J.Newman and D.Hendren

Barnett yielded the gloves to Barnes and Hassett opened the bowling. His first ball in England would have been called a wide if Keeton had not stretched out and edged it to be caught at slip. When Fleetwood-Smith came on, he had an easy time against the slow-footed home batsmen. Hardstaff played himself into better form and was still in when the county were all out at 4.30pm.

In Parliament, the Secretary to the Treasury, Captain Ewan Wallace, was asked to repay the Entertainment Tax on the Manchester Test. Mr Montague (Labour, Islington West) asked, "Does the Minister consider that the National Religion ought to be taxed?" Viscountess Astor (Conservative, Sutton Plymouth): "What is the National Religion?" Chorus of Members: "Cricket".

Lord's July 16 to 19: Middlesex's Gain is England's Loss

The confrontation between the previous year's winners and runners-up was not without incident. Saturday was cold and cheerless and the wicket wet. There was a ridge just on a length and any ball just short of it bounced high. Walter Robins put the champions in and Sutcliffe was brilliantly caught in the gully. Then Hutton received a blow on the fingers from Edrich and was bowled next ball. Mitchell was caught on the leg-side. Gibb (for whom the regular wicketkeeper, Wood, was rested from the team) saw several balls fly past his head then ducked into one which bounced normally. It hit him on the head and went to square cover for four. Gibb went to hospital but was back on the ground at lunchtime. Yardley, dropped twice off Edrich, was caught in the slips off his glove and Barber was caught at short leg. In the rain and drizzle after lunch, Sellers was rapped three times on the knuckles by Jim Smith. Leyland shaped well until he was bowled through the gate. Smailes hit well but Yorkshire were all out for 144, Smith and Gray taking 7-73 between them. Yorkshire took the field without Gibb and Hutton, whose finger was found to be broken. Barber kept wicket and Wood and Turner fielded. Middlesex made 56-2 by the close.

Leyland did not field on Monday because it transpired that he had fractured his left thumb, although he was prepared to bat if necessary. A Middlesex player had to be used as third substitute and at Robins' suggestion, Arthur Wood was allowed to keep wicket. The Middlesex batting struggled hard. Hulme got a nasty blow on the knuckles from Bowes. With five runs needed for the lead, at 140-6, Robins came in to join Edrich. The Middlesex captain had earlier made a remark to Sellers that Leyland would get no sympathy, even if he batted with his arm in a sling. Bowes treated him to some intimidatory bowling, causing him to play a rather eccentric innings, backing away towards square leg (as Bradman had done against body-line). He hit one ball back over the 'keeper's head for four. Then he ran down the pitch, ran back again

Yorkshire's Paul Gibb is hit on the head by a delivery from Jim Smith during the Championship game against Middlesex at Lord's. The wicketkeeper was ruled out of the Fourth Test.

but too late to divert the ball from his stumps: 165-7. Edrich was out at 173 and his was a brave 53, considering that he had been knocked out by Farnes only four days before.

After lunch, Smith smote 26 despite breaking a bat and Middlesex took a lead of 61. Sutcliffe started Yorkshire's second innings with a series of hooks but was caught at short leg at 31. Barber attacked and Mitchell took several blows on the body from Smith, who passed his 100 wickets for the season. At their best point, Yorkshire were 28 runs ahead with five wickets standing. Leyland came in but was hit on the thumb again and retired after one ball. Middlesex needed only 43 to win.

If Middlesex were delighted at their eight-wicket victory, their former captain, Sir Pelham Warner, the Test selector, might be excused for not joining in. For on the Sunday during the match he had to announce the 13 for the Fourth Test at Leeds. Of the 13 who attended at Manchester, Nichols and Smailes were dropped and Hutton omitted because of his injury on Saturday. They were replaced by Mr K.Farnes (Essex), W.E.Bowes (Yorkshire) and Mr.N.W.D.Yardley (Cambridge University & Yorkshire). Because of doubts about Gibb, W.F.Price (Middlesex) was put on stand-by. Farnes strode back in, and Bowes

MIDDLESEX v YORKSHIRE

Played at Lord's, on July 16, 18, 1938.
Middlesex won by eight wickets.

YORKSHIRE

H.Sutcliffe	c Robertson b Gray	0	c Peebles b Edrich	22
L.Hutton	b Edrich	13	absent hurt	0
A.Mitchell	c Gray b Smith	8	(2) c & b Peebles	30
Mr P.A.Gibb	retired hurt	4	absent hurt	0
Mr N.W.D.Yardley	c Compton b Gray	11	(4) b Smith	6
M.Leyland	b Smith	25	(8) retired hurt	1
W.Barber	c Hulme b Gray	3	(3) b Smith	23
*Mr A.B.Sellers	b Smith	36	(5) b Gray	9
T.F.Smailes	c Robins b Smith	16	(7) b Smith	2
H.Verity	not out	10	(9) c Edrich b Gray	5
W.E.Bowes	c Compton b Peebles	2	(6) not out	4
Extras	(B 5, LB 3, W 2, NB 6)	16	(LB 1)	1
Total		**144**		**103**

Fall: 1st inns 1/3, 2/25, 3/25, 4/44, 5/62, 6/84, 7/131, 8/133, 9/144.
2nd inns 1/31, 2/76, 3/80, 4/85, 5/89, 6/98, 7/103.
W.Barber and A.Wood kept wicket for Yorkshire.

MIDDLESEX

J.D.Robertson	b Bowes	16	c Sellers b Yardley	26
W.J.Edrich	c sub b Smailes	53	not out	11
S.M.Brown	c Sellers b Verity	4	c Mitchell b Bowes	0
D.C.S.Compton	lbw b Bowes	24	not out	1
G.E.Hart	c Mitchell b Verity	17		
J.H.A.Hulme	c sub b Smailes	31		
†W.F.Price	lbw b Bowes	0		
*Mr R.W.V.Robins	b Bowes	13		
C.I.J.Smith	c Mitchell b Smailes	26		
Mr I.A.R.Peebles	c sub b Bowes	12		
L.H.Gray	not out	1		
Extras	(B 4, LB 3, NB 1)	8	(B 4, W 1)	5
Total		**205**	(2 wickets)	**43**

Fall: 1st inns 1/23, 2/34, 3/69, 4/98, 5/140, 6/140, 7/165, 8/173, 9/196, 10/205.
2nd inns 1/37, 2/42.

MIDDLESEX	O	M	R	W	O	M	R	W
Smith	23	6	45	4	17	5	33	3
Gray	15	4	28	3	11.2	2	40	2
Edrich	15	3	47	1	5	1	14	1
Peebles	2.3	0	8	1	4	0	15	1

YORKSHIRE	O	M	R	W	O	M	R	W
Bowes	33.1	14	67	5	5	2	17	1
Smailes	23	7	68	3	2	0	20	0
Verity	25	6	62	2				
Yardley	-	-	-	-	2	1	1	1

Umpires: E.J.Smith and C.W.L.Parker.

finally satisfied the selectors of his fitness, so that England at last had the best two opening bowlers together. Yardley was in as a middle-order batsman, thanks largely to his performance for the Gentlemen. Edrich was retained as an opener and, ironically, he probably owed his further chance to the ball he bowled which hit Hutton's finger. Hardstaff stayed in ahead of Fagg and Bartlett, and Wright was preferred to Peter Smith. On Tuesday it was clear that Gibb would not be fit and Price took over. England were certainly not awash with talented wicketkeepers at this time, although Arthur Wood and A.E.Wilson of Gloucestershire were in the running.

In the county matches of July 16-19, at The Oval, Brooks, in his benefit match, stumped Frank Woolley at the start of the third day and the great all-rounder departed to a standing ovation. Surrey were set 207 in 165 minutes. Fishlock was run out off a no-ball when he jumped out to drive, his bat broke and the ball spun back for Levett to run him out. But Surrey won by six wickets. At Bristol Washbrook scored 219 not out but Lancashire came up against Walter Hammond, who cruised to 271 in 390 minutes and passed 2,000 runs on the same day as Bradman. The drawn match produced 1,092 runs for 20 wickets. At Colchester, where Essex beat Sussex by an innings and 13 runs, Peter Smith became another 100-wicketeer, and Nichols reached 98. The top four places in the table were unchanged: Yorkshire average 9.00, Middlesex 8.85, Lancashire 8.47, Surrey 7.20.

Frank Woolley, on his last first-class appearance at The Oval, plays a ball from Watts on to his wicket and is out for 63. In the second innings the great man was caught at the wicket and departed to a standing ovation.

July 20 to 22: No Triple This Time

The groundsman at Headingley, Dick Moulton, said that the outfield was not quite dry near the boundary and there was still a little life in the wicket. He predicted that Bradman would not score a third triple century in a Leeds Test. But with the weather settled, no rain since Sunday and the forecast good, there was a general feeling that the Test would be inconclusive and that The Oval would decide the Ashes. Indeed, no Headingley Test had produced a result since 1929.

The teams practised in the same nets and whilst the Australian selectors conferred in their team hotel at Harrogate, the other tourists kicked a rugby ball around on the Stray, the spa town's popular 200-acre common, and local boys and girls joined in. Kenneth Farnes announced his engagement to Miss Margaret Stapley of Hatten, Essex. For the Test, all reserve seats (3,400 per day) were sold out.

In the county matches which finished on the first day of the Test, Yorkshire displayed their reserve strength. With six enforced changes from the team that lost to Middlesex, they beat Hampshire at Portsmouth. Frank Wilkinson, an in-swinger brought up from the 2nd XI, took 7-68 on the first day. At Bristol, Gloucestershire scored 487-5 declared (Emmett 165 not out) and Surrey replied with 462, seven men passing 40. Then Stan Squires bowled out Gloucestershire for 114. Needing 140 to win in 90 minutes, Surrey triumphed by five wickets with ten minutes to spare (Squires 65 not out). Essex were all out for 58 on the first morning at Worksop, but a century by Sonny Avery and splendid bowling and fielding gave them victory over Notts by 11 runs. Kent started their Maidstone Week by beating Glamorgan and so many people had asked Frank Woolley to reconsider his retirement that he had to make a statement that he had not changed his mind.

Fourth Test at Leeds
Friday 22 July: England Lose Their Sparkle

Queues had started at 4am and there was a very heavy dew and an early morning haze. Hammond and two members of the selection committee, Warner and Perrin, had a good look at the wicket at 10am. At the ground were not only the England 13 but also the injured Hutton, Gibb, Ames and Leyland. The teams were exchanged. England left out Yardley and Goddard. Australia had one change from the Lord's Test: Chipperfield dropped out to give Waite a well-deserved chance. After the toss, Hammond was able to announce to the crowded dressing-room, "Gentlemen, we have won the toss." A cheer went up. "What a player!" someone said. Hammond was tempted to let Bowes loose in the heavy grey atmosphere but decided against batting last on a wicket likely to wear.

So it was McCormick who opened the bowling from the Football Stand (or Pavilion) End with the shaded faces of the crowd and no sightscreen behind him. He bowled to four slips and two short legs and opened with two uneventful maidens. Waite, from the Kirkstall Lane End, got some late outswing with his medium pace. Barnett edged him for four and two through the slips and at 14, when he was nine, he steered a full-toss to square leg where O'Reilly dropped it. Waite changed to McCormick's end and at 19, O'Reilly came on and made the ball turn slowly. Then Barnett gave another chance off Waite to Brown at second slip. Edrich, too, looked uneasy and stayed on six for 20 minutes. After 55 minutes play, only 29 runs were on the board. Then Edrich survived a big lbw appeal against O'Reilly, but next ball the googly bowled him via his pads. A quarter of an hour later, Barnett pushed O'Reilly to mid-on, called Hardstaff for a single, then sent him back. Hardstaff flung himself to the turf but O'Reilly had whipped off the bails from Hassett's throw and England were 34-2 in 70 minutes.

O'Reilly bowled six successive maidens and the 24,000 crowd were not best pleased at this display from Barnett and Hammond. After all, this was not the Roses Match, merely a Test Match. When Fleetwood-Smith came on and Hammond hit a full toss for four, the cheer was more ironic than appreciative. Lunch came at 62-2, O'Reilly having figures of 14-11-4-1, which said more about England's batting than his bowling.

After lunch, with the Princess Royal and her husband, the Earl of Harewood, present, Hammond made an effort to entertain. He drove a no-ball by McCormick straight into the Football Stand for six, and found the boundary ropes off Fleetwood-Smith. But at 88, Barnett failed in his attempt to play and miss against McCormick and edged a catch behind the wicket. He had scored 30 in two and a half hours, the outward shell of the man who made 98 before lunch at Trent Bridge. At 88-3, it was Paynter joining Hammond again — only Compton and the tail to follow.

The sun was now shining and the scene seemed set fair for a Hammond century. O'Reilly had to fall back on leg theory but two lovely cover drives took Hammond past 50. Paynter was the solid henchman. Then Waite relieved O'Reilly and Hammond drove his first ball so hard that the umpire's life flashed before him as he flung himself sideways. A respectable 68 had accrued in the hour after lunch before drinks were brought out by a steward and four waitresses. At 142, Hammond pushed forward and missed O'Reilly's sharp off-break; he was out for 76 in 140 minutes with a six and ten 4's. Compton soon edged O'Reilly between 'keeper and slip for four. There was the one four from Paynter, whilst Compton defended, and England were muddling through somehow. It was flat beer for the Yorkshire crowd, not champagne. Just before tea, though, the struggle was thrown away. Paynter lost his concentration, jumped out to Fleetwood-Smith, overbalanced and was stumped for 28 in 100 minutes. Young Compton followed without addition, mystified by O'Reilly. Tea was taken, the batting shaken to its foundations at 171-6 and O'Reilly the destroyer: 26.5-15-38-3.

One run was added when Price — no Ames, he — prodded forward and edged to slip. Wright and Verity were an unlikely pair to launch a counter-attack but they did, adding 41 in 30 minutes, as the bowling wilted and the field scattered. There were some good shots by Wright and two 4's in an over by Verity off Fleetwood-Smith. There was also some farce, Bradman catching Wright off a no-ball by O'Reilly, then trying to run him out. Fleetwood-Smith got Wright out, skying a catch to Fingleton at deep mid-off, and Farnes was out in the same way, this time Fingleton having to run backwards.

Bowes swung myopically at O'Reilly and was bowled. England were all out at 5.35pm, for 223 in 298 minutes off 98.1 overs, a rate of only 44.89 runs per hour, 2.27 runs per over. Australia bowled 19.76 overs per hour. O'Reilly was back to his best form, conning the batsmen into believing that the slow easy pitch was something of which to be scared; Fleetwood-Smith was at his most accurate, and Waite had bowled well without luck. Only Hammond had played an innings worthy of memory.

Australia had to face Farnes and Bowes and 45 minutes of worsening light. Farnes opened from the shady Football Stand End. In his first over he beat Fingleton. In his fourth he bisected Brown's bat from his body and the ball went through for four runs. Bowes, from his usual Kirkstall Lane End, had less venom, and the batsman grew into their task as the clouds lifted. At 28, Wright replaced Bowes and his very first ball was short and nipped off the pitch. Brown tried to pull it and his leg-stump was knocked back. Barnett came in a nighwatchman and Wright nearly yorked him but he survived. Australia closed the day — a gruelling one for England supporters — at 32-1 (Fingleton 9 not out, Barnett 1 not out) off 13 overs. The day's attendance was 24,000, of whom 15,803 paid £2,888 2s 6d.

It was disclosed that the Mrs Bradman, McCabe and Jeanes would arrive in London on 16 September from the ship *Strathmore.*

Saturday, 23 July: Dancing in the Dark

Barnett had to hit the ball twice to avoid playing on to Wright and Fingleton nearly played on to Bowes but, apart from that, the overnight pair experienced little difficulty. Bowes switched to the Football Stand End and bowled better, having Fingleton play and miss. It was not until 12.55pm, after the gates had been closed, that Verity pushed one through and Fingleton disgusted himself by replicating Brown's mode of dismissal the previous evening. The crowd gave him an appreciative cheer for his fighting innings of 30 in 130 minutes. Bradman settled in quite quickly and cover-drove two 4's off Bowes.

Farnes came on at 116, for a pre-lunch spell, and Barnett hit two leg-side 4's off him. But, at 128, he flashed outside the off-stump and gave Price his first Test victim. He had scored 57 in 130 minutes. McCabe had to face four torrid balls from Farnes, survived two lbw appeals, and Australia went to lunch at 128-3 (Bradman 17 not out).

Soon after lunch, McCabe's off-stump was uprooted by Farnes. Badcock was bowled, making a sad attempt at a stroke: 145-5. The light was now so poor that Bradman batted without a cap; as the afternoon wore on a Davey lamp might have been appropriate. He kept the bowling at bay and the scoring ticking along and hit a four off Verity for his 50 in 92 minutes. Hassett pushed and prodded like a tailender and scored 13 out of 50 in an hour before Wright had him caught at slip. When Waite reached the middle, he spoke to his captain. "Is that you, Don?" he might have said; but Bradman seemed to enjoy the challenge of batting in the twilight, smiling and talking between overs. Remember that there was no sightsceen in the Football Stand. No appeal was made against the light, for Bradman feared that the lowering clouds might deposit their contents on the wicket and thought that it was easier to score in bad light — which also handicaps the fielders — than on a wet wicket. As it happened the rain contained itself. At any time after 3.30pm, an interruption in play could activate the tea interval. At last, at 3.57pm, as Farnes prepared to menace them with the new ball, the batsmen appealed against the light, and tea was taken, with the score 205-6 (Bradman 71 not out). The stoppage lasted 22 minutes. Then Bradman drove Farnes for three 4's and edged Bowes through the slips for the first-innings lead. Waite, having survived 45 minutes in all, was caught behind at 232. In the next over, Bradman passed 100 — his 12th of the tour — and settled down to squeeze out some more runs before the close. But his concentration lapsed for a second and he allowed Bowes to bowl him, taking his eye off the ball and trying to cut a delivery on the stumps. He was backing away towards the pavilion as he played the stroke and he continued his walk off almost in one movement. Even so, his unsupported innings on a slow turning wicket in light which veered from poor to atrocious, was worth as much as his triple centuries in previous Leeds Tests: 103 out of 153 in 178 minutes with nine 4's and no chance.

When the left-handed O'Reilly edged Farnes, Hammond darted across five yards to hold a right-handed catch inches from the turf, one of his most memorable slip catches. Fleetwood-Smith was dropped off a skier by Farnes mid-wicket. Then Bowes ended the innings by bowling McCormick, giving Australia a lead of 19. The innings of

242 which lasted 315 minutes and 98.4 overs, a rate of 46.09 runs per hour and 2.45 per over. England bowled 18.79 overs per hour. The bowling had been tight and very pertinent all day. Some criticised Hammond for under-using Wright. Verity thought that he should have been allowed to bowl over the wicket because he saw a spot near the leg stump. Australia had had the worst of the batting conditions so far and their slender lead was an act of 'daylight' robbery by Bradman.

Edrich and Barnett ventured forth at 5.20pm and before McCormick bowled a ball they appealed successfully against the light. They were back out ten minutes later and, in light better than at any time since before lunch, scored 49 without loss in 55 minutes off 18 overs (Edrich 25, Barnett 20). When four, Edrich was dropped by Fleetwood-Smith at slip off McCormick. Then he drove McCormick confidently straight for four to give England the lead. Barnett recovered his touch and at the close England were usefully placed. A capacity crowd of 33,000, of whom 23,227 paid, saw — or tried to see — an absorbing day of modern Test cricket.

Monday, 25 July: The Crunch Comes

On Sunday it rained everywhere around Leeds, but nothing fell on the most important 22 yards in Yorkshire and by Monday morning, sun shone on the queues waiting to go through the turnstiles. Brown and Fingleton practised and the English Barnett took a net practice to Verity's bowling, assisted by some small boys as fielders.

Under a patchy cloud, Barnett cut McCormick's second ball for a single to bring up the 50. O'Reilly opened from the other end and at once obtained lift and turn, although neither was excessive. Incoming spectators were abused with cries of, 'Sit down', and the umpires spoke to the police about the noise, which gradually eased with the closing of the gates.

Barnett pulled a no-ball by O'Reilly for four, then McCormick troubled Barnett with one short ball and in his next over pitched one half way: Barnett hooked too early and edged upwards; his namesake ran ten yards to hold the catch: 60-1. (It turned out to be the highest partnership of the match).

In the same over, Edrich played a ball down and back on to his wicket but a committee of inspection decided that the bail was not disturbed. The fast bowler rapped Edrich on the knuckles as a parting gesture. O'Reilly took his end and Fleetwood-Smith took on the Kirkstall Lane End.

Edrich survived a big lbw appeal from the 'chinaman' bowler and Hardstaff looked uncomfortable until O'Reilly was called for a no-ball which he swept for four. O'Reilly was angry. His next ball was a fast leg-break that took the off bail, the sort of delivery that is so

O'Reilly bowls to Joe Hardstaff during England's second innings in the Headingley Test. Hardstaff hit a 4 off a no-ball but was then clean bowled.

Edrich enjoys some good fortune when a ball from McCormick hits the stumps but does not dislodge the bails. Shortly afterwards, however, Edrich was stumped off Fleetwood-Smith.

good it seems almost unfair. As he departed, Hardstaff said to umpire Chester, "What chance have you got against a ball like that?" The next ball, to Hammond, was a googly which the captain turned around the corner and Brown took the catch low with his left hand and leapt in the air: 73-3. Paynter saw out the over within a ring of fielders. Edrich pushed out to Fleetwood-Smith's googly, lifted his right foot and Barnett neatly stumped him: 73-4. It was only 12.30pm and the last recognised batsman were at the crease. Paynter hit two 4's in an over off O'Reilly and Compton did the same. They added 23 in 20 minutes, then Compton swept at a ball down the leg-side which kicked a little, brushed it with his glove or bat handle and was caught behind: 96-5. The new batsman brought with him the drinks steward and his retinue of waitresses. Paynter watched every ball as if it were his first and last and Price adhered for 20 minutes. The crowd voiced relief at every defensive stroke. Price was lbw to Fleetwood-Smith: 116-6. Paynter nearly played on — another committee was convened to examine the bails — and without addition Fleetwood-Smith bowled Verity and had Wright caught at slip. Farnes stopped the hat-trick with a drive for four, then glanced a three. O'Reilly bowled him. As Bill Bowes was cheered to the wicket, O'Reilly asked the umpire how many balls were left in the over. "Just two," he was told. "That's enough," said O'Reilly.

Paynter told Bowes to push right forward to every ball. Bowes forgot himself and played his first ball from the crease and that was that. Paynter was left high and dry for 21 not out in 65 minutes, with four 4's, runless since Price left. England were all out five minutes before the scheduled lunch hour for 123 in 171 minutes off 50.5 overs (a rate of 43.16 runs per hour, 2.42 runs per over; Australia bowled 17.84 overs per hour). This day, England had made 74 runs for ten wickets in 115 minutes.

Apart from changing ends at 63, O'Reilly had bowled continuously in the session for figures of 15-4-45-5. Twelve of the runs had come from three no-balls. In the morning, Fleetwood-Smith had 12-0-21-4. Both men had bowled beautifully on a helpful wicket. The ball turned, but England's batting was abject and the hard work of the summer had been thrown away on one pleasant Leeds morning. Only the left-handed Paynter seemed to have a clue. He could have played a match-winning innings if anyone had bothered to stay with him. Instead, the Ashes were half-way down the sink.

Australia could not take their task for granted as they started after lunch needing only 105 to win. Forty more runs would have made all the difference. Farnes and Bowes opened to Fingleton and Brown. Every hint of a false stroke was seized on by the crowd. Four byes were given away. A primeval moan rose up when Bowes bowled a no-ball and Brown hit it for four. But they stood up in joy when at 17, Farnes had Brown lbw with a ball that skidded through. Bradman walked out with an unusually serious face. He survived one very good over by Farnes which contained a big shout for lbw, then glanced a four. Verity came on for Farnes and in his first over Fingleton was bamboozled by a ball that popped: 32-2 in 45 minutes. 14 runs were conceded in Verity's next over and Bowes, at mid on, a poor fielder, was twice to blame. Trying to gather in Barnett's throw in with his boot, he conceded four overthrows. Then he allowed Bradman three instead of a single when the ball sped past him. Wright bowled in place of Bowes and in his first over, Bradman edged for two, then steered the next ball low into the hands of Verity at second slip: 50-3 in 53 minutes. Bradman, uncharacteristically, just stood at his wicket. Umpire Frank Chester said to him, "You've been out a fortnight." The air was rent with cheering.

Dark clouds assembled. In the poor light, Hammond brought back Farnes for Verity. Hassett seized on a no-ball by Wright and hit it for four. The next ball he edged into the slips but Verity moved the wrong way. 60 up in an hour. McCabe, who could have resolved the issue in a few overs, got a bad ball, a rank long hop from Wright, and pulled it straight to mid wicket: 61-4. Any result except a draw now seemed possible. Wright was spinning the ball prodigiously and seemed the main danger. The light was getting worse and an elusive drizzle was in the air. The insupportable tension was relieved when a black dog ran on the field, like the clown scene in a Shakespearean tragedy.

Hassett took a calculated gamble. He thumped a good length ball by Wright and it went for three. This made Wright try harder and he dropped short. He was taken off for Bowes at 68. Hammond switched his four bowlers regularly and relied mainly on the pace men. Hassett saw rain in the offing and resolved that valour was the better part of discretion. He hooked Bowes for four and drove Verity for four. Badocck was strokeless but safe, except when Wright nearly bowled him. In the dressing-room, 'Tiger' O'Reilly was pacing up and down with his pads on, Bradman eating and drinking tea to occupy himself, neither able to watch play. The manager could not bear even to stay in the ground and had gone out to the road where queues of people were milling around, unable to get in.

Hassett shepherded the score to within 14 of victory then he slashed at Wright and was caught at short cover. He had made a priceless 33 in half an hour. Rain was now falling. The new batsman, Barnett, swished a Wright full toss away for four. The rain grew into a shower and at 3.50pm, England induced the umpires to come off, with nine needed. The spectators preferred to get soaked than to leave their places. By 4pm the rain had passed over and sunshine was hinted at. England asked for sawdust; they had not given up the war of nerves. Farnes bowled two maidens. Bowes conceded three singles. Barnett cut Farnes square for four, edged the next ball to the boundary and at 4.15pm

Denis Compton hit two 4s in one over off O'Reilly but was then caught at the wicket off his gloves and England were 96 for five.

Farnes prevented the hat-trick but was soon comprehensively bowled by O'Reilly, leaving England 123 for nine.

Spectators examine groundsman Dick Moulton's 'undoped' Headingley pitch.

Australia retained the Ashes at the end of the most nerve-stretching Test in England since The Oval Test of 1926. Badcock, still there at the end, had done his bit. The players indulged in the usual scramble for stumps and bails. The crowd swept over the ground and stood in front of the dressing-rooms in the pavilion, calling for Bradman. Australia made 107-5 in 110 minutes off 32-3 overs (58.36 runs per hour, 3.29 runs per over, 17.72 overs per hour).

The captains, both changed into ordinary clothes, appeared together on the balcony, smiling happily, posed for photographs, shook hands, waved to the crowd and retired. As the spectators filed out of the ground, newspaper boys were shouting, "Bad news from The Oval", where Yorkshire were struggling against Surrey. Some 36,000 people watched the last day's play in the Test; the aggregate attendance for three days was 99,614 and the total receipts were £14,190.

It was asking too much for England to recover from the batting collapse of the morning. The lead was just too small to defend. The bowling and fielding was not open to criticism. Of course, Hammond's tactics were again questioned. Some said he was right to bring back Farnes and Bowes when the light failed, but that he should not have put on Bowes for Wright at 68-4. Bowes, who did not bowl quite as well as in the first innings, later wrote that he had suggested to Hammond that a spinner should always to kept on at one or both ends. In the final analysis, England would have won if the batsmen had showed the proper technical application in each innings. They tended to play O'Reilly and Fleetwood-Smith from the crease and batsmen who had plenty of strokes were too timid to use them. Australia won, despite poor light in both their innings, thanks to Bradman and O'Reilly. Bradman's century, although one of special skill even by his standards, was par for a Test; O'Reilly's ten-wicket performance was a birdie, perhaps even an eagle.

The groundsman, Dick Moulton, with his natural 'undoped' wicket, had allowed the public to witness one of the most challenging encounters between bat and ball for many years.

During the victory celebrations after the match, Sid Barnes and Jack Badcock went for an impromptu drive in one of the team's cars. An on-coming car with only one headlight forced them off the road and their vehicle turned over. Neither man was hurt. They decided to leave the car where it was and hitched a lift back to the hotel in Harrogate. When Barnes was sneaking up the back entrance he was spotted by Mr Jeanes, who said, "Hullo, what's happened to you?" "I fell over a rake in the back garden," was Barnes' improvised explanation for his peculiar appearance.

ENGLAND v AUSTRALIA

Fourth Test at Headingley, Leeds.

Friday 22nd, Saturday 23rd and Monday, 25th July 1938.
Umpires: E.J.Smith and F.Chester.

ENGLAND First Innings (won toss)		mins	bls	4/6
W.J.Edrich b O'Reilly	12	57	67	1
C.J.Barnett c Barnett (wkt) b McCormick	30	143	134	1
J.Hardstaff run out (Hassett-O'Reilly)	4	9	10	1
*Mr W.R.Hammond b O'Reilly	76	136	149	10/1
E.Paynter st Barnett b Fleetwood-Smith	28	101	108	3
D.C.S.Compton b O'Reilly	14	43	36	2
†W.F.Price c McCabe (slip) b O'Reilly	0	8	8	0
H.Verity not out	25	47	54	4
D.V.P.Wright c Fingleton (long off) b Fleetwood-Smith	22	28	27	3
Mr K.Farnes c Fingleton (long off) b Fleetwood-Smith	2	1	2	0
W.E.Bowes b O'Reilly	3	8	3	0
Extras (LB 4, NB 3)	7			
Total (All out — 98.1 overs)	**223**	298	598	

Nine no-balls were bowled.

Bowling	O	M	R	W
McCormick (NB 3)				
lunch	11	4	21	0
tea	20	6	46	1
end	-	-	-	-
Waite				
lunch	12	4	23	0
tea	18	7	31	0
end	-	-	-	-
O'Reilly (NB 6)				
lunch	14	11	4	1
tea	26.5	15	38	3
end	34.1	17	66	5
Fleetwood-Smith				
lunch	4	2	11	0
tea	17	4	49	1
end	25	7	73	3
McCabe				
lunch	-	-	-	-
tea	1	1	0	0
end	-	-	-	-

Timetable Of The Innings

Time	Score	Mins	Overs	
11.30 Friday start				
12.27 Edrich out	1-29	57	19.5	Barnett 15
12.38 Hardstaff out	2-34	68	23.1	Barnett 16
1.15	51	105	34.5	
1.30 to 2.17 Lunch	62	120	41	Barnett 25 Hammond 18
2.40 Barnett out	3-88	143	48.3	Hammond 39
3.01	103	164	55	
3.43 Hammond out	4-142	206	69.5	Paynter 17
3.52	152	215	71.5	
4.23 Paynter out	5-171	246	81.5	Compton 14
4.28 Compton out	6-171	251	82.5	Price 0
4.28 to 4.47 Tea (rain)				
4.52 Price out	7-172	256	84.5	Verity 1
5.12	203	276	91.1	
5.22 Wright out	8-213	286	95.3	Verity 20
5.25 Farnes out	9-215	289	95.5	Verity 20
5.34 Bowes out	10-223	298	98.1	

Individual Targets
Hammond 52 94m 100b

AUSTRALIA First Innings		mins	bls	4/6
J.H.Fingleton b Verity	30	127	117	1
W.A.Brown b Wright	22	30	30	1
†B.A.Barnett c Price (wkt) b Farnes	57	131	140	6
*D.G.Bradman b Bowes	103	178	184	9
S.J.McCabe b Farnes	1	14	9	0
C.L.Badcock b Bowes	4	11	12	0
A.L.Hassett c Hammond (slip) b Wright	13	55	52	1
M.G.Waite c Price (wkt) b Farnes	3	47	35	0
W.J.O'Reilly c Hammond (slip) b Farnes	2	12	6	0
E.L.McCormick b Bowes	0	7	5	0
L.O'B.Fleetwood-Smith not out	2	5	4	0
Extras (B 2, LB 3)	5			
Total (All out — 98.4 overs)	**242**	315	594	

New ball at 209. Two no-balls were bowled.

Timetable Of The Innings

Time		Score	Mins	Overs	
5.47	Friday start				
6.17	Brown out	1-28	30	9.1	Fingleton 6
6.30	Close	32	43	13	Fingleton 9 Barnett 1
11.30	Saturday start				
12.01		50	74	22.1	
12.54	Fingleton out	2-87	127	39.4	Barnett 35
1.09		100	142	44.5	
1.29	Barnett out	3-128	162	51.2	Bradman 17
1.32	to 2.15 Lunch	128	165	52	Bradman 17 McCabe 0
2.27	McCabe out	4-136	177	55.2	Bradman 24
2.39	Badcock out	5-145	189	59	Bradman 29
2.45		150	195	60.2	
3.35	Hassett out	6-195	220	78.4	Bradman 63
3.48		203	258	82	
3.57	to 4.19 (bad light)	205	267	85	Bradman 71 Waite 2
4.30	First Innings lead	226	278	88.3	
4.46	Waite out	7-232	294	93.5	Bradman 97
4.58	Bradman out	8-240	306	97	O'Reilly 2
5.00	O'Reilly out	9-240	308	97.1	McCormick 0
5.07	McCormick out	10-242	315	98.4	

Bowling	O	M	R	W
Farnes				
close	7	1	21	0
lunch	13	2	40	1
tea	19	3	56	2
end	26	3	77	4
Bowes				
close	4	0	11	0
lunch	18	4	41	0
tea	29	5	63	1
end	35.4	6	79	3
Wright (NB 2)				
close	2	2	0	1
lunch	12	4	32	1
tea	15	4	38	2
end	-	-	-	-
Verity				
close	-	-	-	-
lunch	9	3	13	1
tea	19	6	30	1
end	-	-	-	-
Edrich				
tea	3	0	13	0
end	-	-	-	-

Individual Targets

Barnett	51	125m	130b
Bradman	52	92m	88b
	100	170m	173b

ENGLAND Second Innings (19 in arrears)		mins	bls	4/6
W.J.Edrich st Barnett b Fleetwood-Smith	28	111	110	3
C.J.Barnett c Barnett (wkt) b McCormick	29	77	69	5
J.Hardstaff b O'Reilly	11	23	23	2
*Mr W.R.Hammond c Brown (short leg) b O'Reilly	0	1	1	0
E.Paynter not out	21	64	60	4
D.C.S.Compton c Barnett (wkt) b O'Reilly	15	19	20	3
†W.F.Price lbw b Fleetwood-Smith	6	20	14	1
H.Verity b Fleetwood-Smith	0	5	5	0
D.V.P.Wright c Waite (slip) b Fleetwood-Smith	0	1	1	0
Mr K.Farnes b O'Reilly	7	3	6	1
W.E.Bowes lbw b O'Reilly	0	1	1	0
Extras (LB 4, W 1, NB 1)	6			
Total (All out — 50.5 overs)	**123**	171	310	

Five no-balls and one wide were bowled.

Bowling	O	M	R	W
McCormick (NB 2)				
close	6	2	12	0
end	11	4	18	1
Waite				
close	2	0	9	0
end	-	-	-	-
O'Reilly (NB 3)				
close	6	4	11	0
end	21.5	8	56	5
Fleetwood-Smith (W 1)				
close	4	0	13	0
end	16	4	34	4

Timetable Of The Innings

Time		Score	Mins	Overs	
5.20	Saturday (Players appeared, bad light, ball not bowled)				
5.35	start				
6.00	England take lead	22	25	8.1	
6.30	Close	49	55	18	Edrich 25 Barnett 20 extras 4
11.30	Monday start				
11.31		50	56	18.2	
11.52	Barnett out	1-60	77	24.1	Edrich 26
12.17	Hardstaff out	2-73	102	32.2	Edrich 28
12.20	Hammond out	3-73	105	32.3	Edrich 28
12.26	Edrich out	4-73	111	33.5	Paynter 0
12.46	Compton out	5-96	131	40.3	Paynter 8
12.53		101	138	42	
1.08	Price out	6-116	153	47.2	Paynter 21
1.15	Verity out	7-116	160	49.1	Paynter 21
1.18	Wright out	8-116	163	49.2	Paynter 21
1.23	Farnes out	9-123	168	50.4	Paynter 21
1.26	Bowes out Lunch	10-123	171	50.5	

AUSTRALIA Second Innings
(needing 105 in 600 mins)

		mins	bls	4/6
J.H.Fingleton lbw b Verity	9	42	43	0
W.A.Brown lbw b Farnes	9	15	12	1
*D.G.Bradman c Verity (slip) b Wright	16	35	31	1
S.J.McCabe c Barnett (mid-on) b Wright	15	17	16	1‡
A.L.Hassett c Edrich (cover) b Wright	33	32	36	5
C.L.Badcock not out	5	46	42	0
†B.A.Barnett not out	15	20	18	3
Extras (B 4, NB 1)	5			
Total (5 wickets — 32.3 overs)	**107**	108	198	

Three no-balls were bowled.
‡McCabe hit one five (due to four overthrows).

Timetable Of The Innings

Time	Score	Mins	Overs	
2.15 Monday start				
2.30 Brown out	1-17	15	4.5	Fingleton 4
2.57 Fingleton out	2-32	42	13	Bradman 10
3.07	50	52	15.2	
3.07 Bradman out	3-50	52	15.3	McCabe 12
3.16 McCabe out	4-61	61	17.4	Hassett 8
3.41 Hassett out	5-91	86	25.5	Badcock 4
3.49 to 4.02 rain	96	94	28.1	Badcock 4 Barnett 5
4.15	103	107	32.2	
4.16 Australia win	107	108	32.3	

Australia won by five wickets and kept the 'Ashes'.

Bowling

	O	M	R	W
Farnes				
rain	9.1	2	9	1
end	11.3	4	17	1
Bowes (NB 1)				
rain	9	0	32	0
end	11	0	35	0
Verity				
rain	5	2	24	1
end	-	-	-	-
Wright (NB 2)				
rain	5	0	26	3
end	-	-	-	-

County matches July 23 to 26: Yorkshire Falter

Yorkshire's strength of reserve failed them at The Oval. With five top players absent, fortune did not smile on them. Smailes broke down with leg trouble in Surrey's opening innings of 264. Yorkshire collapsed in reply — Turner retiring after being injured when he tried to hook Watts — to be 36-6 at the close. The lame Smailes led a recovery to 100 all out on Monday. Surrey elected to bat again and made 383-3 declared in 83 overs, Whitfield 174 not out. Holmes declared, giving his side an hour plus the last day to bowl out Yorkshire, which they did by 3.35pm on Tuesday with 232 runs to spare. It was Surrey's fifth consecutive win. Lancashire beat Sussex in two days at Hove, Len Wilkinson taking a hat-trick. Middlesex lost unexpectedly to Kent at Maidstone in two days as Arthur Fagg took his tally of runs for July to 974. Stan Worthington hit two centuries in Derbyshire's win over Notts. Each of the eight county matches yielded 12 points for somebody. Yorkshire's dominance was now under threat. They averaged 8.66 from 18 matches and had to share the lead with the trans-Pennine enemy.

Hammond and Bradman acknowledge the crowd after the Australians had retained the Ashes.

The Three-Nations Tour

July 27 to 29: 'Shake the Hand That Bowled Bradman'.

A LARGE, expectant crowd of 8,000 turned up at Taunton, where the wicket was soft but easy and the outfield wet. Somerset, though, batted as if there were hidden terrors. Even Harold Gimblett — he was having a bad season — coming in at 41-4 after a 20-minute stoppage for rain, played a very poor shot and skied a catch to cover. Andrews drove Fleetwood-Smith for six into the River Tone, but after lunch he was caught and bowled by Ward, although some thought it was a bump ball. Wellard lapped two 6's and cover-drove a four in one over by Ward. The forgotten man, Edward White, got some turn and took 3-8. There was an unpleasant wind in mid afternoon but, opening with Walker (back after injury), Badcock batted as if he were back home in Adelaide, making 67 out of 106-0 at tea, when rain put paid to the day.

On Thursday, Walker was bowled after five minutes and the star attraction came in. Although troubled by Andrews' in-swingers and tied down by Wellard's off-breaks, Bradman made 72 by lunch. Meanwhile, Badcock was smartly run out from gully for a scintillating 110 in 155 minutes. After lunch, Bradman motored on to 100 in 150 minutes; 75 minutes later he was 202. Then he threw his wicket away and Bill Andrews was able to patent a greeting which he could use for the rest of his life: "Shake the hand that bowled Bradman." McCabe hit eight 4's before the tea-time declaration.

Before the Somerset innings could begin, a single policeman had to shoo off the hordes of spectators who had congregated around the square. The county again collapsed, to 119-6 at the close. Gimblett fell to a wild stroke, but Bertie Buse hit seven 4's and Andrews, who hit two more 6's off Ward, lived to fight again on Friday. However, he was out in the first over of the morning and Somerset presumed upon only 25 minutes of the third day. Fleetwood-Smith took 4-9 in 25 balls and McCabe fielded, despite trouble with his legs.

SOMERSET v AUSTRALIA

Played at Taunton, on July 27, 28 and 29.
Australia won by an innings and 218 runs.

SOMERSET

Mr M.D.Lyon	c Ward b Fleetwood-Smith	26	c Walker b White	2
F.S.Lee	c Chipperfield b McCabe	0	c Chipperfield b White	4
H.T.F.Buse	run out	0	lbw b O'Reilly	33
Mr R.J.O.Meyer	c Barnes b Fleetwood-Smith	7	c Badcock b O'Reilly	17
*Mr E.F.Longrigg	b White	7	c Chipperfield b Fleetwood -Smith	23
H.Gimblett	c Badcock b Fleetwood-Smith	7	c Hassett b Ward	6
W.H.R.Andrews	c & b Ward	19	c Walker b Fleetwood-Smith	20
Mr C.J.P.Barnwell	b O'Reilly	11	b Fleetwood-Smith	18
A.W.Wellard	b White	20	lbw b Fleetwood-Smith	6
†W.T.Luckes	not out	5	b Fleetwood-Smith	1
H.L.Hazell	c Hassett b White	3	not out	1
Extras	(B 1, LB 1, NB 3)	5	(B 4, NB 1)	5
Total		**110**		**136**

Fall: 1st inns 1/2, 2/2, 3/16, 4/41, 5/49, 6/49, 7/81, 8/85, 9/106.
2nd inns 1/5, 2/6, 3/31, 4/70, 5/85, 6/86, 7/120, 8/130, 9/131.

AUSTRALIA

†C.W.Walker	b Andrews	37
C.L.Badcock	run out	110
*D.G.Bradman	b Andrews	202
S.Barnes	lbw b Wellard	9
A.L.Hassett	c Gimblett b Buse	31
A.G.Chipperfield	b Wellard	10
S.J.McCabe	not out	56
E.S.White	not out	2
Extras	(B 4, LB 1, W 1, NB 1)	7
Total	(6 wickets, declared)	**464**

Fall: 1st inns 1/108, 2/202, 3/225, 4/289, 5/316, 6/445.
F.Ward, W.J.O'Reilly and L.O'B.Fleetwood-Smith did not bat.

SOMERSET	O	M	R	W	O	M	R	W
McCabe	2	2	0	1				
Hassett	6	3	14	0	4	0	8	0
O'Reilly	15	5	22	1	6	1	17	2
Fleetwood-Smith	13	3	40	3	11.1	1	30	5
White	8.3	4	8	3	12	6	13	2
Ward	2	0	21	1	15	2	63	1

AUSTRALIA	O	M	R	W
Wellard	39	8	146	2
Andrews	24	2	108	2
Meyer	17	3	54	0
Buse	12	1	82	1
Hazell	11	1	57	0
Lyon	2	1	10	0

Umpires: C.N.Woolley and E.Cooke.

During the week the selectors made the first batch of invitations to tour South Africa during the winter. They were Hammond, who accepted the captaincy, Hutton, Edrich, Paynter, Compton, Gibb, Yardley, Ames and Farnes. Compton was contracted to play for Arsenal and was consulting with the manager, George Allison, about his availablility. (Two weeks later he announced that he would not be able to tour.)

At Lord's, MCC and the Australian Board met to discuss the problem of time limits on Tests. The Australians wanted to have all timeless Tests in England as well as Australia, and cited the first two Tests in support of their case. The English suggested a 30-hour limit for all Tests (five days of six hours in England, six days of five hours in Australia).

Yorkshire badly needed 12 points against lowly Northamptonshire at Scarborough and just scraped home, although Cyril Turner became another casualty when he broke his nose via the edge of his bat. By the time Verity had bowled out Northants a second time, only two hours remained to score 128. Rain stopped play for a time and threatened to return, so Leyland made sure that they scored the last 87 in 45 minutes to win with half an hour to spare. The fielding captain, Robert Nelson, allowed the match to carry on in rain. Lancashire got no points in a rain-affected draw against Essex. Surrey suffered their first defeat since 20 June, by ten wickets at The Oval, where Perks took 12-145 and Gibbons scored 178 for Worcestershire. Middlesex had no match. At Leicester against Sussex, Les Berry scored 172 in 260 minutes with two 6's. One broke the pavilion window and the other hit an attendant, who was not hurt. Yorkshire were back on top, Lancashire now third. The big-four positions were: Yorkshire, played 19, average 8.84; Middlesex played 15, average 8.26; Lancashire played 19, average 8.21; Surrey played 18, average 7.33.

Fighting broke out between Russia and Japan on the Manchuquo border. On Friday, 29 June, Parliament adjourned for the summer recess and was not due to meet again until 1 November.

July 30 to August 2: Disappointment in the Valleys.

The keen cricketing public of South Wales were cruelly deprived of the highlight of their season, the Bank holiday match against the Australians, while most of England basked in 85 degrees sunshine. Three thousand braved a dark, umpromising Saturday at St Helen's, Swansea. On a soft wicket, Dyson and Emrys Davies scored 38 in an hour before rain drove the spectators across the grass to shelter in the big stand. The mist and drizzle set in for the day and the Mumbles lighthouse was seen flashing.

Sunday was a good day and Arthur Mailey, the former Australian leg-spinner who was on the tour as a journalist, took some of the younger Australians on a picnic. One of them reported back to Jack Fingleton: "It started very brightly. We had several cars, some very nice lasses and there was nothing wrong with the day. We got well out in the country and Arthur picked a grand spot. We all agreed it would be a lovely spot in which to have lunch and then Arthur said, 'Good Lord, I forgot all about the picnic basket'."

On Bank Holiday Monday, 15,000 went in and sat impatiently in the sun until play started at 12.35pm. Twenty-five minutes and 71 deliveries, from Waite and White, elapsed before E.Davies cut a two, the first runs of the day. The sun disappeared after lunch and Davies soldiered on to score 58 in 160 minutes. A collection for his benefit raised £75. Rain and thunder ended the day at 4pm, a bitter disappointment to the now-record Welsh crowd of 20,000, who had paid £2,360 in the hope of seeing Bradman bat. They did, however, see a smart display of Australian fielding. Barnes once chased a ball to the boundary, could not apply the brakes in time and ran into the crowd. His boots tore up the trousers of one of the spectators. Barnes told him to see him at the end of the match and arranged to get him a new £2 suit.

Despite hot sun and wind on Tuesday, the wicket did not dry very quickly. Bradman was unwilling to play but agreed to start at 4pm and Glamorgan declared at the overnight score. After being approached twice, Mr Jeanes agreed to reduce the admission price to 6d and 3,000 people were admitted. Sixty-one runs were scored in 90 minutes before as the match drew peacefully to a close.

Although without Hutton, Smailes and Turner, Yorkshire were back to reasonable strength for the Roses Match at Old Trafford. On a dull Saturday, before a disappointing crowd, Lancashire's batsmen were once again overawed by their opponents, although the sight of Yardley opening the bowling can hardly have filled them with trepidation. Only Len Hopwood (45) batted with any gallantry and the off-spinner Ellis Robinson took 5-57. Lancashire were all out at 4pm for an unmemorable 133. Yorkshire were not of a mind to throw away the gift and batted carefully for 123-1 at the close.

On Monday the sun shone and 30,000 flocked in. Sutcliffe was out early for 61. Gibb, secure and painstaking, made 78 and Yorkshire added a steady 109 before lunch. At 285-5, Leyland was joined by Sellers and they punched home the advantage in a partnership of 108. Leyland was out on the stroke of tea for 135 but Sellers did not declare and was still in on 82 when the innings ended at 453, a lead of 320. Albert Nutter took 5-68 and Paynter fielded untiringly. Lancashire finished 69 for the loss of Washbrook, lbw ten minutes before the close, but whatever chance they had of a draw dissolved in the rain overnight. The ball turned from the start and only Paynter — 58 in 90 minutes — displayed the proper technique and the Red

GLAMORGAN v AUSTRALIA

Played at Swansea, on July 30, August 1, 2, 1938.
Match drawn.

GLAMORGAN

A.H.Dyson	c Bradman b Waite	27
E.Davies	c Walker b Waite	58
T.L.Brierley	c Barnes b Waite	22
D.Davies	c Brown b Waite	11
*Mr M.J.Turnbull	st Walker b White	11
C.Smart	not out	8
Extras	(B 5, LB 5, NB 1)	11
Total	(5 wickets, declared)	**148**

Fall: 1st inns 1/71, 2/116, 3/117, 4/132, 5/148.
Mr J.C.Clay, Mr W.Wooller, J.Mercer, E.C.Jones and †H.G.Davies did not bat.

AUSTRALIA

W.A.Brown	c Dyson b E.Davies	8
J.H.Fingleton	c H.Davies b Wooller	1
*D.G.Bradman	st H.Davies b Clay	17
A.L.Hassett	not out	26
S.Barnes	not out	5
Extras	(B 2, W 2)	4
Total	(3 wickets)	**61**

Fall: 1st inns 1/3, 2/21, 3/43.

A.G.Chipperfield, M.G.Waite, †C.W.Walker, E.S.White, F.Ward and E.L.McCormick did not bat.

AUSTRALIA	O	M	R	W
McCormick	14	2	43	0
Waite	36.1	17	45	4
White	23	10	49	1

GLAMORGAN	O	M	R	W
Mercer	6	3	4	0
Wooller	10	6	9	1
Clay	10	4	15	1
E.Davies	4	0	21	1
Jones	2	0	8	0

Umpires: J.Hardstaff and J.Smart.

SCOTLAND v AUSTRALIA

Played at Broughty Ferry, on August 4, 5, 1938.
Match drawn.

Australians 213 (Barnes 31, Fingleton 30, McCabe 62, Waite 30, Mr.J.N.Symon 5-33, G.Hunt 2-28) and 320 (Badcock 42, Fingleton 69, Waite 43, Ward 71, Mr W.D.Laidlaw 5-128, — Wass 2-21). Scotland 88 (Mr.P.A.Gibb 26, Fleetwood-Smith 4-21, Fingleton 2-17, Barnes 2-17) and 185-8 (Mr.K.R.Davidson 40, — Walker 44, Mr W.D.Laidlaw 36*, Ward 4-50).

SCOTLAND v AUSTRALIA

Played at Glasgow, on August 6 1938.
Australians won by 61 runs.

Australians 143 (Barnes 49, McCabe 38, Mr A.Paris 3-24, Mr.J.N.Symon 3-44). Scotland 82 (A.F.Wensley 20, O'Reilly 7-39, White 2-18).

Rose withered for 120, Verity 20-8-21-5. As Cardus wrote: 'The crowd went home carrying their lunch parcels.'' It was 1910 since Yorkshire last beat Lancashire twice in a season.

Middlesex, 118 behind on the first innings at Hove, needed 300 to beat Sussex. Early on the third day, at 210-4, Jim Smith was promoted and made 57 in 35 minutes and they won by three wickets. Surrey secured only four points from a high-scoring draw at home to Notts. Kent beat Hampshire in two days at Canterbury and Fagg, making 42 in his only innings, passed 1,000 runs for the month of July. Poor George Paine had an unfortunate benefit match for Warwickshire against Derbyshire. He bagged a 'pair' and took 1-102. Essex won again, at Worcester and Farnes took 12-119 in his second county match of the season.

Leslie Ames' finger was out of plaster and he hoped to be fit again in ten days. Somerset Wanderers CC arrived in Berlin to play four club matches. Welcomed by Herr Felix Mensel, the Reich sports leader (who later scored 27 in his side's total of 46 against them) appealed to MCC to set up an international European cricket cup.

August 3 to 5: I Left My Appendix in Dundee

Wednesday 3 August meant, for the Australians, a day's train journey from South Wales to Eastern Scotland, to Dundee on the northern bank of the Firth of Tay. Bradman left the train at Perth to holiday with friends. The rest were met at their destination by a kilted Ben Barnett, who had gone on ahead. Chipperfield alighted from the train a sick man, but it was not fatigue from the journey. He had to enter Dundee Royal Infirmary for an emergency appendicitis operation. On Thursday, the Australians batted on a perfect wicket at Broughty Ferry, a resort a few miles east of the city and made 213. Symon, a Portsmouth footballer and G.Hunt, the Aberdeen professional from Bermuda, bowled well at fast-medium pace. The fielding was excellent, although Paul Gibb, brought up to captain the Scots, missed two stumpings. After Scotland collapsed, McCabe did not enforce the follow-on and the second day crowd were treated to 299 runs in 129 minutes, with nine 6's and five dropped catches. W.D.Laidlaw, a leg-spinner, conceded 128 runs in 15 overs. The innings of 320 came off only 53 overs. Scotland then managed to play out time, despite losing Gibb in the first over. Barnes had four stumpings, and eight Australians bowled.

Yorkshire won at Leicester by an innings and 74 runs, helped by rain on Thursday night. Lancashire succumbed to Kent at Canterbury, where Fagg was the third man to reach 2,000 runs for the season. Needing 289 to win on the last day, overnight rain and hot sun made the pitch treacherous, Lancashire did well to last until 1.20pm, Paynter making a masterly 47 in 65 minutes. Middlesex had an easy win at

Edgbaston, Edrich scoring 159 in four hours. Essex beat Notts at Chelmsford by 197 with five minutes to spare, their sixth win in seven matches. At Bristol, Hammond scored his 14th century of the season, going one ahead of Bradman. He was on course to beat Jack Hobbs' 1925 record of 16 centuries in a season. The top four Championship positions were unchanged but Lancashire's average was slipping. Len Hutton's finger was X-rayed and the bone had healed.

The British Government sent an envoy to Prague. He was Lord (Walter) Runciman, a former Liberal MP and Minister in the National Government. Runciman was to be a standing adviser to the Czech Government in its Sudeten negotiations. On Friday, 5 August, 24 years and one day after Britain declared war on Germany, the RAF staged a mock invasion exercise; bad weather delayed its start and in the fog, six men were killed.

August 6 to 9: Elementary for Holmes and Watts

In a one-day match at Glasgow, Gibb put the Australians in on a soft wicket and they were all out in two and a half hours, Barnes having batted for two hours. The pitch was easier when Scotland batted but then O'Reilly got to work on them. McCormick had some fun with the crowd. As he bowled they chorused, 'Nae ball!', so he ran up deliberately way past the line. 'Nae ball', they shouted but he had not let the ball out of his hand and he held it aloft in triumph.

On Monday, at Sunderland, the Australians started a two-day game against the second-class county, Durham. Fog delayed the start until 2.30pm. 'Bagga' Barnes and 'Musso' Badcock, as they called each other, enjoyed themselves in a stand of 170 in 85 minutes. Ten thousand people watched. On Tuesday, Durham were all out twice in three hours.

Yorkshire achieved their fourth victory in a row, their 16th of the season, by 210 runs in two days in a low-scoring game at Sheffield against Derbyshire. Surrey beat Middlesex at The Oval, thanks to some great catching; Middlesex dropped Errol Holmes twice and Eddie Watts during a partnership of 109 for the eigth wicket in Surrey's first innings. Lancashire made 442-6 declared at Trent Bridge (Paynter 140 in four hours) but with Wilkinson not finding a length they could not bowl out Notts twice. On the first day of Hastings Week, Bartlett gave value to the holiday crowd with 114 including four 6's, one of which broke a window in the South Terrace, and Kent were bowled out twice by James Langridge. Gloucestershire began the Cheltenham Festival with a 44-run win over Hampshire. The match aggregate was 504 runs for 40 wickets and Tom Goddard, with a semi-circle of short legs, took 7-26 in the second innings of 58, bowling unchanged with Sinfield.

DURHAM v AUSTRALIA

Played at Sunderland, on August 8, 9, 1938.
Australians won by an innings and 179 runs.

Australians 380-5dec (Brown 48, Barnes 140*, Waite 34, Badcock 103*, Mr J.Grigor 3-82). Durham 105 (J.Carr 29, Fleetwood-Smith 6-53, O'Reilly 4-32) and 96 (J.Carr 29, Fleetwood-Smith 4-37, O'Reilly 6-35).

The July unemployment figures were 1,773,116, down since June, but nearly half a million more than in July 1937.

August 10 to 12: Futility at The Oval

It seemed an odd piece of planning that the Australians should play a second match against Surrey at The Oval only a week before the Test there. After the long journey from Sunderland they were probably not prostrate with grief when overnight rain caused the whole of the first day's play to be lost.

On Thursday, when play started at 2.15pm under a hot sun, Brown and Fingleton were suspicious of the pitch and of the array of slips. Fingleton was first out at 64, after passing his 1,000 runs, caught ten feet off the ground by the tall Alf Gover at square leg, in the shadow of the gasometer. McCabe showed his class in a chanceless innings of 67 in 105 minutes but a quick return by Fishlock, at cover, to Brooks ran him out. On Friday morning, the last six wickets fell for 93 in 73 minutes. Barnes hit five 4's in a stylish 63. Surrey were 16-0 at lunch, then O'Reilly took 3-0 in three overs either side of a thunderstorm. McCormick, who had tried out his long run but was no-balled, took a great diving catch at first slip. Parker stroked 4's off Fleetwood-Smith and McCormick, and was going well when two more bouts of rain ended the match early. Some 12,000 people had watched the two days' play.

Yorkshire put Warwickshire in to bat at Headingley and established a strong position despite resistance from Dollery, 126 not out in 280 minutes. Mitchell scored a century and Leyland 98, but a cloudburst after 15 minutes' play on Friday morning flooded the ground. Middlesex beat Kent by an innings after a blank first day at Lord's, with Jim Smith taking 9-90 in the match; Ames returned to the Kent side as a batsman, so it was Levett standing behind the wicket when Smith hit a ball straight up in the air and gave one of those awful steepling catches, which Levett dropped as he fell over the stumps. Lancashire encountered a treacherous third-day wicket at Weston-super-Mare and were all out for 139, losing to Somerset by ten wickets. Surrey had no match. Derbyshire beat Worcestershire at Derby and rose to fifth place above Essex, who drew an fairly even contest with Northants. Not a ball was bowled between Glouscetershire and Nottinghamshire at Cheltenham.

SURREY v AUSTRALIA

Played at The Oval, on August 10, 11, 12, 1938.
Match drawn.

AUSTRALIA

W.A.Brown	lbw b Squires	39
J.H.Fingleton	c Gover b Watts	27
*S.J.McCabe	run out	67
A.L.Hassett	lbw b Gregory	11
S.Barnes	run out	63
M.G.Waite	c Holmes b Squires	5
†B.A.Barnett	lbw b Parker	26
E.S.White	b Garland-Wells	14
W.J.O'Reilly	not out	23
E.L.McCormick	c Gover b Parker	0
L.O'B.Fleetwood-Smith	b Garland-Wells	7
Extras	(B 12, LB 2, W 1)	15
Total		**297**

Fall: 1st inns 1/64, 2/74, 3/97, 4/190, 5/209, 6/232, 7/260, 8/268, 9/278.

SURREY

R.J.Gregory	lbw b O'Reilly	6
L.B.Fishlock	c McCormick b O'Reilly	9
H.S.Squires	c McCormick b O'Reilly	9
T.H.Barling	lbw b O'Reilly	0
J.F.Parker	not out	36
E.W.Whitfield	lbw b Fleetwood-Smith	10
Mr H.M.Garland-Wells	c O'Reilly b Fleetwood-Smith	14
*Mr E.R.T.Holmes	b Fleetwood-Smith	8
E.A.Watts	not out	0
Extras	(B 4, LB 5, NB 4)	13
Total	(7 wickets)	**105**

Fall: 1st inns 1/16, 2/17, 3/17, 4/44, 5/79, 6/97, 7/105.

†E.W.Brooks and A.R.Gover did not bat.

SURREY	O	M	R	W
Gover	13	2	41	0
Watts	11	4	18	1
Parker	17	4	58	2
Squires	22	5	69	2
Gregory	26	7	70	1
Garland-Wells	10	3	26	2

AUSTRALIA	O	M	R	W
McCormick	10	2	21	0
Waite	4	1	8	0
O'Reilly	12	6	25	4
White	8	6	3	0
Fleetwood-Smith	8	1	35	3

Umpires: T.Oates and C.N.Woolley.

At Hove, Sussex hit 597-7 declared against Leicestershire and John Langridge and Jim Parks scored 295 in less than four hours before a wicket fell. Then Jim Hammond hit four 6's, one of which struck a car headlamp. Leicestershire made 379 at second attempt but still lost by an innings.

Len Hutton's finger was pronounced fit and he was ready to return to county cricket on Saturday.

Russia and Japan agreed a cease-fire. And Lord Runciman persuaded the Sudeten German leaders to talk directly to the Czech Government.

August 13 to 16: Happy Days at Canterbury

Canterbury, where the Australians next went, escaped the severe thunderstorms which had afflicted London and the North of England on Friday, but the wicket was soft. Fingleton scored four 4's in 23 out of 25, until Alan Watt changed ends because of the breeze and had him 'plumb' lbw. Bradman, in his first innings for 11 days, was nearly caught at short leg at once, then settled down to reach 50 in even time; but before lunch he drove off the back foot slightly off balance and was caught at cover.

Because of a farewell lunch for Frank Woolley, the afternoon started 15 minutes late. Ten thousand voices cheered when he came on to bowl in his familiar ritual, the left arm coming from behind his back and flowing high past his ear, the ball dropping on to a perfect length. Badcock succumbed to the new ball after hitting ten 4's in 135 minutes. Waite was in a hitting mood and he nearly put a hole through Chalk's chest as the fielder caught him at cover. Barnes and Barnett added 101 in an hour. Barnes, though dropped three times, played some lovely strokes, but he did nothing more popular than to pop up a catch at silly point off Woolley. Walker and White got stuck in a lull and the crowd barracked when Walker called for a new bat, then turned to laughter when they saw Fingleton appear with six bats and a golf club. The score at the close was 450-8; Kent's attack had been handicapped by Wright's erratic length.

After rain on Sunday, the hot sun returned. Bradman batted on while the wicket was still placid so that Kent would have use of it at its worst. Woolley and Fagg came out to bat through a line of applauding spectators and off the first ball of the innings, Woolley played in front of him and set off for a single; Walker raced up from behind the stumps and hit the bowler's wicket underarm; Wooley had not grounded his bat and he was out.

Waite, from the Nackington Road End, switched to off-breaks around the wicket and took 3-3 in eight overs as Kent slumped to 57-5 at lunch. White switched to left arm over and took 3-8. Although, Wright and Levett put on 31 for the last wicket, punishing loose bowling by Fleetwood-Smith, Kent followed-on 371 behind.

KENT v AUSTRALIA

Played at Canterbury, on August 13, 15, 16, 1938.
Australia won by ten wickets.

AUSTRALIA

J.H.Fingleton	lbw b Watt	23		
W.A.Brown	lbw b Watt	4		
*D.G.Bradman	c Todd b Watt	67		
C.L.Badcock	c Davies b Todd	76		
S.Barnes	c Todd b Woolley	94		
M.G.Waite	c Chalk b Todd	18		
B.A.Barnett	c Chalk b Todd	54		
†C.W.Walker	c Fagg b Watt	42		
E.S.White	c Todd b Wright	52	(1) not out	0
F.Ward	c Valentine b Todd	16		
L.O'B.Fleetwood-Smith	not out	0	(2) not out	6
Extras	(B 24, LB 7, NB 2)	33	(NB 1)	1
Total		**479**	(No wicket)	**7**

Fall: 1st inns 1/31, 2/38, 3/152, 4/211, 5/243, 6/345, 7/380, 8/437, 9/474.

KENT

F.E.Woolley	run out	0	c Bradman b Ward	81
A.E.Fagg	c Brown b Waite	14	st Walker b Ward	11
L.E.G.Ames	st Walker b White	30	b Waite	139
Mr B.H.Valentine	lbw b Waite	1	lbw b Waite	36
*Mr F.G.H.Chalk	b Waite	11	lbw b Fleetwood-Smith	7
L.J.Todd	b Ward	0	b Waite	26
Mr C.H.Knott	b Waite	4	not out	17
Mr J.G.W.Davies	c Waite b White	2	st Walker b Ward	9
D.V.P.Wright	not out	21	b Waite	5
A.E.Watt	b White	8	c Barnes b Waite	9
†Mr W.H.V.Levett	b Fleetwood-Smith	15	b Fleetwood-Smith	7
Extras	(B 1, LB 1)	2	(B 16, LB 14)	30
Total		**108**		**377**

Fall: 1st inns 1/0, 2/28, 3/34, 4/52, 5/53, 6/62, 7/64, 8/64, 9/77.
2nd inns 1/76, 2/109, 3/204, 4/243, 5/315, 6/326, 7/337, 8/346, 9/366.

KENT	O	M	R	W	O	M	R	W
Watt	35	7	102	4				
Todd	40	10	145	4				
Davies	26	3	75	0				
Wright	16.3	0	77	1				
Woolley	14	1	47	1				
Levett	-	-	-	-	0.3	0	6	0

AUSTRALIA	O	M	R	W	O	M	R	W
Waite	22	7	43	4	32	4	85	5
White	17	7	35	3	18	3	78	0
Ward	7	1	14	1	24	2	92	3
Fleetwood-Smith	3	0	14	1	26.3	3	92	2

Umpires: F.Chester and J.Smart.

Woolley started with two 4's off Waite, two drives off White, successive 4's off Fleetwood-Smith, and went to 50 in 40 minutes. After tea, he on-drove Ward for six, then drove at him again, but checked his shot and gave a low catch to mid on. He hit 81 out of 109 in 66 minutes, with the six, one five and 13 4's. The crowd rose to him in thankfulness. Valentine hit two 6's in one over, Ames reached 100 in 100 minutes with three 6's and Kent were 265-4 at the close.

Tuesday was grey and windy and only a few came to watch. The new ball had no effect but Waite eventually bowled Ames with the 'arm' ball, for 139 in 165 minutes. The follow-on was avoided and Kent were all out at 1.20pm, six runs ahead. Rain fell during lunch, after which Levett doffed his pads and opened the bowling. Fleetwood-Smith put his pads on. The first ball was a bread roll; 'no-ball' was called but not recorded. Then he bowled a conventional no-ball, then Fleetwood-Smith hit a two and a four to end a happy match.

England named 14 for The Oval Test. Hutton and Ames were back. Fagg's runs in July and his 2,169 (average 55.61) so far in the season were acknowledged. Leyland (1,347 runs, average 40.69) was called up at last. Edrich and Hardstaff were relieved to hear their names again, and Charles Barnett was the only lamb to be sacrificed for England's poor batting at Leeds. Wright retained his place, though some thought Peter Smith of Essex deserved a chance. As from the XI who played at Leeds, out went Barnett and Price; in were L.Hutton (Yorkshire), A.E.Fagg (Kent), M.Leyland (Yorkshire), L.E.G.Ames (Kent) and T.W.J.Goddard (Gloucestershire).

Australia had all their players fit except Chipperfield, who was recovering well in a Dundee Nursing Home.

Fagg, Wright, Goddard and Verity were, at the same time, invited to join the team to tour South Africa, as also were B.H.Valentine, Perks and Wilkinson (L).

Yorkshire inserted Leicestershire at Bradford; Verity came on at 23-0 and ended with 15-5-18-7 in a total of 62. Sutcliffe made the 142nd century of his career and the leaders won with minimum trouble in two days. Middlesex had little difficulty in beating Somerset. (In the Middlesex first innings of 267, Arthur Wellard had the extraordinary figures of 31-2-140-7; what a contrast with Verity!). Lancashire ended a bad run with victory at Birmingham, Paynter making two hundreds in a match for the first time. At Westcliff, Essex beat Surrey and Morris Nichols' undefeated 133 brought him the all-rounder's double. For the fourth successive season he was first to that target. Sussex enjoyed their fourth win in a row at Portsmouth. Derbyshire consolidated fifth place by winning at Nottingham, and Alderman took a memorable catch off the Notts captain, Heane, running round the boundary to hold it right-handed high above his head.

Yorkshire now had an average of 9.16 points with four matches to play. Middlesex averaged 8.60 with three matches left. Lancashire averaged 7.16 with five to play, Surrey 7.04 with five. Yorshires worst average at the end of the season would be 7.86. Middlesex's best would be 9.04, and Lancashire and Surrey could only get to 8.00. No other county had any chance of the Championship.

In Germany, reservists were called up for Army manoeuvres.

August 17 to 19: Stop That Train

On Wednesday and Thursday, the Australians played a friendly game against the Army at Aldershot. The Army were 78-2 at lunch. Fingleton at mid-on, hit the stumps at both ends with one throw but nobody was out. Steele, the army chaplain and Hampshire player, was smartly run out by Barnes when he had a misunderstanding with Knapp. The Army collapsed in an hour after lunch. Australia countered with 229, Fingleton hitting five 4's, McCabe scoring 23 in 15 minutes and Barnes 58 in 80 minutes. The Army were routed again, by O'Reilly's flight, though Stephenson of the Middlesex Regiment and Essex drove freely. The match finished before tea on Thursday.

Unlike the previous four Tests, the final 'timeless' Test was due to start on a Saturday. Australia had a free Friday but the England players were not so lucky. Six of the 14 were playing in the Gloucestershire-Yorkshire match at Scarborough which could last until 6pm on Friday evening, in which case they would have to catch a train at 8.05pm, arriving at Kings's Cross London at 3.15am on Saturday. The two captains, Hammond and Sellers, one the Test captain, the other a Test selector, made no arrangement for changing the hours. The LNE Railway company announced that, if necessary, the Newcastle-King's Cross train could stop to pick them up at 7.48pm, arriving in London at 10.15pm.

Fortunately Yorkshire beat Gloucestershire in two days. Put in on a difficult wicket, Sutcliffe made a masterly 37, twice being hit on the body, and paved the way for Yardley, 97, Leyland, 79 and even Bill Bowes who hit two 6's off Goddard. The total of 346 was too much for both Gloucestershire innings. Verity took 10-83 in the match and they were bowled out twice on the second day before a 12,000 holiday crowd. Essex could not recover from bad batting on the first day at Lord's and Denis Compton made the highest score of his short career, 180 not out in only 150 minutes with 25 4's — 12 points to Middlesex. Surrey were unable to capitalize on first-innings points at Birmingham. Lancashire also only had four points when rain deleted the third day at Swansea. Kent won, playing away to Leicestershire at Oakham, Valentine scoring 242. He came in at 22-2 on the first morning and was 237 at tea. But Les Ames got another bang on his unlucky finger when keeping wicket, and Doug Wright was also hurt. Both had to withdraw from the Test team. Somerset lost at Worcester, but Frank Lee was on the field for every ball, scoring 109 not out and 107. Derbyshire won for the third time in a row. The top of the table read as follows:

	Played	Average	To Play
Yorkshire	25	9.28	3
Middlesex	21	8.76	2
Lancashire	25	7.04	4
Surrey	22	6.90	4
Derbyshire	22	6.36	3
Sussex	25	5.60	4
Essex	23	5.56	3

As Yorkshire's worst possible average was now 8.29, and Middlesex's best was 9.04, Lancashire's best was 7.72, and Surrey's best was 7.69, the Yorkshiremen now had only one county to fear.

THE ARMY v AUSTRALIA

Played at Aldershot, on August 17, 18 1938.
Australians won by an innings and 67 runs.

The Army 113 (Mr L.T.Grove 26, Mr C.P.Hamilton 33, McCormick 3-16, McCabe 2-6, Fleetwood-Smith 4-62) and 119 (Mr.M.N.Harbottle 28, Mr J.W.A.Stephenson 25*, O'Reilly 7-33). Australians 299 (Fingleton 64, Brown 31, Barnes 45, Barnett 58, Mr R.E.Osborne-Smith 4-64, Mr T.H.Knapp 3-52).

Maurice Leyland, Yorkshire's leading middle-order batsman who scored 1,884 runs as his county retained the Championship. Called into the England team for the Fifth Test.

The Final Test

THE Saturday start was proving to be a real headache for England. Both Ames and Wright were unfit. To replace Ames behind the wicket, the 39-year-old Arthur Wood of Yorkshire was called up. Wood, a popular and effervescent 'keeper, was certainly a better choice than Gibb or Price. The selectors 'unofficially' notified Morris Nichols to report to The Oval on Saturday morning and also suggested to Peter Smith, the leg-spinner, that he might like to be in the vicinity. Both these Essex men had been playing at Lord's on Friday and had no match on Saturday. The selectors were certainly taking a 'belt and braces' approach to the 'Timeless Test'.

On Friday, a meeting of the Advisory County Cricket Committee and the Board of Control decided that the Tests against South Africa in 1940 should last four days. Until now, no Test in England against countries other than Australia had lasted more than three days.

When Wood was contacted on Friday evening he was in Nottingham, where Yorkshire were due to play on the morrow. His cricket gear was, at that moment, on its way from Scarborough and when it arrived at 8.45pm, it was too late to catch a train to London. So Wood decided to travel in style, by taxi. When the driver woke him up at the England team hotel, the 360-room Great Central at Marylebone Station (room and breakfast 13s 6d a night) and told him how much money was on the clock, Wood said, "I could 'a' bought taxi for less."He had to borrow the money from his Yorkshire colleagues. It cost him £7 10s. The forecast for Saturday was not all that good: cool with sunny periods and showers.

In Germany it was decreed that Jewish people could not attempt to disguise their origin by using 'Aryan' Christian names.

Fifth Test at the Oval
Saturday 20 August: 'They'll Get a Thousand.'

'Bosser' Martin, the rotund groundsman at The Oval, had heard a lot of talk about the perfect wicket at the Trent Bridge Test and was determined to do better on his own patch. He was ferociously proud of his work and said that this one would last until Christmas. When Wood pretended to see some holes on the track, Martin said that the only holes were the three at each end where the stumps went. Umpire Frank Chester was reminded of a strip of velvet when he looked at it. Bill O'Reilly claimed that he could smell the 'cowyard confetti'.

With so many changes it is as well to remind ourselves who the England hopefuls were on the morning. There were eight batsmen: Hutton, Fagg, Edrich, Hammond, Paynter, Leyland, Hardstaff and Compton; wicketkeeper, Wood; two fast bowlers, Farnes and Bowes, with Nichols on stand-by; and two spinners, Verity and Goddard, with Peter Smith not knowing what he was. The selectors were deciding whether to play seven batsmen and three bowlers, or six and four. There was a chance that Fagg might be chosen as the man in form and that either Hardstaff or Edrich would be omitted, or even Hutton, who had not found his form after returning from injury. Hutton's tally for the season so far was only 1,201 runs (average 48.04); Hardstaff's 1,282 (average 47.48). Fagg had 2,275 (average 54.16). Only Hammond, Paynter and Wood were certain to play.

Australia had the problem of Badcock, but he was still in form in county matches, as was Sid Barnes who had done enough to get a chance. McCormick was rumoured to have neuritis in the shoulder, but he bowled well in the Friday nets and told vice-captin McCabe that he was fully fit.

The gates were opened at 9am and entrance through the turnstiles was available for about 20,000, which was half the ground's capacity. As Test cricket was back in London, television returned and 'Teddy' Wakelam was joined in the commentary box by Todd Rich. Radio had Howard Marshall, of course, but this time, for the sake of variety, the National Programme planned to broadcast, from time to time, the Australian radio commentary of Erich Sholl, Chester Wilmot, W.A.Oldfield and A.E.R.Gilligan. Some 4,500 were first in when the gates opened. A couple from Canterbury and a group of youths from Northampton were among the 50 or so who had queued all night. It was a fresh morning, breezy, with patchy cloud, cool but with no sign of rain.

England left out Fagg and Goddard, thus playing seven and three. Australia caused a surprise by leaving out McCormick, due ostensibly to the inflammation in his shoulder. The truth was probably that they anticipated, as did England, a long game that would be decided on batting strength. From the Leeds Test, Barnes for McCormick was the only change. It meant that McCabe (13 wickets, average 31.00) and Waite (53 wickets, average 20.64) would have to do what they could to look like a fearsome new-ball attack. The 12th men were Fagg (England) and White (Australia).

It is often said that Bradman expected to win the toss, having lost the previous three, but I cannot believe that so well-ordered a brain as his could fall for the old myth; a coin has no memory and the chance of winning the toss on any one occasion is always 50-50. It is true that when they tossed, Hammond was in blazer and flannels, Bradman in a suit, but that was the case at the Lord's Test as well. Watched by the Oliver Hardy figure of Bosser Martin in his three-piece suit and Homburg hat, Bradman called heads but the coin came up tails and, of course, Hammond elected to bat. Back in the dressing-room he reminded Hutton and Edrich that this was a timeless Test: "Be there at the lunch *and* tea interval."

The ground was quiet and less than half full when Waite opened with a maiden to Hutton from the Vauxhall End. McCabe conceded a single to Edrich in his first over and, as he took his sweater from umpire Chester, said, "Frank, they'll get a thousand." Both openers had an optimistic two slips and a gully. Hutton was off the mark in the fourth over. A quiet start. Then in the eighth over, McCabe conceded eight runs, four from a wristy late cut by Hutton, which were the first runs on the off-side. The first half-hour saw 20 runs and a forlorn lbw appeal against Edrich.

Then the Test really started. O'Reilly came on at Waite's end, with his usual two short legs, and his first delivery, a no-ball, was lofted for two. Fleetwood-Smith trotted in from the Pavilion End. At the start of O'Reilly's third over, Edrich faced him for the first time. The last ball was quicker, well pitched up; Edrich played back to it was rapped on the pad and given out lbw. After 45 minutes, England were 29-1. Poor Bill Edrich had missed his golden opportunity and he was in purgatory. His nightmare must have been to see himself constantly selected for England and constantly failing to make runs.

Nobody knew who was number-three: Hammond? Hardstaff? There was no mistaking the broad behind, sloping shoulders and sturdy walk of Maurice Leyland under the angled Yorkshire cap. "It's that Yorkshire bastard again," mumbled the man who had just taken his 100th English Test wicket. Leyland walked up to Hutton and said, "Keep it up young Leonard," then settled down to drive a single to get off the mark and played and missed once at Fleetwood-Smith. Hutton, firmly anchored in the crease, drove O'Reilly for four to bring up the 50. Leyland used his feet to off-drive two lovely 4's off Fleetwood-Smith. There was not much sign of any turn and O'Reilly asked of Chester: "Where's the groundsman's hut? If I had a gun, I'd shoot him!" But when in his annoyance he dropped a shorter, faster ball, Leyland ducked and deposited his cap very close to the wicket. Oh, for a burst of McCormick, neuritis or no! Lunch came at 89-1 in two hours (Hutton 39 not out, Leyland already 35).

In the second over after lunch, at 91, Hutton went down the pitch to cover-drive Fleetwood-Smith, the ball swung in late then turned

Using a sixpence found on the floor of the dressing-room, Hammond tossed and Bradman called incorrectly. So, like F.S.Jackson in 1905, Hammond had gained England the choice of innings in all the Tests. Of course, there was no toss for the Third Test at Manchester which was wiped out by rain. Note the poor state of the outfield.

Edrich turns for the pavilion, lbw to O'Reilly's for 12. England are 29 for one after 45 minutes' play.

Leyland is bowled by O'Reilly off a no-ball. He had a similar escape later in the day.

away and Barnett missed the stumping chance. The scoring rate increased. Leyland was first to 50 in 95 minutes. Hutton's half-century came in 140 minutes. Waite tried coming around the wicket and mixed up his bowling styles; Leyland nearly played on to him when 70, but versatility was no substitute for class. Leyland heard a no-ball call off O'Reilly, swung across the line, was bowled — and had a good laugh. At last the sun peeped out. Not more than 20,000 people had peeped into the ground — many who feared a lock-out had settled for watching football instead. The English soccer season was starting with 44 friendly matches played for the Football League's Jubilee Fund, which attracted about half a million spectators up and down the country.

At 178, Barnes was allowed to reveal for the first time in England that he bowled right-arm leg-breaks. When 86, Hutton edged a Fleetwood-Smith full toss close to first slip. The latter's erratic length helped Hutton to streak through the 90s to his second Test hundred of the summer, after 212 minutes of vigilance. All that passed for life in the wicket was now gone. The Australians were bowling on a billiard table and with a billiard ball. Waite came and went with the new billiard ball and Leyland passed his 100 in 202 minutes with an easy off-drive that kicked up dust. Two minutes later, at 4.25pm, a shower passed overhead and tea was taken, the score 242-1. The session had yielded 153 runs in 130 minutes, a decorous, gentle slaughter. During the tea interval, the doyen of cricket writers, a hard man to please, saw Leyland and said, "Even you, Maurice, are perpetuating the stonewall game." "Aye, but Mister Cardus, tha must remember as I'm playing for me place in team."

The shower was quite heavy for a while but play resumed at 4.45pm. It assisted Waite to get one ball head high against Leyland and O'Reilly to rap Hutton on the knuckles. But the wicket was only having its little joke and soon subsided into good behaviour. As he moved into the 140s, Hutton took a fancy to the lofted on-drive and Hammond appeared on the balcony (pads on) before the ball had reached the ropes, to gesture a 'calm down' message. The crowd roared when the 300 came up at 5.30pm, then the partnership nearly ended with the proverbial run out. Leyland hit Waite to extra cover and ran. Badcock pounced and threw to the bowler, but Waite had backed into the stumps and Leyland was safely in before he could advert to rule 20: 'The wicket shall be 'down' . . .if both bails be off, when a stump is struck out of the ground.'

A voice below the gasometer warned, "Pull yourself together Yorkshire, play a bit careful please." In the long evening shadows, Barnes made Leyland play and miss once. Hutton late-cut a four so delicately that he brush-stroked Barnett's gloves with the end of his bat. O'Reilly and Fleetwood-Smith ended the day bowling as well and as ineffectually as they had begun.

The score was 347-1. Hutton was 160 in 355 minutes with 15 4's. Leyland 156 in 309 minutes with 14 4's in a stand of 318. It had been an undemanding day for the scorecard printer: 'Edrich W.J. lbw b O'Reilly 12' was the only entry. It seems a lot of runs until one realizes that no less than 131 overs were bowled, as follows:

Waite 33-5-62-0; McCabe 17-4-45-0; O'Reilly 35-10-79-1; Fleetwood-Smith 35-3-121-0; Barnes 11-2-21-0.

Bradman's tactics during the day had been to change the bowling around and to set defensive fields. Apart from the missed stumping and run out, the fielding had been excellent all day.

As Hutton walked off he knew he had two people to thank: Jim Wright, the Yorkshire masseur, and Maurice Leyland who had supported him and who kept the bulk of O'Reilly's bowling to himself. During the last session, Leyland told Hutton: "I'll tell you something, I've got O'Reilly taped. And I'll tell you something else, he knows it."

The official attendance figures were 16,500, of whom 12,999 had come through the turnstiles. It was a cool day, maximum temperature 66° F.

Bradman spent Sunday as guest of Walter Robins in his home in Buckinghamshire. They played golf, sheltering from a rainstorm under the trees. After a good night's sleep, Hutton was taken by Hedley Verity to lunch at a friend's house in Bognor Regis and they played cricket on the beach. Maurice Leyland played golf. The forecast for Monday was good.

Monday 22 August: Paynter Wins a Bet

By 8am there were about 1,500 people queuing at the turnstiles. A sharp shower came at 7.15am and again just after the wicket was rolled, lasting 15 minutes. At 11.55am the players emerged, the crowd slightly bigger than at the same time on Saturday. The spinners opened, Fleetwood-Smith from the Pavilion End. In a few minutes the stand passed 323, which was the record set for any wicket by England against Australia, by Hobbs and Rhodes at Melbourne in 1911-12 . The crowd had read their morning papers and clapped. Under grey clouds the Yorkshiremen carried on quietly, scoring mostly by cuts and drives. When O'Reilly, after being called for a no-ball, dropped the faster ball short, Leyland cheekily cut over the head of slip for four. Both men were on 174 when Fleetwood-Smith beat Leyland with a ball that popped over the stumps. When both were 187, Hutton pushed O'Reilly down to deep mid off and ambled a single. Hassett fumbled the ball, they went for a second. Hassett threw to the bowler's end, Bradman dashed in from mid-on and removed the bails with Leyland just out of his ground. The time was 1.07pm and he was out for 187 out of a stand of 382 in 381 minutes with 17 4's and one possible stumping chance at 63.

When Leyland came in, the great England bowler, S.F.Barnes, came into the dressing-room and said, "Well played, that was a good knock, but not as good as the innings you played in that charity game before the war." He was referring to the time when 12-year-old Leyland had come to watch his father play in a charity match with some league professionals. Father Leyland's team were a man short and young Maurice was put in at number-11. In partnership with his father he put on 28 runs against the bowling of Barnes and Cecil Parkin. "I said then that you would make runs for England one day." The two had not met since and Leyland was astonished that Barnes remembered.

Meanwhile, on the field, Hammond straight drove and swept 4's and took 12 in an over off Fleetwood-Smith. He was already on 20 at lunch, when England were 434-2. Hutton (191) had added only 31 in 95 minutes. It seemed a big score but England had scored 400 before and lost, even in a four-day Test, when 'you-know-who' was batting on the other side.

Hammond obviously took that view, because he and Hutton slowed down after lunch. Hammond drove and missed twice at Waite and went into a cocoon. After 468 minutes, Hutton reached England's third 200 of the summer with a late cut at 447 and then greeted O'Reilly's return with a couple of 4's off Waite, but otherwise not much happened. The match drifted on. Suddenly — and for no apparent reason — Fingleton doubled up with what looked like an attack of cramp. In fact a muscle in his left leg had snapped. With some wry amusement, his colleagues carried him part of the way to the boundary's edge and deposited him there, but unlike Polar explorers they did not mark the spot with a cross. From there, Fingleton hopped up the pavilion steps and was not seen again. White, the 12th man, stepped on to a Test field for the first time.

The hour after lunch produced only 43 runs, Hammond scoring 17 of them, as O'Reilly and Waite bowled a series of maidens. The crowd, now 27,000 of them, sat stoically under the clouds. It was like watching a cathedral being built. Drinks were served at 485-2 and the 500 was posted in 525 minutes. Fleetwood-Smith, having rested since lunch, came on and kick-started the game into life, finding the edge of Hutton's bat with a googly and beating Hammond twice in an over. Hutton's engine ticked along at an unchanging pace, passing Hammond's 240 at Lord's to become England's highest scorer in an home Test against Australia. Hammond rejoindered with his 50 in 110 minutes. What attacking strokes there were seemed to be played at random. At 4.15pm Hammond tried to turn to leg a ball that went straight through and was lbw to the deserving Fleetwood-Smith. He had made 59 in 141 minutes, 39 in two hours since lunch, and hit four 4's, one of them since lunch.

Just before Hammond was out, Eddie Paynter suggested to Compton that the pair of them were so mentally attuned to sitting in the dressing-room that they would not make ten runs between them. A wager of £1 was put on it. For Paynter's arrival, Bradman created the illusion of a batting collapse by posting a silly mid-on and silly mid-off for O'Reilly. Paynter fulfilled his part of the prophecy when O'Reilly's top-spinner had him lbw. Compton faced the same field, in quite poor light, but survived to tea, at 553-4. Hutton now had 263 in 585 minutes.

A little rain extended the tea interval to half an hour and at 5pm the Australian fielders gamboled out as if born again. Waite bowled from the Pavilion End and in his first over, Compton played forward and found himself yorked by an in-swinger. Everyone marvelled at the turn of events: a batsman had let a ball pass through his bat and pad on to the stumps; three wickets had fallen for nine runs; Compton was a pound poorer; Hutton could go at any time due to sheer fatigue.

Suddenly, England were grateful to have a batsman at number-seven in the person of tall, handsome Joe Hardstaff. On his way to the Vauxhall End wicket he presented his compliments to Len Hutton and umpire Chester: "These Aussies have had their games with me and now it's my turn to have a game with them." Hardstaff brought a breath of fresh air to the game as he stroked Waite wristily to leg for four and played some flashing off-drives that seemed to come from his father's era.

One hard drive hit McCabe's leg at silly mid-on. During the delay while McCabe recovered, Hutton lay down on the grass. His target now was the 287 of R.E.Foster at Sydney 1903-04 — England's highest score against Australia. Cricketers' penchant for landmarks and records was useful in giving him something to aim for and saved him from seeing only an unending purposelessness. He passed that score with a single off Fleetwood-Smith, at 5.39pm, and the same event brought up the 600 and a great cheer. At 6.17pm Hutton, with yet another late cut for a single off O'Reilly, reached his 300 and with no more mountains to be climbed that night, the batsmen appealed against the light and departed. The score at the close was 634-5 (Hutton 300 not out, Hardstaff 40 not out) in 662 minutes off 243.2 overs. The day had witnessed 287 runs for four wickets in 307 minutes off 112.2 overs. The bowling and fielding had remained commendably tight, Bradman, especially, at mid-off and mid-on, never gave up. The bowling figures for the day were:

Waite 28-8-59-1; McCabe 12-4-14-0; O'Reilly 31.2-9-65-1; Fleetwood-Smith 35-5-114-1; Barnes 6-0-19-0.

Hutton had a thorough massage from Surrey's Sandy Tait, read a telegram from Mrs S.Foster: "Cordial congratulations from the mother of R.E.Foster and all Aberdovey sportsmen." R.E., of a famous Worcestershire family, had died of tuberculosis in 1914. Hutton told Howard Marshall on the radio: "I'm looking forward to a good night's rest," and finally sank back into a chair in the Great Central Hotel, where Hedley Verity brought him a stout and port. Meanwhile, Bradman was telling Fingleton that he would have to bat, even if on crutches. Psychologically, England had already won the match.

Tuesday 23 August: Onward and Upward

Hutton had a sleepless night and woke with aching stiff limbs. He had two more records in his sights: 334, by Bradman at Leeds in 1930, the highest innings in Anglo-Australian Tests; and 336 not out by Hammond at Auckland in 1932-3, the highest in all Test cricket. In the public mind it was the former that mattered. His opponents' plan was to exploit any tension this prospect might create. O'Reilly and Fleetwood-Smith bowled tight to a leg-side field and all were on their toes.

Hardstaff cut O'Reilly gracefully for his 50 but that seemed irrelevant. When Hutton was 311, he was nearly bowled by Fleetwood-Smith. At 670, Waite and McCabe took the new ball but not for long. After an hour's play Hutton was only 321, then he hoisted the 700 in 730 minutes with a late cut off Waite for four. The spinners came back. Fleetwood-Smith, from the Vauxhall End, had two lbw appeals against Hutton. The first, as Barnett confirmed, snicked the bat, the second umpire Chester thought too high. A boundary and a single brought Hutton to 331. The Surrey CCC head waiter appeared on the steps with drinks and E.W.Swanton (correspondent of the *Evening Standard*) sensibly put out a staying hand. For O'Reilly, from the Pavilion End, Bradman spent some time setting the field and put himself at silly mid off and Brown at silly mid on. O'Reilly bowled a no-ball, Hutton swung and missed it completely.

A single in that over brought him to face Fleetwood-Smith. The fifth ball was shortish, on the stumps but the googly, so Hutton stepped back towards the leg side and cut it with the spin, a gentle caress but with good enough timing to speed it to the boundary. Hutton ran to the other end and as he turned he saw that the ball was crossing the rope. Bradman came up and shook his hand and gently tapped him on the arm. Hardstaff was next. Some 30,000 people stood up and cheered and a cornet, sounding from below the gasometer led them into singing *For he's a jolly good fellow*. Umpire 'Fanny' Walden said, "Thank God that's over, the last few overs have been a nightmare." All the Australians congratulated Hutton except Bill O'Reilly, who lay down on the ground, no doubt thinking what Lancastrian Dick

Don Bradman is the first to congratulate Len Hutton after his record-breaking score. Hutton's partner, Joe Hardstaff, is next in line to shake his hand.

Tyldesley said in 1930 when asked his opinion of Bradman: "He's no bloody use to me." The drinks waiter was now allowed to go out. The time was now 12.47pm, and Hutton was 336 out of 711 after 739 minutes. Bradman's 334 had taken 383 minutes and a 14-year-old Leonard Hutton was in the crowd at that occasion. A few moments later came the second curtain call, when he passed 336 and became the maker of the highest score in all Tests.

The next landmark was the passing of 729-6 declared by Australia at Lord's 1930, which was the biggest innings in any Test between England and Australia and in any Test in England. There were no further alarms or excursions up to lunch at 758-5 (Hutton 361, Hardstaff 96). The English balloon was floating ever upward. Among the many telegrams received during the day was one from Herbert Sutcliffe, Hutton's mentor and county partner: "Heartiest congratulations. There is no one more pleased than I. Go for Bradman's 452 record. Congratulations to Maurice."

In the first over after lunch, off Fleetwood-Smith, Hardstaff's typical cover-drive brought four runs and his first Test hundred against Australia, in 192 minutes. Then at 2.30pm the incredible happened, the unending ended, the unbeatable was beaten. Hutton drove O'Reilly uppishly and was caught by Hassett at cover. For the eighth time he walked off the field and for the first time he was alone. Up the pavilion steps into the Long Room he was then shepherded by his fellow Yorkshiremen to the bar where Maurice Leyland ordered two bottles of champagne, "one for thee and one for me." He had been batting for three days and three hours, in actual playing time 13 hours and 17 minutes (797 minutes), with 35 4's, 15 3's, 18 twos and 143 singles and, incredibly, only one actual chance, a stumping at 41. He scored 364 out of 770. It was not an innings to be remembered for great stroke-play, or excitement, but it was an edifice unsurpassed in its assuredness, security and concentration. Most of his runs came from nicely-timed cuts, exquisite off-drives and on-side placements. Lest it be thought that Hutton had sunk into a mere sheet-anchor role, note that only Leyland of his partners had noticeably outscored him. For instance, in the stand of 215 in 206 minutes, Hutton made 100, Hardstaff 101.

The score was now 770-6 on the third afternoon and Cardus wrote: "A new game had been invented using the implements of cricket."

Next in was Arthur Wood, who since the innings began had had a new England cap specially made by the manufacturers to fit his $6^5/_8$ head. He came out with a spring in his step and meant to play strokes. Hardstaff was now at a standstill, frozen in time like Miss Havisham in *Great Expectations,* scoring four runs in half an hour after Hutton left him. The bowling was now in the hand of Barnes and Hassett. At 798 Bradman permitted himself the indulgence of a bowl, enjoyed his two overs with boyish enthusiasm, and sent down a maiden to Hardstaff. When the 800 came up, such a first digit was not in the compass of the scoreboard and a little figure eight was eventually unearthed and hung up.

Hardstaff was still playing a game of his own, stroking the ball as and when the mood took him. Wood tried harder and hit seven 4's in his first 36, but he did not have the ability to take total command. The crowd voiced impatience. Wood, partial to the sweep, was dropped at square leg when 47, which was, believe it or not, the first clearly missed catch of the innings. At 4.04pm, Wood pulled a full toss from Barnes, got it high in the splice and was caught by the bowler. He had hit eight 4's in 92 minutes. Back in the pavilion he uttered a legendary quip: "Just like me, getting out in a crisis."

With Verity in, Australia had broken through to the tail. Bradman bowled again from the Vauxhall End, but some ironic mischief of fate decreed that in fielding a hard drive by Hardstaff he should turn over his ankle in one of the huge craters in the crease which had been chiselled out by the spinners' continual bowling. It was soon clear that the Australian captain could not walk, never mind play on. After a few minutes, White and Fleetwood-Smith carried him off towards the pavilion, past the figure of Bill O'Reilly lying flat out on the grass and waving Bradman away. It was a tragedy, not in removing any spark of contest in the match, for that had long since gone, but in that one would ever know how, and how well, Bradman would face up to the challenge of batting against such a total.

The rest was anti-climax: no antics from Farnes and Bowes, no chasing of the thousand, no dramatic declaration. The players went off for tea and then the rolling of the pitch told the crowd that England had declared. Bosser Martin was crestfallen: "They should have gone on to make a thousand."

Hardstaff was left undefeated on 169, made in 326 minutes with one five and 20 4's. The innings of 903-7 dec lasted 917 minutes — or 15¼ hours, about the same length as Wagner's operatic cycle *Der Ring des Nibelungen*, off 335.2 overs. England scored at 59.09 runs per hour, 2.69 runs per over. Australia maintained a rate of 21.98 overs per hour. At least one Yorkshireman had been at the wicket throughout. Even more amazing than the monumental batting was the unflagging sharpness of the fielders, nursed and inspired by Bradman and the fact that only one catch, one stumping and one run out were counted as definite chances. No doubt the relatively cool weather helped to sustain them, though on this day the temperature reached 70°F. The bowling figures for the day were:

Waite 11-3-29-0; McCabe 9-0-26-0; O'Reilly 18.4-7-34-1; Fleetwood-Smith 17-3-63-0; Barnes 21-1-44-1; Hassett 13-2-52-0; Bradman 3-2-6-0.

The innings was the biggest in Test cricket, beating 849 by England v West Indies at Jamaica 1929-30 and 729-6 declared by Australia v England at Lord's 1930. It was the biggest in first-class cricket in England, beating 887 by Yorkshire v Warwickshire at Birmingham 1896.

Australia batted at 5pm and Farnes and Bowes set foot on the field for the first time. Farnes, from the Pavilion End with three slips and a gully, bowled a maiden to Brown. In Bowes' first over, poor Jack Badcock pushed a tame catch to short mid on. McCabe played his shots with an air of impermanence until he hooked hard to Edrich's left at square leg and was well caught: 19-2, or in effect probably 19-4, taking into account Bradman's and Fingleton's injury. Hassett was undaunted. He punished Farnes on the leg side and did the same to Edrich, who replaced him. He slashed Edrich over the slips for four, then square cut him properly for two. Sadly, in the same over, he hooked down Compton's throat at long leg. Hassett had made 42 out of 51 in 35 minutes, the brightest innings of the match. Barnes emulated him. Verity posed no problems, Farnes and Bowes were tried again, and even Leyland bowled his left-arm wrist spin with three short legs, but no further break came. Australia closed the day at 117-3 in 90 minutes (Brown 29 not out, Barnes 25 not out) off 29 overs.

A sunny, pleasant historic day had been watched by 28,928 people, of whom 26,428 paid, amongst them a party of lads from Leeds who decided to come on Monday evening and who had to be back at work at 7am on Wednesday.

The reactions and post mortems now started to flood in, for the match was as good as over and everyone was thankful that an end was in sight. Indeed, it is said that the remaining Australian batsmen were told to ensure that they did not make England bat again — some hope of that! — for their bowlers' sake. Bradman left the ground ten minutes after close of play in a car with other members of the team and the pain of the injury showed in his face. When at last the car got through the pressing crowd he went to his room in the hotel and his ankle was X-rayed. Mr Jeanes announced that a fracture of the tibia was revealed. "Bradman is quite cheerful and is now having dinner with me in my room at the hotel. His leg is not in plaster as it does not necessitate it at this stage. The surgeon is seeing him in the morning."

Leonard Hutton, just a respected young cricketer three days before, was a national hero, his name now on the lips of people who knew nothing of cricket. After he was out, he climbed up to the perch on top of the Ladies' Stand to be interviewed for radio by Howard Marshall. Hutton gave two more radio interviews and one with Leslie Mitchell on television, and made a modest little speech for the cinema newsreels, recalling that he had watched Bradman's 334 at Leeds in

1930: "Little did I realize then that eight years later I should have the chance of beating it." For the 7.30pm news on the Regional Programme, he said, "It was a very tiring and hard job. The Australian bowlers bowled very well and they did not give any runs away at all. I am really pleased that it is all over. The feeling I had at about 332 — well, I really don't know what they are, but I waited for a loose ball to come along so that I could crack a four and before long it came along and I managed to pierce the fielders. It was very difficult to get those last few runs and I was glad when it was all over."

The Mayor of Pudsey reported that nobody there had worked, all had been listening to the radio. His telegram read: "25,000 people were filled with pride. It is a great achievement and the joy bells are ringing in Pudsey." This was literally true: a peal of 364 chimes. He and the deputy town clerk arranged for a Len Hutton banquet for a date in October. Hutton's mother heard it all on the radio: "What with all the excitement I don't know where I am; of course I am pleased, but I knew he would do it."

His father, a stonemason, was working on a new telephone exchange at Laisterdyke and a boy kept him up to date by running to and from a nearby house where there was a wireless set. Mr Hutton's cousin, John Daniel Hutton, was buried on the day of the record, at Wilmslow, Cheshire, having died on the Saturday, aged 65. A few hours before his death, he had asked how Len was getting on .

Telegrams and statements came from Yorkshire captain A.B.Sellers, from A.W.Carr, a former England captain, from Jack Hobbs, and even from the headquarters of the Boys' Brigade (Len was a former member of the 2nd Leeds Company). One county colleague suggested he might repeat the feat in the second innings. Australian messages tended to emphasize the headaches he would give Australian bowlers in years to come. Arthur Chipperfield was reported to be listening in the Dundee nursing home, and able to get out of bed, no doubt able to see the bright side of his illness. At the Radiolympia exhibition, and at a television theatre at Kingsway, off The Strand, crowds watched the match. The record innings created a big interest in television sets.

Wednesday 24 August: 'Just Say I Am Pleased'

The fourth day was fine and warm but only 8,000 were at the turnstiles when they opened. The first news was that Bradman was definitely out of the match as well as Fingleton. Bradman issued a statement to the Press: "I am keenly disappointed I cannot carry on . . .but I appreciate very much the many messages of sympathy [one from the MCC president and former Prime Minister Earl Baldwin] which have been sent to me in my misfortune. I am feeling quite cheerful otherwise."

There were no more than 10,000 present when Brown and Barnes resumed. They negotiated the early overs of Farnes and Bowes easily enough, then Barnes chopped a Bowes inswinger on to his stumps. He had made a chirpy 41 out of 75 in 70 minutes, with five 4's. In the same over, Barnett edged and Wood took quick steps to his right to hold the catch and made sure everyone knew about it — his first Test victim on the eve of his 40th birthday. Waite hit two 4's off Bowes, then played all round a yorker. O'Reilly entered to a special cheer but he soon waved his bat outside the off stump and gave Wood a low catch. The day was only just starting and already Bowes had twice taken two wickets in an over, and last man Fleetwood-Smith was at the crease.

Brown passed 50, took 4, 2 and 3 off Edrich, then a curiosity occurred. Brown cut the last ball of an over and took a single to keep the strike. Hutton chased the ball from slip and kicked it over the boundary. In accordance with MCC instructions to umpires ('The runs which have been arranged for a boundary hit (four) are to be added to the runs already made, should a fielder wilfully cause the ball to reach the boundary') Frank Chester awarded five to Brown and directed that he should stay at the end to which he had run. When Hutton returned to his place in the slips, Hammond was seen to say something to him.

Fleetwood-Smith played a few 'air' shots but he also smashed a four, cross-batted over the bowler's head, and hooked another four. Leyland came on to bowl and then Hammond, whom he also hit for four. Ironically, it was Brown who was out, in a rather unreal way, befitting the mood of the game. He swept at Leyland, punted the ball up in the air off the end of his bat and Hammond made the catch at second attempt. The innings thus ended at 201, all out with only eight wickets down, Brown, first in last out, had 69 with six 4's. It lasted 166 minutes and 52.1 overs. That was a rate of 72.65 runs per hour, 3.85 per over and 18.85 overs per hour.

No doubt Brown kept his pads on as it was certain that Australia would be asked to follow-on, 702 behind. Badcock avoided the ultimate indignity of a 'pair' but after a couple of hard hit off-drives he played back to a good length ball and lost his off stump. McCabe was again unable to discern any useful function for himself and glanced down the leg side, where Wood turned and pounced on the ball, his back to the batsman. Only Brown seemed to know what he was there for. At lunch he had ten out of 31-2.

In the first over after lunch, Bowes got his seventh wicket of the match, Hassett lbw to a ball that kept low. Then Brown was unlucky to get a ball from Farnes that kicked high and was caught at short leg off the shoulder of the bat. The end could not be long delayed. Left-handed Barnett, joining Barnes, thought that he might as well play his natural game. He hit five 4's in his first 22 runs, off 11

Ben Barnett is bowled by Farnes in Australia's second innings.

balls, three of them pulls in one over by Farnes. Verity and Leyland checked the scoring. Farnes came back and both batsman got 4's off him. After they added 74 in 49 minutes, Barnes tried to pull Verity on to the roof of Archbishop Tennyson's Grammar School, and was lbw. Waite was caught at silly mid off, first ball. That was the end of Verity's over and when Farnes bowled Barnett (for 46 in an hour), bringing in Fleetwood-Smith, it was feared than Verity might not have the chance to finish the match with a hat-trick. But the last man played out Farnes' over without difficulty. Verity bowled his 'hat-trick ball' to O'Reilly, but it was too far up and O'Reilly had no problem.

At 123, O'Reilly swiped Verity to long leg for a catch to Hardstaff. Wood pulled up the stumps and prepared to bolt for the pavilion — but Hardstaff dropped the catch. However, in Farnes' next over from the Pavilion End, Fleetwood-Smith hoicked in the air to mid on, watched Leyland catch it, then turned to grab a stump, and they all ran off. The match ended at 3.40pm, Australia all out at 123-8 in 112 minutes off 34.1 overs (65.89 runs per hour, 3.60 runs per over, and 18.30 overs per hour). Bill Brown had been on the field for all but the last 65 minutes of a match lasting 1,195 minutes. The police were unable to prevent spectators from running on to Bosser Martin's much prized square but the players got off safely with their trophies.

The day's attendance was a disappointing 15,000, of whom 12,981 had paid. The aggregate for the four days was 94,212, of whom 81,336 paid £19,176 3s 6d — record receipts for a Kennington Oval Test.

On the Saturday morning, Hammond in his flannels and blazer, had tossed the coin with the Australian captain in a suit. Now he appeared on the balcony in the same attire, shaking hands with the Australian vice-captain McCabe, in a suit. Hutton too came out to accept the cheers and a voice started the crowd in singing *On Ilkley Moor baht 'at.*

Hammond could not be persuaded to talk the Press. "You know I never say anything," he told a would-be interviewer, "Just say I am pleased." He declined to give his opinion on timeless Tests. Once again, for at least the third time during the summer, there was an inquest on whether, and what, time limit there should be. From early on the second afternoon this match had ceased to be a meaningful contest and become a one-sided accumulation of records. England's batting had not been particularly slow, but in the context of the situation it gave the impression at times of having come to a standstill.

Badcock looks back to see his off stump go flying out of the ground after playing back to a good-length ball from Bowes.

The crowd swarm on to The Oval playing area after Leyland's catch helped dimiss Fleetwood-Smith to end the 'Timeless Test'.

Well done! England skipper Wally Hammond is congratulated by Australian vice-captain Stan McCabe.

England, and Hammond in particular, were delighted to inflict on the Aussies the humiliation that had been suffered by England at The Oval in 1930 and 1934. It was not pretty to watch, but many people felt better for having seen it done. If Australia had won the toss the pattern might have been the same, though they would probably scored the runs much more quickly. One thing was fairly sure: timeless Tests on artificially prepared perfect batting strips were not a good idea. The side that wins the toss tries to grind the opposition into submission. In fairness to Bosser Martin, there was life in the pitch on the first morning and Australia had no quick bowler to take advantage of it.

ENGLAND v AUSTRALIA

Fifth Test at Kennington Oval.

Saturday 20th, Monday 22nd, Tuesday 23rd and Wednesday, 24th August 1938.
Umpires: F.Chester and F.Walden.

Saturday

ENGLAND First Innings (won toss)		mins	bls	4/6
L.Hutton not out	160	355	387	15
W.J.Edrich lbw b O'Reilly	12	45	59	0
M.Leyland not out	156	309	347	14
Extras (B 5, LB 10, W 1, NB 3)	19			
Total (1 wicket — 131 overs)	**347**	355	793	

New ball at 206. Seven no-balls and one wide were bowled.

Timetable Of The Innings

Time	Score	Mins	Overs	
11.30 Saturday start				
12.15 Edrich out	1-29	45	19	Hutton 16
12.45	52	75	30.4	
1.30 to 2.15 lunch	89	120	48	Hutton 39 Leyland 35
2.23	102	128	51.1	
3.06	150	171	66.3	
3.41	201	206	78.2	
4.25 to 4.45 (rain) tea	242	250	94.2	Hutton 111 Leyland 104
4.56	250	261	97.1	
5.35	300	300	111.2	
6.30 Close	347	355	131	

Bowling	O	M	R	W
Waite (W 1)				
lunch	15	3	19	0
tea	27	5	46	0
close	33	5	62	0
McCabe				
lunch	7	4	10	0
tea	13	4	28	0
close	17	4	45	0
O'Reilly (NB 7)				
lunch	13	6	28	1
tea	26.2	8	62	1
close	35	10	79	1
Fleetwood-Smith				
lunch	13	2	29	0
tea	24	3	79	0
close	35	3	121	0
Barnes				
lunch	-	-	-	-
tea	4	0	12	0
close	11	2	21	0

Individual Targets			
Hutton	50	142m	173b
	100	212m	254b
	151	331m	362b
Leyland	50	94m	110b
	103	202m	218b
	153	299m	331b

Monday

ENGLAND First Innings (continued)		mins	bls	4/6
L.Hutton not out	300	662	718	27
W.J.Edrich lbw b O'Reilly	12			
M.Leyland run out (Hassett-Bradman)	187	381	438	17
*Mr W.R.Hammond lbw b Fleetwood-Smith	59	141	153	4
E.Paynter lbw b O'Reilly	0	4	4	0
D.C.S.Compton b Waite	1	13	14	0
J.Hardstaff not out	40	71	86	6
Extras (B 10, LB 18, W 1, NB 6)	35			
Total (5 wickets — 243.2 overs)	**634**	662	1472	

New ball at 436. Twelve no-balls and one wide bowled so far.

Timetable Of The Innings

Time	Score	Mins	Overs	
11.55 Monday start (rain)				
11.57	350	357	132	
1.00	402	420	156.5	
1.07 Leyland out	2-411	427	159.3	Hutton 188
1.30 to 2.15 lunch	434	450	167	Hutton 191 Hammond 20
2.40	451	475	176.3	
3.32	500	527	194.4	
4.15 Hammond out	3-546	570	210.4	Hutton 257
4.20 Paynter out	4-547	575	211.4	Hutton 258
4.26	553	581	213	
4.30 to 5.00 Tea, rain	553	585	214	Hutton 263 Compton 1
5.05 Compton out	5-555	590	215.5	Hutton 265
5.39	600	624	228.4	see note 1
6.17 Close (bad light)	634	662	243.2	see note 2

1. Off this ball Hutton reached 288 beating R.E.Foster's record score for England v Australia. 2. Off this ball Hutton reached 300.
Shortly before 3.00 Fingleton retired hurt and E.S.White fielded as substitute.

Bowling	O	M	R	W
Waite (W 1)				
lunch	42	8	73	0
tea	54	11	102	0
close	61	13	121	1
McCabe				
lunch	-	-	-	-
tea	29	8	59	0
close	-	-	-	-
O'Reilly (NB 11)				
lunch	47	13	104	1
tea	59	16	132	2
close	66.2	19	144	2
Fleetwood-Smith (NB 1)				
lunch	50	7	167	0
tea	61	7	209	1
close	70	8	235	1
Barnes				
lunch	-	-	-	-
tea	-	-	-	-
close	17	2	40	0

Individual Targets			
Hutton	200	468m	516b
	253	563m	616b
	288	624m	685b
	300	662m	718b
Hammond	50	111m	117b

Tuesday

ENGLAND First Innings (continued)		mins	bls	4/6
L.Hutton c Hassett (cover) b O'Reilly	364	797	847	35
W.J.Edrich lbw b O'Reilly	12			
M.Leyland run out	187			
*Mr W.R.Hammond lbw b Fleetwood-Smith	59			
E.Paynter lbw b O'Reilly	0			
D.C.S.Compton b Waite	1			
J.Hardstaff not out	169	326	400	20‡
†A.Wood c and b Barnes	53	92	95	8
H.Verity not out	8	25	19	1
Extras (B 22, LB 19, W 1, NB 8)	50			
Total(7 wkts, dec — 336 overs minus 4 balls)	903	917	2029	

Mr K.Farnes and W.E.Bowes did not bat.

New ball at 670. Seventeen no-balls and one wide bowled in the innings.

‡Hardstaff hit one five.

The 333rd over was incomplete because Bradman retired hurt after bowling two balls.

Timetable Of The Innings

Time		Score	Mins	Overs	
11.30	Tuesday start				
11.54		650	686	252.2	
12.35		700	727	267	
12.47	Bradman 334 passed	711	739	270.5	Hutton 336
12.55	Hammond 336 passed	715	747	272.3	Hutton 340
1.07	Australia 729 passed	730	759	276.4	
1.23		750	775	283.3	
1.30	to 2.15 lunch	758	782	286	Hutton 361 Hardstaff 96
2.30	Hutton out	6-770	797	291.3	Hardstaff 101
3.00		801	827	303.3	
3.42	England 849 passed	850	869	318.3	
4.03	Wood out	7-876	890	326.4	Hardstaff 150
4.21	Bradman off	887	908	332.2	
4.30	Tea, innings declared	903	917	336	900 up off last ball

Bowling

	O	M	R	W
Waite (W 1)				
lunch	66	14	135	1
end	72	16	150	1
McCabe				
lunch	38	8	85	0
end	-	-	-	-
O'Reilly (NB 14)				
lunch	79	24	161	2
end	85	26	178	3
Fleetwood-Smith(NB3)				
lunch	81	10	281	1
end	87	11	298	1
Barnes				
lunch	22	2	54	0
end	38	3	84	1
Hassett				
lunch	-	-	-	-
end	13	2	52	0
Bradman				
lunch	-	-	-	-
end	2.2*	1	6	0

*incomplete 3rd over

Individual Targets

Hutton	336	739m	794b
	340	747m	798b
	350	762m	812b
Hardstaff	51	92m	113b
	101	192m	236b
	150	298m	367b
Wood	50	74m	78b

AUSTRALIA First Innings

Batsman	Runs	mins	bls	4/6
W.A.Brown c Hammond (short leg) b Leyland	69	166	153	6‡
C.L.Badcock c Hardstaff (silly mid-on) b Bowes	0	4	3	0
S.J.McCabe c Edrich (short leg) b Farnes	14	10	15	2
A.L.Hassett c Compton (long leg) b Edrich	42	33	41	5
S.G.Barnes b Bowes	41	68	72	5
†B.A.Barnett c Wood (wkt) b Bowes	2	2	3	0
M.G.Waite b Bowes	8	10	8	2
W.J.O'Reilly c Wood (wkt) b Bowes	0	2	3	0
L.O'B.Fleetwood-Smith not out	16	26	20	3
Extras (B 4, LB 2, NB 3)	9			
Total (All out for 8 wickets — 52.1 overs)	**201**	166	318	

J.H.Fingleton and *D.G.Bradman (absent hurt) did not bat. Five no-balls were bowled. ‡Brown hit one five, awarded by the umpire when the fielder (Hutton) kicked the ball over the boundary.

Timetable Of The Innings

Time		Score	Mins	Overs	
5.00	Tuesday start				
5.04	Badcock out	1-0	4	1.3	Brown 0
5.15	McCabe out	2-19	15	4.5	Brown 4
5.38		51	38	11.2	
5.50	Hassett out	3-70	50	15	Brown 12
6.10		102	70	21.4	
6.30	Close	117	90	29	Brown 29 Barnes 25
11.30	Wednesday start				extras 7
12.00	Barnes out	4-145	120	39.2	Brown 41
12.04	Barnett out	5-147	124	39.5	Brown 41
12.10		152	130	41.3	
12.15	Waite out	6.160	135	43.1	Brown 45
12.19	O'Reilly out	7-160	139	43.4	Brown 45
12.45		200	165	51.2	
12.46	Brown out	8-201	166	52.1	

Bowling

	O	M	R	W
Farnes				
close	9	2	42	1
end	13	2	54	1
Bowes				
close	9	0	21	1
end	19	3	49	5
Edrich (NB 4)				
close	4	0	27	1
end	10	2	55	1
Verity				
close	5	1	15	0
end	-	-	-	-
Leyland				
close	2	0	5	0
end	3.1	0	11	1
Hammond (NB 1)				
close	-	-	-	-
end	2	0	8	0

Individual Targets
Brown 51 144m 123b

AUSTRALIA Second Innings (follow on 702 behind)

Batsman	Runs	mins	bls	4/6
C.L.Badcock b Bowes	9	17	29	2
W.A.Brown c Edrich (square leg) b Farnes	15	47	27	1
S.J.McCabe c Wood (wkt) b Farnes	2	1	2	0
A.L.Hassett lbw b Bowes	10	10	12	1
S.G.Barnes lbw b Verity	33	64	74	4
†B.A.Barnett b Farnes	46	55	50	7
M.G.Waite c Edrich (silly mid-off) b Verity	0	½	1	0
W.J.O'Reilly not out	7	10	7	1
L.O'B.Fleetwood-Smith c Leyland (mid-on) b Farnes	0	6	3	0
Extras (B 1)	1			
Total (All out for 8 wickets — 34.1 overs)	**123**	112	205	

J.H.Fingleton and *D.G.Bradman absent hurt.

Timetable Of The Innings

Time		Score	Mins	Overs	
1.00	Wednesday start				
1.17	Badcock out	1-15	17	5.5	Brown 5
1.20	McCabe out	2-18	20	6.2	Brown 6
1.30	to 2.15 lunch	31	30	9	Brown 10 Hassett 9
2.17	Hassett out	3-35	32	9.5	Brown 13
2.32	Brown out	4-41	47	14.1	Barnes 4
2.36		51	51	15	
3.15		100	90	29	
3.23	Barnes out	5-115	98	31.5	Barnett 45
3.25	Waite out	6-115	100	32	Barnett 45
3.29	Barnett out	7-117	104	32.4	O'Reilly 1
3.37	Fleetwood-Smith out	8-123	112	34.1	

England won by an innings and 579 runs

Bowling

	O	M	R	W
Farnes				
lunch	5	1	17	1
end	12.1	1	63	4
Bowes				
lunch	4	1	13	1
end	10	3	25	2
Leyland				
lunch	-	-	-	-
end	5	0	19	0
Verity				
lunch	-	-	-	-
end	7	3	15	2

Don Bradman turns his ankle in attempting to field a drive from Hardstaff.

The Australian captain is carried from the field. An X-ray revealed that he had fractured a tibia.

Bradman, on crutches and staying for the next few days at the team hotel, told the Press that he was doubtful whether there would be any arrangement for a timeless Test on Australia's next tour in 1942. And the chairman of the England selectors said that he thought four or possibly five days should be enough to decide any Test. He also responded to a lot of letters, some of them anonymous, criticising the omission of Hutton and Leyland in the Leeds Test, by saying that both were then unfit (a rather debatable claim in the latter's case).

Len Hutton issued a Press statement: "There is no truth whatever in the report in a London newspaper that I am engaged to Miss Dorothy Dennis of Harehill, Leeds". Miss Dennis, daughter of a former Yorkshire cricketer, was suffering a seige by the Press at her place of work, Marshall & Snellgrove, Bond Street, Leeds.

August 20 to 23: Traditional Gesture from Charlie Barnett

A win for Yorkshire at Nottingham in the fixture which coincided with the first three days of The Oval Test would have brought the Championship title very close. After scoring 320 on the first day, the effect of the absence of the players at The Oval told in the bowling on an easy pitch. Notts played a solid, defensive riposte, Charlie Harris making 103 in four hours, and although Robinson took 7-122, Yorkshire could not start their second innings until well into the final day, 83 behind, and Sellers was never in a position to set a target. Middlesex had no match. Surrey came up against Frank Lee's continuing run of form at Taunton — 141 in 255 minutes — but half of the match was lost to rain and Surrey were glad not to reach a first-innings decision. At Manchester, Lancashire gave a debut to Richard Parkin, son of Cecil, who scored 60, but they lost to Gloucestershire in two days by ten wickets. Charlie Barnett gave in this match the traditional two-fingered reply to the Test selectors by scoring 168 in 280 minutes and taking 5-63 and 6-40 with his awkward medium-pace swing.

Question: Where was the first ever County Championship match off mainland Great Britain played? Answer: Newport, Isle of Wight, where Hampshire beat Northants with McCorkell hitting the winning six with five minutes to spare.

Oddly, the rain virtually wiped out play in the South on Monday, from Cardiff to Eastbourne, but left The Oval almost untouched. Yorkshire (average 8.92) and Middlesex (average 8.76) each had two matches to play.

In Europe, the Runciman negotiations were said to be at a serious stage. The Spanish Nationalists rejected the British plan for withdrawal of foreign troops.

August 24 to 26: Wells Farrago

In the round of county matches which started on Wednesday, the last day of the Test, Yorkshire were fortunate to be hosting a friendly game against Scotland at Harrogate. As Middlesex reached no decision against Lancashire at Manchester, the top two kept the identical average, although Middlesex now had only one more match to play, and that against Surrey. Surrey beat Hampshire by three wickets at Bournemouth in a game of poor batting. At Eastbourne, Sussex moved from 32-0 to 540-6 declared on the second day. John Langridge was dropped four times in making 215 in even time, but Glamorgan's dogged Yorkshire opener Arnold Dyson ensured a draw with 96 and 170 not out. Worcestershire were sinking to defeat at Nottingham when last man Reg Perks, just selected for the South African tour, roused the crowd with 75 out of 84 in 30 minutes. Notts, though, still won.

Put together Somerset and Kent on the small ground at Wells and the result could only be a farrago of 6's. For Somerset, Arthur Wellard went to town on the county that had rejected his services. As well as taking 7-65 and 6-50, he hit 57 in 37 minutes with seven 6's, and 37 with four 6's. In the first inning he gorged himself in one over by Frank Woolley. The first five balls went for 6,6,6,6,6, three landing in neighbouring gardens. Off the sixth ball he was dropped by Valentine near the sightscreen and took a single. Valentine (114 with four 6's and 14 4's) and Knott (65 with two 6's and nine 4's) added 180 in two hours. In the Kent second innings, Woolley hit three 6's. The result, by the way: Somerset won by 27 runs.

Wednesday, the last day of the Test, marked the opening of the annual Radio Exhibition at Olympia. The crowds were attracted to the special television area, where, as well as seeing play from The Oval, they could see programmes being made and participate in 'Come and be Televised'. You could buy a Pye model 817 (4 x 3 $^{3}/_{8}$ inch screen) for 21 guineas, a GEC Vision Unit (7¼ x 5¾) for 23 guineas, or for prestige or commercial use a Marconiphone radio and TV (22 x 18) for 200 guineas.

Things seemd to be going well in Czechoslovakia. Lord Runciman acquired the epithet, 'Duchacek' ('the man who gets things done') and the Government said it was willing to discuss greater autonomy for the minorities. But on Friday, the Sudeten German leaders stated that their people were 'free to act in self-defence if attacked'; and the German Press stepped up its attacks on Czech 'atrocities' and British 'procrastination'.

The Crisis

August 27 to 30: The County Climax

THE Australians came back into earthly time when they resumed their county matches at Hove. There were six more games and three weeks of cricket to face and Bradman, Fingleton and Chipperfield unlikely to play in any of them. Fortunately, McCormick was fit enough. As usual, the first day of the English League football season heralded beautiful summer weather; 800,00 people watched 44 matches, with 58,000 at Arsenal to see the champions beat Portsmouth 2-0.

Sussex, without the injured J.H.Parks, tied the batsmen down by good bowling, but Hassett scored 50 in an hour and they reached 131-4 at lunch. After lunch the ever-adhesive Brown made his usual contribution, 75 in 165 minutes with two 4's. White drove powerfully for seven 4's in 45 minutes. McCormick bowled off his long run as Sussex made 43-0 by the close.

Monday was dull and chilly, but the good crowd who came were magnificently rewarded. Hugh Tryon Bartlett came in at 12.30pm and made his usual agonising start: four runs in 15 minutes. Twenty minutes and three 6's later he passed 50. In one over by Ward there were 22 runs, Bartlett hitting 4,4,6,6. One six off Ward carried 125 yards over long on, down the Hove slope to land on a grass island near the secretary's office at the South Gate. All Bartlett's shots were perfectly timed. The century came in 57 minutes with six 6's and 11 4's, beating E.R.T.Holmes' 65-minute 'crawl' for Surrey against Sussex, to become the fastest of the season so far. He was 104 at lunch, then he hit another seven 4's and had made 157 in 125 minutes when he perished nobly, caught at deep mid on. He gave one chance in the gully just before he was dismissed. Bartlett and the self-effacing James Langridge, also a left-hander, put on 195 in 110 minutes against wholly defensive fields.

Another hitter, George Cox junior, came in and drove Barnes and Ward straight for 6's, making 74 in 100 minutes. If this sort of punishment had been meted out to the Australians earlier in the tour it would have seriously deflated their morale. Ward purchased wickets like a millionaire with six months to live: he finished with 36.1-6-184-6. Australia went in again, 117 behind, and seemed to be

SUSSEX v AUSTRALIA

Played at Hove, on August 27, 29, 30, 1938.
Match drawn.

AUSTRALIA

	1st innings		2nd innings	
†C.W.Walker	b Hammond	7	(11) not out	2
C.L.Badcock	c Jas.Langridge b Wood	22	(4) c Holmes b Wood	58
A.L.Hassett	b Hammond	74	(9) c J.Cornford b Wood	56
S.Barnes	lbw b Jas.Langridge	24	(3) b Wood	44
*S.J.McCabe	b Wood	3	(6) b Hammond	16
W.A.Brown	b Wood	75	(2) c W.Cornford b Hammond	23
B.A.Barnett	c Hammond b John Langridge	17	(5) lbw b Hammond	53
M.G.Waite	c Stainton b J.Cornford	46	(7) b Hammond	9
E.S.White	c Stainton b Wood	44	(8) b Hammond	15
F.Ward	c Hammond b J.Cornford	2	(1) c W.Cornford b J.Cornford	0
E.L.McCormick	not out	8	(10) lbw b Jas.Langridge	2
Extras	(B 6, LB 5, W 3)	14	(B 13, LB 8, W 1)	22
Total		**336**		**300**

Fall: 1st inns 1/24, 2/46, 3/105, 4/110, 5/162, 6/191, 7/262, 8/309, 9/313.
2nd inns 1/5, 2/55, 3/91, 4/174, 5/200, 6/200, 7/233, 8/240, 9/276.
Barnett deputized as wicketkeeper when Walker was injured

SUSSEX

	1st innings		2nd innings	
John G.Langridge	st Walker b Ward	32	st Barnett b Ward	13
Mr R.G.Stainton	lbw b Ward	58	b McCormick	10
H.W.Parks	lbw b White	12	not out	29
Mr H.T.Bartlett	c Barnes b Ward	157		
Jas.Langridge	st Barnett b Barnes	68		
G.Cox	b Ward	76		
*Ft-Lt.A.J.Holmes	c Barnes b White	13		
H.E.Hammond	c McCormick b White	8		
D.J.Wood	st Barnett b Ward	1		
†W.L.Cornford	not out	12		
J.H.Cornford	st Barnett b Ward	1		
Extras	(B 4, LB 10, NB 1)	15	(W 1)	1
Total		**453**	(2 wickets)	**53**

Fall: 1st inns 1/72, 2/93, 3/109, 4/304, 5/364, 6/411, 7/429, 8/447, 9/451.
2nd inns 1/12, 2/53.

SUSSEX	O	M	R	W	O	M	R	W
J.Cornford	29	4	84	2	26	6	55	1
Hammond	32	6	86	2	34	4	107	5
Wood	25.4	1	96	4	25.4	3	81	3
Jas.Langridge	18	4	49	1	19	7	35	1
John Langridge	2	0	7	1				

AUSTRALIA	O	M	R	W	O	M	R	W
McCormick	24	1	86	0	6	0	18	1
Waite	17	4	55	0	4	2	5	0
McCabe	2	0	6	0				
Ward	36.1	6	184	6	4.4	0	19	1
White	33	13	75	3				
Barnes	6	1	32	1				
Brown	-	-	-	-	3	0	10	0

Umpires: A.C.Russell and H.W.Lee.

saving the game when Badcock, who was suffering from lumbago, and Barnett added 83. In poor light on the final afternoon, Barnett was lbw when hit on the boot and Badcock caught in the gully off a full-blooded shot. Jim Hammond took the new ball and bowled McCabe off his pads playing no stroke. Waite and White added 30 but at 3.30pm, Australia were only 123 ahead with two wickets left and Hassett batting with an injured hand. McCormick hung on whilst Hassett batted brilliantly for 56 out of 67 in 65 minutes. Walker, who had damaged his hand earlier in the match, batted last. Sussex needed 184 in 50 minutes to win. If Bartlett had not strained a muscle they might just have gone for it, but as it was they had to settle for a moral victory.

The Australian injury list was now beyond a joke. Besides Bradman, Fingleton, Badcock, Hassett and Walker, Fleetwood-Smith was also suffering from lumbago.

In the County Championship, Yorkshire were at full strength at last — although Gibb was preferred to Sutcliffe and Barber — at Dover. Middlesex were at home to Surrey. If Yorkshire won, Middlesex had to win to stay in the race.

Kent brought in Ames as a batsman, but Wright was still unfit. Yorkshire won the toss and batted, making a steady unspectacular start. Yardley, dropped twice, played some delicate shots. In the afternoon the reflection of the sun on car windows caused a short stoppage. Mitchell made 73 in 225 minutes and at 280-8, Verity joined Sellers. At the close it was 326-8 and although Sellers was on 93, he declared overnight.

Monday was a duller day as Fagg and Woolley put up the 50 in half an hour. Verity came on at the Railway End and soon had Fagg caught at slip and Woolley dropped at mid-on, where Yardley took the ball on the mouth. Kent collapsed to 136-5 at lunch. The dismissal of Valentine ended the resistance and Kent followed-on 158 behind. The Yorkshire fielders were back on the field before the spectators had finished their perambulations around the middle. Woolley went for a doubtful second run and was thrown out by Leyland from square leg. Fagg cut Verity straight to slip and Valentine was lbw: 19-3. Chalk was dropped off Verity, square leg running round in circles until he fell down on his behind, and then Chalk pulled Verity for six. But Verity was getting just enough turn and lift to suit him and with Robinson's and Leyland's assistance he ensured that Kent were all out for 109 and the match was won at 5.20pm on the second day. Now the onus was on Middlesex.

Scores:— Yorkshire 326-8 dec (A.Mitchell 73, Mr N.W.D.Yardley 43, Mr A.B.Sellers 93*, L.J.Todd 5-64). Kent 168 (A.E.Fagg 42, Mr B.H.Valentine 45, H.Verity 5-42) and 109 (Verity 4-53, M.Leyland 2-4). Yorkshire (12 pts) won by an innings and 49 runs.

At Lord's, Middlesex made only 241 on Saturday in an uninspired display. A bright 40 by Edrich ended when he backed up too far to Compton's off-drive. Compton played a two-minded shot against Garland-Wells and was caught and bowled. Allen took three hours to score 40 and Smith made 25 before being caught in the deep off one of his better shots. For Surrey, Fishlock was dropped at third slip before bad light stopped play at 18-0.

Monday was heartbreak for Middlesex. Play started at 2.45pm and their only 'success' all day was when Fishlock retired hurt after a second blow on the knuckles. Robins found the pitch too slow and Allen bowled too short. Gregory reached 100 in two and a half hours and Surrey were 225-0 at the close. On Tuesday, Squires passed 100 with one of his many sweeps. Middlesex batted again in mid-afternoon, 155 in arrears. They lost their sense of direction now that the title was beyond their grasp. Robertson and Compton batted well but Compton's indecisiveness ran out Robertson and nearly did the same for Allen. They fell to 92-5 with 75 minutes left. Allen and Robbins defended, but both were lbw to Squires and Middlesex became 135-8, 20 behind with 40 minutes left. Robins hit out against Gregory and Squires, and Smith drove Gregory for six. At 6.15pm the Surrey captain called it a day. The Middlesex challenge petered out as in 1937 and the title stayed up north where it seemed to belong.

Scores:— Middlesex 241 (W.J.Edrich 40, D.C.S.Compton 52, Mr G.O.Allen 40) and 183-8 (J.D.Robertson 43, Mr R.W.V.Robins 38*, H.S.Squires 4-60). Surrey 396 (L.B.Fishlock 58, R.J.Gregory 129, H.S.Squires 116, Mr I.A.R.Peebles 6-76). Drawn (Surrey 4 pts).

At Clacton, the wicket sweated under the covers and Farnes took 7-75 and 8-38, unchanged in each innings, and Essex beat Glamorgan in two days. Derbyshire, put in by Leicestershire at Ashby-de-la-Zouch, also won with a day to spare. Lancashire could not force a win against Warwickshire at Blackpool. Hampshire, set 243 to beat Notts at Bournemouth, collapsed and Ronald Giles, a slow left-armer, in his first match of the season, took the last two wickets with the last two balls of the match. Unlucky Northants came so close to the cherished ambition at Worcester when the home county, chasing 237 in a day and a bit, fell to 91-6 but Martin and Singleton guided them to an exciting two-wicket victory.

Winston Churchill, speaking at Theydon Bois, warned of German Army manoeuvres and said that the threat of war was close but not inevitable. The British ambassador in Berlin came home for consultations. Sir John Simon, Chancellor of the Exchequer, reaffirmed Britain's moral, although not binding, obligation to support the only democracy in Eastern Europe.

August 31 to September 2: Bartlett Loses a Trophy

Arriving at Blackpool in the early hours of Wednesday morning, eight fit and three unfit Australians took on a motley collection of county and Lancashire League cricketers billed as an England XI. The latter included Leslie Warburton, a League all rounder, Amar Singh, India's best quick bowler, P.T.Eckersley, former Lancashire captain and now MP for Manchester Exchange, and the great George Duckworth, retired Lancashire and England wicketkeeper. McCabe put them in on a slow, soft wicket. O'Reilly took 3-0 in four overs and 'England' were all out in 145 minutes. Amar Singh bowled well, unchanged for 140 minutes, keeping the ball up and swinging it late. Off the fifth ball of an over he had Brown out lbw to a typical ear-splitting Duckworth appeal. Hassett went first ball. Off the first ball of the next over, George Pope bowled Badcock. Ward used his own peculiar pull shot to give the Australians the lead. The England XI lost Edrich before the close, so that in a six-hour day, 6,000 people saw 21 wickets fall for 339 runs.

Bill O'Reilly in action against an England XI at Blackpool. He took 4 for 30 as the England XI slumped to 132 all out.

Armar Singh, India's best quick bowler, sends one down for the England XI. Singh, who took 6 for 84, was playing in League cricket that summer.

England XI openers Denis Smith (left) of Derbyshire and Bill Edrich of Middlesex.

On Thursday early rain delayed the start for an hour and the Australians practised to entertain the 2,000 spectators. Howorth needed three runs to complete the double but he was out to a running catch off the first ball of the day. England were 76-7 at lunch, and apart from an enterprising 15 by Duckworth, that was that. The match was over at 3.20pm on the second day, hardly what the organizers hoped for, but at least it gave the embattled tourists an extra day to travel to the South Coast.

There was some good news for Lancashire CCC when the Government conceded that whatever the ticket-holders got for their money in the Manchester Test it would not be classified as entertainment and no tax would be levied. Arthur Fagg withdrew from the tour to South Africa and Hugh Bartlett was selected to replace him. The South African Board agreed to MCC's request that the Fifth Test at Durban be played to a finish if one side did not lead by more than one Test.

Yorkshire continued their South Coast sojourn at Hove. On the first morning, helped by the sea fret they bowled out Sussex for 77. Arthur Mitchell made 100 in the indecent time of 140 minutes. Yorkshire collapsed in the sea fret on Thursday morning, but gained a lead on 253. Coming in with Sussex at 82-4, George Cox caused an embarrassment. On the previous day, Bartlett (not playing in this match) had been presented with a cup for the fastest 50 at Hove. Cox, who had just come into form, raced to 50 in 28 minutes and Bartlett had to hand the cup back. Then, after being dropped off Verity at 69, Cox threatened to really rub it in by beating Bartlett's 57-minute century. On 95 in 53 minutes, he pulled Leyland in the air but the ball landed just inside the rope and a single resulted. Then James Langridge was out and 60 minutes had elapsed before Cox could get to three figures. In hot sun after overnight rain, Yorkshire struggled to make the 70 needed to win on the last day but Gibb guided them to a four-wicket victory.

Lancashire, who had won once since 25 July, ended the season on a high note against Surrey. Needing 240 to win, Washbrook and Paynter put on a remarkable show of running between the wickets, almost hit-and-run, to clinch it by eight wickets. But thanks to first-innings points Surrey were not supplanted by Lancashire from their place. Essex made their highest total of the season, 553 at Gloucester, in an easy victory and Nichols scored 159 and took 9-37 and 6-128. Somerset beat Leicestershire in two days thus achieving their highest-ever number of wins in a Championship season. Leicestershire, once fourth in the table, had not won a game since 30 June. Kent folded up in two days at Dover against Notts; after making 18 in his last innings for Kent, Frank Woolley was presented with a silver coffee set by the Mayor.

AN ENGLAND XI v AUSTRALIA

Played at Blackpool, on August 31 and September 1, 1938.
Australia won by ten wickets.

AN ENGLAND XI

W.J.Edrich	b O'Reilly	31	lbw b O'Reilly	9
D.Smith	b O'Reilly	26	c Hassett b White	26
T.S.Worthington	c McCabe b Ward	45	(4) c Brown b Ward	7
L.F.Townsend	c Badcock b O'Reilly	0	(5) lbw b O'Reilly	1
A.J.Croom	st Barnett b Ward	0	(6) c Badcock b O'Reilly	4
L.Warburton	st Barnett b Ward	1	(7) not out	11
R.Howorth	c McCabe b Ward	5	(3) c Hassett b O'Reilly	8
Amar Singh	c Waite b Ward	7	c Brown b Ward	0
G.H.Pope	b Ward	10	c Badcock b Ward	6
*Mr P.T.Eckersley	lbw b O'Reilly	2	c Brown b Ward	0
†G.Duckworth	not out	0	b O'Reilly	15
Extras	(B 1, NB 4)	5	(B 8, LB 3, NB 1)	12
Total		**132**		**99**

Fall: 1st inns 1/52, 2/61, 3/65, 4/70, 5/72, 6/86, 7/95, 8/121, 9/126.
2nd inns 1/15, 2/33, 3/60, 4/61, 5/67, 6/67, 7/67, 8/78, 9/78.

AUSTRALIA

C.L.Badcock	b Pope	14	not out	29
W.A.Brown	lbw b Amar Singh	11	not out	15
A.L.Hassett	c Worthington b Amar Singh	0		
S.Barnes	b Pope	23		
†B.A.Barnett	b Amar Singh	9		
*S.J.McCabe	lbw b Amar Singh	11		
M.G.Waite	lbw b Amar Singh	22		
E.S.White	b Warburton	16		
W.J.O'Reilly	b Amar Singh	17		
F.Ward	b Warburton	31		
E.L.McCormick	not out	1		
Extras	(B 5, LB 13, W 1)	19	(B 8, LB 6)	14
Total		**174**	(No wicket)	**58**

Fall: 1st inns 1/26, 2/26, 3/26, 4/39, 5/65, 6/99, 7/101, 8/124, 9/173.

AUSTRALIA	O	M	R	W	O	M	R	W
McCormick	5	1	22	0	2	1	4	0
Waite	10	1	31	0	2	1	6	0
O'Reilly	19	11	30	4	16	6	44	5
Ward	13.5	0	44	6	8	1	20	4
White					7	4	13	1

AN ENGLAND XI	O	M	R	W	O	M	R	W
Amar Singh	25	2	84	6	7.1	1	16	0
Pope	18	4	44	2	3	1	2	0
Warburton	6.1	2	10	2	2	0	15	0
Edrich	2	0	17	0				
Worthington	2	2	0	0				
Howorth	-	-	-	-	2	0	11	0

Umpires: A.Dolphin and G.Best

The Czech Government proposed to set up autonomous cantons and President Benes met two Sudeten German leaders, but not Henlein who drove to Berchtesgaden to consult with Hitler. Italy decreed that all Jews who had immigrated since 1918 had to get out.

September 3 to 6: The Australians Limp On

Another England XI, quite strong, met the Australians at Folkestone. Jack Fingleton rose like Lazarus and limped out to bat on the first morning and stayed for 45 minutes. Barnett hit well on the leg side for 82 in 90 minutes. In three hours, Barnes missed his first century of the tour by nine runs. Later, O'Reilly batted with delicacy. At 366-8, the players went off in light that was not very dim and they did not return.

On Monday, the England XI started badly. Ward bowled Paynter with his first ball, a full toss. Compton played an odd innings, trying to step back and force the ball away on the off side, until he was bowled with a poor stroke to another Ward full toss. Only Ames knew how to use his feet against Ward's clever flight. George Pope slowly compiled the 17 he needed for his 1,000 runs, but brother Alfred became O'Reilly's 100th victim of the tour. Australia batted again at 4.15pm and McCabe played his first decent innings for a long time. He gave a stumping chance off Wilkinson at 39, then hit 22 in an over by him. When he was beautifully caught in the gully by Valentine he had hit 17 4's in 75 minutes. The Australians were 204-5 at a sunlit close of play. On Tuesday morning, Barnett was dropped in the gully by Valentine then caught there next ball. The Australians batted on idly. When Fingleton reached 50 in 90 minutes, scarcely a hand was clapped. Many of the crowd were on their way home. A declaration did not come until lunch time, when the England XI were set the completely unrealistic target of 495 in three hours.

Woolley received three cheers when he came out to open with Fagg, but there was nothing to do but play out time and even with Woolley at the crease, nobody was sorry when rain ended the match early. Fortunately this was not his last first-class match. There are two views on how festival cricket of this kind should be played: either seriously to win, or light-heartedly to entertain. The Australians were disappointing their many admirers by doing neither. No doubt there were two good reasons for that. First, the Oval Test had sapped their will to play competitive cricket and reduced their pool of fit players to soldier on. Second, as Fingleton wrote in his diary: "So far as the Australians are concerned, the three Festival games at the end of the tour are misnomers and unpopular. They come at the end of over four months of hard play, six days a week from eleven in the morning (*sic*) to six-thirty in the evening. Each Festival side,

AN ENGLAND XI v AUSTRALIA

Played at Folkestone, on September 3, 5, 6, 1938.
Match drawn.

AUSTRALIA

W.A.Brown	b A.V.Pope	3	c Levett b A.V.Pope	22
C.L.Badcock	run out	21	(3) c Woolley b Wilkinson	39
A.L.Hassett	b Todd	18	(4) b Wilkinson	18
S.Barnes	c Woolley b Todd	91	(5) lbw b Wilkinson	15
J.H.Fingleton	b Compton	12	(8) not out	51
†B.A.Barnett	b G.H.Pope	82	c Valentine b Todd	29
*S.J.McCabe	st Levett b Wilkinson	26	(2) Valentine b Todd	91
M.G.Waite	c Levett b Todd	60	(7) c G.H.Pope b Compton	42
E.S.White	lbw b G.H.Pope	27	not out	5
W.J.O'Reilly	not out	40		
F.Ward	c Levett b Todd	2		
Extras	(B 2, LB 6)	8	(B 6, LB 9)	15
Total		**390**	(7 wickets, declared)	**327**

Fall: 1st inns 1/4, 2/37, 3/46, 4/74, 5/206, 6/245, 7/262, 8/317, 9/386.
2nd inns 1/45, 2/139, 3/173, 4/196, 5/203, 6/232, 7/285.

AN ENGLAND XI

F.E.Woolley	c Badcock b Waite	5	not out	16
A.E.Fagg	c White b Waite	22	not out	20
E.Paynter	b Ward	14		
D.C.S.Compton	b Ward	17		
L.E.G.Ames	c & b Ward	78		
*Mr B.H.Valentine	st Barnett b Ward	15		
G.H.Pope	not out	41		
L.J.Todd	b Ward	13		
A.V.Pope	lbw b O'Reilly	5		
†Mr W.H.V.Levett	b Ward	3		
L.L.Wilkinson	b Ward	0		
Extras	(B 4, LB 4, W 1, NB 1)	10	(LB)	2
Total		**223**	(No wicket)	**38**

Fall: 1st inns 1/10, 2/39, 3/48, 4/89, 5/150, 6/163, 7/203, 8/212, 9/223.

AN ENGLAND XI	O	M	R	W	O	M	R	W
A.V.Pope	23	2	73	1	21	7	60	1
Todd	31.4	4	97	4	16	3	69	2
Wilkinson	28	8	75	1	19	3	86	3
G.H.Pope	24	2	101	2	20	3	64	0
Compton	5	0	19	1	6	1	18	1
Woolley	9	0	17	0	3	0	11	0
Ames	-	-	-	-	1	0	4	0

AUSTRALIA	O	M	R	W	O	M	R	W
Waite	10	1	28	2	4	1	10	0
McCabe	4	0	12	0				
O'Reilly	21	4	54	1				
Ward	26.3	3	112	7	4	0	11	0
White	6	2	7	0	7	2	15	0

Umpires: F.Chester and E.J.Smith

also, amounts to an English Test eleven . . .These Festival games would approach more to the nature of their name if the competitive aspect were dropped and players mingled for the choosing of two teams."

Only one county match remained to be played, at Gloucester, where Hammond made his 100th century for his county, in Reg Sinfield's benefit match against Sussex. Basil Allen set Sussex 304 to win in four hours. John Langridge was dropped three times and Harry Parks and Holmes, batting with a runner, led Sussex home with time to spare, ending a very disappointing season for the western county. There was plenty of festival atmosphere at Scarborough, tents, flags and bands, but not much of it was evident on the field where Yorkshire and MCC drew. Frank Smailes completed the first 'double' by a Yorkshire player since 1926.

On Monday, Hitler arrived at Nuremberg for the start of the highly frenetic Party Rally. French reservists were called up because of German border activity. The Czech Government was communicating its 'definitive' reply to the Sudeten demands. The Air Minister, Sir Kingsley Wood, inspected the manufacture of barrage balloons. Mr Lyons said that Australia 'stands four-square with Great Britain.'

September 7 to 9: Farewell to Woolley

Two Festival matches were played whilst the tourists rested. At Folkstone, England Past and Present (ten Test men, captained by Hammond, with Woolley, Patsy Hendren and Percy Chapman of the Past) got the better of Sir Pelham Warner's XI (Kent, Middlesex, Essex, Norfolk's Walker, a Dollery and two Popes) but rain wiped out most of the last day. George Pope bowled Ames to reach the 'double'. Hammond, passing 60 twice, became the only batsman to 3,000 runs. (But for his injury Bradman would have needed to score 571 runs in a maximum of five matches to do it as well). Hendren made 19 and 0, Chapman 33 and 18. Woolley, 22 and 31, received a radio gramophone and Sir Pelham made a nice speech. His last stroke in first-class cricket was caught at deep mid-off, fittingly.

The Gentlemen v Players match at Scarborough was the epitome of high-scoring festival cricket with a manufactured finish. In the Players' first innings of 429 (off 102.2 overs) seven men exceeded 40 and Wellard hit 4,6,4,4,0,6 in one over by F.R.Brown. G.O.Allen dropped a few short balls at Herbert Sutcliffe and the umpire, George Hirst, expressed a pained surprise. The Gents captain set the Players 130 to win in 50 minutes, which they did with no time to spare, thanks to Hardstaff's lofted cover drive.

On 9 September the Australian wives, Mrs Bradman, McCabe and Jeanes, arrived on the *Strathmore* at Marseilles. They could have been in London the next day but the English tour was not over, so they had to complete the sea journey past Gibraltar and the Bay of Biscay.

The Sudetenland Germans abruptly broke negotiations with the Czech Government, objecting that the British had leaked the Czech proposals before the Germans had formally received them. The Prime Minister returned from his holiday in Scotland. On Friday, the Sudetens agreed to return to the talks, and Hitler, in his speech at Nuremberg (to 180,000 Party leaders) made no direct reference to the crisis.

September 10 to 13: Tempers Frayed at Scarborough

After three days' much needed rest, the Australians went to Scarborough and, save for resting Hassett, fielded their strongest available team against Mr Henry Leveson Gower's XI. He had arrayed a very strong team, captained by R.E.S.Wyatt, of ten Test cricketers and Gibb, who was very nearly one. The tourists made a confident start, then Nichols replaced Farnes and he dismissed Fingleton, Brown and Badcock for 22 in 7.1 overs. McCabe pulled Verity for six, then gave a chance to mid on which Leyland dropped at second attempt. After lunch he was caught at slip. Barnes, runless for half an hour after lunch, played a schizophrenic game of frugality and freedom in his three-hour stay. Waite on-drove Verity for six, and hit Bowes for a successive six and four. Nichols bowled at his best and many edges off him never went to hand. He took a brilliant one-handed return catch from Barnes. It was a day competed for like a Test match, enjoyed by 12,000 people in the sun.

Leveson Gower's XI were 31-1 overnight. The wicket was fully covered during the wet Sunday. Even so, McCormick got some lift, until he retired with a strained thigh. Herbert Sutcliffe left at 57. Barnett pulled a six off O'Reilly, his only scoring shot. Hutton and Leyland were together again, adding this time a mere 99 in 80 minutes. Leyland, Wyatt and Hutton departed in quick succession. Hardstaff reached 50 in 37 minutes, Gibb hooked and drove hard for 40 in 65 minutes. In one over after tea, Hardstaff hooked to the boundary for his 100, drove over the sightscreen and was bowled trying to repeat the shot.

Even Verity was hitting the ball so hard that Ward was injured trying to catch and bowl him. When the home team had made 363-8 in 104 overs, after five and a half hours, Wyatt, keen to chalk up a win, declared in order to have a go at the Aussies before the close. McCabe put in Ward and O'Reilly to open. They faced five overs in 15 minutes, scoring no runs and making no attempt to do so. The 15,000 crowd, who had sweltered under a hot sun, barracked. As the players left the field, a friend of Wyatt's came up to him and said, "What's wrong with the Australians?" Wyatt replied, "I supppose they just don't want to be beaten." Some one in the crowd overheard the conversation, and a version of it got back to the Australian manager, in which Wyatt was reported as saying what rotten sports the Australians were. Mr Jeanes tackled Wyatt about the matter, then rang up Mr Leveson Gower and threatened that the Australian team would withdraw from the match. Leveson Gower and Wyatt went to the Australian team hotel. After 20 minutes wait, Mr Jeanes appeared and stood by his attitude. Wyatt demanded to see Stan McCabe and told him, "This is absolute nonsense; I never said anything of the sort." McCabe defused the situation at once: "If you say that, it's good enough for me. We'll play'.' The Press never got hold of the story and nothing appeared in the papers. It would seem on the face of it that Jeanes reacted rather rashly, but one should not condemn him without knowing his side of the event.

On Tuesday, the pitch was still intact. In the first over by Farnes, Bowes caught O'Reilly at square leg. Ward stayed longer but Nichols beat him for pace. The two regular openers, Brown and Fingleton, started a rescue operation, then Bowes came on for Farnes. He had Fingleton caught down the leg-side by Gibb from a full leg glance; Badcock's off-stump was pinged back by a break-back; and a good ball beat McCabe to give Bowes 3-8. Barnes hit across the line of Verity.

Whenever the 1938 Australians collapsed, Bill Brown was usually at the non-striker's end watching, and this day was no exception. At lunch, at 70-6, he was not out 22, having batted most of the session. A pull for four off Bowes, one of his few positive shots, had saved the innings defeat. Brown and Barnett started the second session with a fillip of boundaries. Then Barnett was lbw to Bowes, Waite saw little of his first and only ball, Fleetwood-Smith displayed his eccentric stroke-play for a short while and, with McCormick unfit, Australia were all out at 3.30pm, Brown 38 not out in 165 minutes. The varied pace and swing of Bowes and the needling accuracy of Verity had done for the rest of them. Two Yorkshiremen completed the formality of winning the match when Sutcliffe and Hutton hit off the runs in half an hour, the older man hitting six rock-like 4's on the on side. It was the Oval Test replayed at the seaside and, indeed, they were the 1938 Australians' only two defeats. That evening they crossed the Pennines to catch a ferry from Heysham and were probably not too sorry to escape from the grind and graft of the England tour.

The weekend passed with tension but without incident in Central Europe. Crowds gathered in Downing Street and the Cabinet held an emergency meeting on Monday. Hitler's closing speech to the magnificently orchestrated Nuremberg Rally was bold and vitriolic, full of genuine-sounding indignation and readiness to go to the aid of the 'tortured' Germans in Czechoslovakia in their desire for self-determination. On Tuesday, after unrest in Sudeten areas, the Czech

Mr H.D.G.LEVESON GOWER'S XI v AUSTRALIA

Played at Scarborough, on September 10, 12, 13, 1938.
Leveson Gower's XI won by ten wickets.

AUSTRALIA

J.H.Fingleton	c Farnes b Nichols	17	(4) c Gibb b Bowes	20
W.A.Brown	lbw b Nichols	29	(3) not out	38
C.L.Badcock	c Gibb b Nichols	12	(5) b Bowes	0
*S.J.McCabe	c Wyatt b Nichols	58	(6) b Bowes	1
S.Barnes	c & b Nichols	90	(7) b Verity	1
†B.A.Barnett	c & b Farnes	14	(8) lbw b Bowes	12
M.G.Waite	c Hardstaff b Farnes	77	b Bowes	0
W.J.O'Reilly	c Verity b Farnes	0	(1) c Bowes b Farnes	0
F.Ward	c Bowes b Verity	3	(2) b Nichols	20
L.O'B.Fleetwood-Smith	b Nichols	1	st Gibb b Verity	5
E.L.McCormick	not out	0	absent hurt	0
Extras	(LB 5)	5	(B 2, LB 2, NB 1)	5
Total		**306**		**102**

Fall: 1st inns 1/36, 2/57, 3/64, 4/135, 5/150, 6/274, 7/280, 8/304, 9/306.
2nd inns 1/0, 2/26, 3/52, 4/52, 5/54, 6/55, 7/90, 8/90, 9/102.

MR H.D.G.LEVESON GOWER'S XI

H.Sutcliffe	lbw b O'Reilly	25	not out	36
L.Hutton	c Barnett b O'Reilly	73	not out	9
C.J.Barnett	st Barnett b Ward	6		
M.Leyland	b Fleetwood-Smith	51		
*Mr R.E.S.Wyatt	c Ward b Fleetwood-Smith	1		
J.Hardstaff	b O'Reilly	108		
†Mr P.A.Gibb	lbw b O'Reilly	40		
M.S.Nichols	lbw b McCabe	9		
H.Verity	not out	23		
W.E.Bowes	not out	2		
Extras	(B 15, LB 7, NB 3)	25	(LB 1)	1
Total	(8 wickets, declared)	**363**	(No wicket)	**46**

Fall: 1st inns 1/57, 2/66, 3/165, 4/173, 5/173, 6/288, 7/319, 8/350.
Mr.K.Farnes did not bat.

LEVESON GOWER'S XI	O	M	R	W	O	M	R	W
Farnes	23	3	75	3	8	4	10	1
Bowes	22	5	70	0	16	6	42	5
Nichols	26	1	113	6	14	3	28	1
Verity	10.1	1	43	1	19.2	10	17	2

AUSTRALIA	O	M	R	W	O	M	R	W
McCormick	8	2	28	0				
Waite	20	3	51	0	5	1	24	0
Ward	28	2	92	1	0.2	0	3	0
O'Reilly	25	5	75	4	5	1	18	0
Fleetwood-Smith	17	1	75	2				
McCabe	6	0	17	1				

Umpires: J.Newman and A.Dolphin.

Government imposed martial law there. Henlein delivered an ultimatum demanding withdrawal of State police from German areas. The Services Ministers and Chiefs of Staff met with the Prime Minister at Downing Street.

Wednesday 14 September.

Arriving in Belfast docks in the morning, the visitors were taken to the Grand Central Hotel and given Royal Irish Poplin ties, then motored to see the Stormont building which housed the Parliament of Northern Ireland. Then they went on a tour of the County Down coast, lunching at Royal County Down Golf club. Then it was through the Mountains of Mourne, Silent Valley reservoir, tea at the Great Northern Railway Hotel, Rostrevor, overlooking Carlingford Lough and the independent State on the other side. Jack Fingleton recorded in his diary: "In a lonely thatched cottage on the side of the Mourne Mountains, an aged Irish woman talked remarkably of world politics . . .Her anticipations of world events were proved to be true, and her home was so remote that one wondered how tales of the outside world would ever penetrate there."

The Prime Minister sent a message directly addressed to Hitler in Berlin: "In view of the increasingly critical situation, I propose to come over at once to see you with a view to trying to find a peaceful solution. I propose to come across by air and am ready to start tomorrow . . ." Hitler accepted.

Thursday 15 September

The Australians played a one-day game at Ormeau Road, Belfast, against the Gentlemen of Ireland. The latter included local-born Surrey professional, Thomas McMurray, who was not able to arrive until lunch, when before a crowd of 3,000 the tourists were 116-5. Mailey was impressed by the bowling of James Macdonald, who also took a good catch at mid-off from Barnett. Ireland reached 60 before the

GENTLEMEN OF IRELAND v AUSTRALIA

Played at Belfast, on September 15 1938.
Australians won by 61 runs.

Australians 145 (Waite 30, Mr James Macdonald 5-24, Mr E.A.Ingram 4-46). Gentlemen of Ireland 84 (Mr T.J.Macdonald 28, O'Reilly 3-7, Ward 5-22).

GENTLEMEN OF IRELAND v AUSTRALIA

Played at Dublin, on September 16, 17 1938.
Australians won by an innings and 33 runs.

Gentlemen of Ireland 100 (Mr N.B.Williams 26, O'Reilly 3-7, White 2-12) and 106 (Mr E.D.R.Shearer 56, O'Reilly 5-39, White 3-16). Australians 239 (Fingleton 37, McCabe 62, Badcock 52, Barnes 53, Mr E.A.Ingram 7-83).

fourth wicket fell, but the batting was timid and unenterprising. Billingsley, the last man, batting without gloves, got a hearty cheer when he hit two 4's. With an easy victory under their belts, the Australians caught the 7.10pm train to Dublin, leaving the United Kingdom for the first time in five months. They were entering the State now called, under Mr de Valera's new constitution, 'Eire', and which was still a member of the British Empire but a Republic in all but name. An Australian team had not been in Ireland since 1912, when civil war over Home Rule was close. Now Ireland in both parts was at peace for the time being.

Bradman, still unfit, had been staying since his injury at the Buckinghamshire home of Mr and Mrs Walter Robins, typing out replies to letters of sympathy, playing bridge, reading, playing the piano and hearing of rumours that he was going to take a job in England. He did not go to Ireland because he wanted to greet the wives who arrived at Plymouth on this day. Mrs Jesse Bradman was wearing a fur coat, and said, "If this is what you call warm, what must it be like in winter?"

Mr Chamberlain left from Heston Airport on his first-ever flight with the earnest hopes of the nations heavy on his shoulders. He arrived at Munich and drove through cheering crowds to the German Chancellor's mountain-top villa at Berchtesgaden. Hitler treated him with great respect and they had two hours of discussion in the evening, agreeing to meet again. But the ground was suddenly shifting. Henlein publicly demanded union of the Sudetenland with Germany and this was now the agenda, not self-government, but secession.

Friday 16 September

Australia started a two-day match against Gentlemen of Ireland in the park of the historic Trinity College in the heart of Dublin. Ireland were all out in 105 minutes, then McCabe and Fingleton added 104 in an hour. After tea, at 113-3, Ingram took 5-29 in ten overs. He was on a hat-trick when Barnes came in at number-ten and appealed successfully against the light, Australia closing at 165-8. Five thousand people watched.

The Prime Minister arrived back at Heston, announcing: "I have had a long talk with Herr Hitler, it was a frank talk, but a friendly one." He then drove to Buckingham Palace.

Saturday 17 September

Barnes averted the hat-trick and hit 53 in even time. Badcock took two hours over 52. When they went in again, Ireland offered little resistance apart from Shearer, who used his feet well and was last out. After an informal reception that evening at the Shelbourne Hotel, hosted by Captain Lindsay, president of the Irish Cricket Union, the

Australians left for the boat to England. Hassett and Fingleton stayed on and waved their colleagues away among the crowd singing *Come back to Erin* at the quay-side.

'Our British people' Monday, 19 September.

British and French Ministers had met at Downing Street at the weekend and sent their proposals for settlement to the Czechs. The proposals were not yet published but were believed to be worse than the Czechs feared and thought by the German Press to be a big step forward.

Wednesday 21 September

The Czech Government announced with the greatest reluctance its acceptance of the Anglo-French plan, which involved an orderly secession of the German-speaking areas, provided that its new frontier could be guaranteed. Chamberlain was to fly to Germany on Thursday with an offer of an international commission to fix the new frontiers.

Saturday, 24 September

This was, for most of the Australian party, their last night in England, spent at a sports club dinner in St James' Square. Apart from McCabe, Jeanes and Bradman, they were leaving these shores on Sunday.

Chamberlain arrived home depressed and deflated after two days of talks at Bad Godesberg on the Rhine. Germany was now demanding immediate annexation of most of the disputed areas with plebiscites in the rest; all Czech-built industrial and military installations to be kept intact for the Germans to take over; and the Germans could not be pinned down on a promise to respect the remaining Czech state. The Czech Government, now with a completely new cabinet, rejected it and mobilized the army. In London, trenches were dug in the parks and depots opened for the fitting of gas masks.

Monday, 26 September

In a speech at the Berlin Sportpalast, Hitler demanded cession of the disputed areas by 1 October, his 'last territorial claim in Europe'.

Tuesday 27 September

The Fleet was to be mobilized. Parliament met a month early. The Queen launched a new Cunard liner *The Queen Elizabeth* on the Clyde. She gave a message from the King, absent because of the international situation. He bade the pople to be of good cheer. The Prime Minister broadcast to the nation: "How horrible, fantastic, incredible it is that we should be digging trenches and trying on gas masks here because of a quarrel in a far away country between people of whom we know nothing . . .Armed conflict between nations is a nightmare to me, but if I were convinced that any nation had made up its mind to dominate the world by force, I should feel that it must be resisted."

Most people envisaged that war would herald a rain of bombs on the cities, having images in their minds fixed by the air raids in Spain and by the chilling opening for the film of H.G.Wells' novel *Things to Come.*

Wednesday 28 September

Bradman and the others left en route through France to catch the ship at Toulon, bound for Australia. He said to the Press: "On behalf of the team I should like to express our sincere gratification at the generous hospitality showered on us throughout our tour. My greatest impression is of the magnificent calm and spirit of our British people during these last troublesome days. I know we all fervently pray for peace."

In a long speech in the House of Commons, the Prime Minister reviewed his efforts of the past weeks, and his words were all gloom, save for the announcement that Germany had postponed mobilization for 24 hours. As he spoke, the Foreign Secretary Lord Halifax, watching in the Peers' Gallery, went out. Lord Dunglass (courtesy title of the son of the Earl of Home), the PM's parliamentary private secretary, left the Chamber and returned with two sheets of paper. These were passed to Mr Chamberlain. He read in silence for a minute, finished his review, then said, "This is not all. I have now been informed by Herr Hitler that he invites me to meet him at Munich tomorrow. He has also invited Signor Mussolini and M.Daladier — and I have no doubt M.Daladier will also accept. I need not say what my answer will be." The whole Chamber, all but a few, rose and cheered.

All next day they, the 'Big Four', talked at Munich — the Czechs waiting in the corridor outside the conference room — and at 1.30am on Friday, agreement was announced whereby most of the disputed areas would be handed over to Germany between 1 and 10 October and other parts would be dealt with by international commission and plebiscite. What was left of Czechoslovakia started to be known as Czecho-Slovakia.

The Bradmans were crossing France when the threat of war was lifted at Munich. Bradman felt the strain of his third tour of England and was pretty sure that, war or no war, he had made his last visit to England as Australian captain. But the voyage home did produce one positive result: John Russell Bradman was born on 10 July 1939.

One other happy note: a week before sailing off to South Africa, Len Hutton attended a banquet for him with 300 people at the Albert Hall, Pudsey, having just announced his engagement to Miss Dorothy Dennis. They were married on 16 September 1939.

A Memorable Year

THE 1938 cricket season has gone down in history as one to be remembered, yet in some ways it fell short of the high hopes that attended its beginning. The Test series was the most evenly contested in England since 1926, record crowds watched and there was much good cricket and great stroke-play. The First Test at Trent Bridge and the Fourth at Leeds were as good as one could wish to see. The Second at Lord's became a stalemate too early, although England's second-innings collapse provided a brief period of excitement. The Final Test at The Oval was unique and historic, but for the good of cricket it was as well that it should remain unique.

It was a disappointing series in that Australia were not quite as good a team as expected, yet they did just enough and at the right time to retain the Ashes. England were a better side all round but were frustrated by lapses just at the most crucial moments. One interesting way of assessing their respective talents is to pick an 'eclectic' XI from those who appeared in the four Tests. My choice, based on 1938 performances, would be as follows: Hutton (Eng), Brown (Aus), Bradman (Aus), Hammond (Eng), Paynter (Eng), McCabe (Aus), Ames (Eng), Verity (Eng), O'Reilly (Aus), Farnes (Eng) and Bowes (Eng).

The openers pick themselves, leaving no room for C.J.Barnett (Eng). So do Bradman, Hammond and, on performance, Paynter. McCabe, really on the strength of one innings, makes it only just ahead of England's Compton, Hardstaff and Leyland. If unfit, Ames would yield probably to B.A.Barnett (Aus). The bowlers are a straightforward choice, with McCormick (Aus) and Wright (Eng) the nearest challengers. Whatever XI is chosen, one cannot avoid a heavy preponderance of Englishmen. However, on merit the captaincy would have to be awarded to Bradman, rather than Hammond.

The 'Epitome of the Test Series' in the Appendix also shows that on figures, England were clearly the better side.

On the tour as a whole, the great sucesses were Bradman, less spectacular but if anything even more assured and skilful than before, and an excellent leader; Brown, who played throughout the tour to the utmost of his ability and beyond; and O'Reilly, whose extraction of a little help from the Headingley wicket decided the Ashes and who was always dangerous. Apart from his brilliant innings at Trent Bridge, McCabe had a moderate tour and rarely sparkled. McCormick failed to live up to his billing as a fierce fast bowler and achieved little against the counties, although a couple of spells in the Lord's Test showed what he might have done. He never quite adjusted after the farcical opening at Worcester and Australia were forced to rely on the spinners to carry the attack. Even so, it was still a mistake to leave him out of the Oval Test.

Fingleton never got going with the bat but took credit for his fielding. Badcock mastered the county attacks but, like some Australians before and since, he was below expectation in Test cricket on English wickets. After a good start to the tour, Fleetwood-Smith disappointed, his rare talent being reduced to that of a stock bowler, save for good support bowling in the Headingley Test. Waite was useful but innocuous in the Tests. Chipperfield had done little of note when he was injured at Lord's and then dropped out with appendicitis. Hassett had a good first tour and played a brave part in the Headingley Test. Barnes found his feet quickly after an idle May and June and looked a marvellous prospect for the future; he was also a useful and much-needed deputy wicket-keeper. Ward was unsuccessful in his one Test, but he did play his part by bowling out county sides quickly. Barnett had a good tour under the strain of being the only fit wicketkeeper for much of the time but was unfortunate enough to miss stumping Hutton early in The Oval Test. Walker the reserve 'keeper was too often injured to do himself justice. He and White, who soldiered on dutifully in the county matches, were the only two not to play in a Test.

The fact that a side with so little display of individual brilliance could retain the Ashes against a rising England side, and could win 15 and lose only two first-class matches, was a tribute to Bradman's inspiring and disciplined leadership. Hammond later wrote in his autobiography that the 1938 Australians were a friendly side who mixed more with opponents, players and public than their predecessors. 'Tiger' Smith, who umpired in two Tests, thought them a well-disciplined bunch though guilty of gamesmanship in appealing and in not 'walking'.

Despite the frustrations, England could look confidently to the future. They had settled upon a good captain: Hammond had shown himself to be an expert leader, although not faultless. His batting was at its height and his performances were crucial: a great 240 at Lord's; top-score in the Leeds defeat, and a ship-steadying innings at The Oval; and several slip catches. Compton could be a little impetuous in his youth, but two innings in the first two Tests showed that he had the good fighting spirit when the battle was raging. Hutton, of course, wrote his name indelibly in the book of Test cricket and his supporting hundred on the first day of the series had already established his ability; England missed him at Leeds. Paynter played two golden innings and was left without support in the second innings collapse at Leeds. Leyland did not satisfy the selectors of his fitness until The Oval Test, when he did not disappoint. Hardstaff failed at Leeds but gave nothing away at The Oval. Barnett's opening onslaught in the First Test rocked the Australian bowling back on its heels, which had an important psychological effect, but he was dropped after a timid performance at Leeds. Edrich was the biggest let-down. He failed to get going in every innings; he seemed confident enough, but the luck was not with him; Bob Wyatt thought that he was not keeping his head still.

Farnes was dropped for the abortive Manchester Test after straying in direction at Lord's, but generally he maintained his position as one of the world's best fast bowlers (there was not a lot of competition, to be honest) and when Bowes was selected they made a formidable duo. Verity's best match was at Lord's but otherwise he suffered slightly in comparison with O'Reilly, his arch rival. Wright impressed everyone with his leg-breaks but his talent was a delicate flower which was hard to nurture in the Test arena, and he did not quite establish his position. In the wicketkeeping department England could no longer rely on the perennial Ames to be fit; Wood was a satisfactory replacement, but he was not young enough to be counted as an ideal successor.

In the County Championship, Northamptonshire came last for the fifth year in a row, yet they were not quite as bad as the results suggest. Partridge held their bowling together despite the added duties of opening the batting, but the greatest encouragement came from the solid batting of Dennis Brookes.

Glamorgan dropped to 16th place, due partly to the unavailability for many matches of Clay and Matthews. Wooller made a promising debut in August, but the player of the season was Arnold Dyson, the opening batsman.

Leicestershire were perhaps flattered by a high position in mid-season and then declined steadily to finish 15th. Berry was out of form for most of the season and Dempster's absence in the second-half of the campaign, due to other commitments, was sorely felt. Perhaps the palm should go to George Geary, who ended his long career before going to coach at Charterhouse with a great resurgence in his batting.

Hampshire were too easy to beat and stayed at 14th position. Moore was in great form but could only play a few matches. Arnold lost his strokes and was dropped from the side. Heath bowled with great spirit but the season was most memorable for the achievements of Stuart Boyes, the senior professional, with his slow left arm.

Warwickshire dropped two places from 1937, although Cranmer led with gusto. Mayer and Hollies carried the bowling, but in an ordinary side it was the expert determined batting of Tom Dollery that stood out.

There was no return to the great days for Nottinghamshire. Larwood was never fit and Voce suffered from injury. Keeton, who had an operation after the end of the season, was in moderate form by his own standards. The best feature of the side, although he missed many matches, was the classic batting of Joe Hardstaff.

Worcestershire came 11th. New South African pace bowler Crisp started well but dropped out with shoulder trouble. Bull missed the early part of the season with a fractured finger. Gibbons had another excellent season. Howorth nearly did the 'double', but player of the year was Reg Perks, whose consistent fast bowling earned him a ticket to South Africa.

Gloucestershire caused a great surprise by dropping to tenth place, due to weakness in bowling. Tom Goddard missed some matches through injury and never returned to his usual top-class form. Barnett and Hammond were often lost to representative calls, but the latter batted with all his usual magnificence and was once again the county's greatest jewel. He was appointed to succeed Allen as captain for 1939.

Kent were a team worth watching for their exhilarating batting and rose to ninth place. Woolley made few large scores but was a consistent aggressive opening batsman in his final season. Valentine tore apart many attacks and Ames had a good season, although he was out of action for six weeks after the Lord's Test. Without doubt the season belonged to Arthur Fagg, after a blank 1937, who had a golden July.

Sussex had an equally brilliant batting side in 1938, especially as it was their more fluent stroke-players who reached a peak. James Langridge and Jim Parks fell away slightly from 1937, whilst John Langridge was most consistent and Cox ended the season brightly. Like Kent the bowling lacked penetration. Sussex's cricketer of the summer, although he could not appear in every match, was amateur batsman Hugh Bartlett.

Somerset had their best summer for many years, rising to seventh place. Harold Gimblett had a moderate season, but his opening partner Frank Lee hit 2,015 runs. Buse made a successful comeback. Andrews, who did the 'double', and Wellard formed one of the most spirited new-ball pairs in the country, and the latter, the leading wicket-taker in first-class cricket and renowned six-hitter, carries the prize as Somerset's player of the year.

Essex were being propped up in the table by Northants in mid-season, then Kenneth Farnes came in during the school holidays, Pearce took over the captaincy, and they rose to finish sixth. O'Connor recovered his batting form, but player of the season was Morris Nichols, earliest to the 'double' yet again.

Derbyshire dropped to fifth place but had a reasonable season and were in the title hunt in the closing weeks of the summer. Copson and Mitchell were the leaders of a strong bowling attack, and Worthington had some good sequences with the bat. The best player was George Pope, whose all-round prowess attracted attention from the Test selectors.

Lancashire looked like potential winners in the first half of the season, then after a putrid display in the first Roses Match at Bradford, lost the initiative, but were in with a chance until near the end, finishing fourth. Double defeat in the Roses Matches was a humiliating experience. Pollard was one of the most hard-working opening bowlers in the country, supported by Phillipson (who missed some matches through injury) and Albert Nutter, in his first full season, as was leg-spinner Wilkinson, promising enough to earn a tour to South Africa. The season belonged to Eddie Paynter, whose boyish enthusiasm, whether batting at number-one for the county or at number-five for England, made him one of the stars of 1938.

Surrey showed signs of a return to their golden days with a good run in July which included a win over Yorkshire, and they just withstood Lancashire's late challenge to end in third place. Holmes enthused a good spirit of enterprise and in his absence Garland-Wells (who took over full time in 1939) emulated him. They were helped by the fact that not one man was chosen in an England Test squad. Gover's knee trouble which reduced his stamina was made up for by Eddie Watts' great contribution with the new ball.

Middlesex never quite had enough steam to overtake Yorkshire. They beat Yorkshire in a controversial battle at home, but later suffered the White Rose revenge. The side was packed with young talented batsman, especially Compton and Edrich, who were much missed during the Tests, and Robertson and Brown, who looked good for the future. Walter Robins led as aggressively as ever, and amateur bowlers Allen and Peebles made effective appearances. Jim Smith had a vintage season with the ball, and in short bursts with the bat. Although he fell slightly away later and had a cruel baptism in Tests, Edrich must be Middlesex's man of the year, for his 1,000 runs before the end of May.

The Championship winners were again Yorkshire, the last season to be witnessed by the club president Lord Hawke, who died in October. It was the performance of a strong, experienced and dedicated team with deep enough talent to survive the unusually high losses of players to injury and Test selection. Strangely, the side lacked a regular quick bowler to partner Bill Bowes, who, coming in after knee trouble, went quickly to the top of the first-class averages and stayed there. His greater accuracy and swing compensated for a slight reduction in pace. Verity was, as always, a fixed star in the spin attack and Robinson came on well. In the hands of Herbert Sutcliffe, Barber, Mitchell and, after the University Match, Yardley, the batting was a strong efficient engine. Maurice Leyland played on through shoulder trouble which kept him out of the England side. Hutton we know all about, yet he scored only 631 runs (average 45.01) in Championship matches. Smailes was the first Yorkshire player to do the 'double' since 1926. The disastrous match against Middlesex at Lord's in July, and a big loss against Surrey threatened a fall of the mighty, but they soldiered on through all adversity to take the title quite easily in the end. If one man, above all, is to be credited it is Brian Sellers, who captained boldly, sternly and played to win. His 999 Championshp runs (average 30.27) may not sound much, but he was playing above his natural ability, and utterly selflessly for his side.

The 1938 season can be seen now as the last of an epoch of high-scoring batting, of leg-spin bowling and of the amateur spirit. The following year was so much overshadowed by the assumption of the coming war that it cannot truly reflect a cricketing reality. When the game returned again in 1946, there was, for a few years, a honeymoon between cricketers and the public which developed into the more serious workaday 1950s, when the off-spinner and the seamer were the kings. Cricket has gained a lot and matured in the last 50 years and still holds its own as a glory of our summers, but something of its innocence and sparkle has gone; something that 1938 had, despite the indifferent weather.

Averages in the Test Matches

ENGLAND BATTING

	Pld	*In*	*NO*	*Runs*	*HS*	*Ave*	*100s/50s*	*Mins*	*Balls*	*4s/6s*	*Runs /hour*	*Runs/ 100 balls*
M.Leyland	1	1	0	187	187	187.00	1/0	381	438	17	29.4	42.7
L.Hutton	3	4	0	473	364	118.25	2/0	1042	1093	50	27.2	43.3
E.Paynter	4	6	2	407	216*	101.75	1/1	762	796	53/2†	32.0	51.1
J.Hardstaff	2	3	1	184	169*	92.00	1/0	358	433	23†	30.8	42.5
Mr W.R.Hammond	4	6	0	403	240	67.17	1/2	721	776	50/1	33.5	51.9
A.Wood	1	1	0	53	53	53.00	0/1	92	95	8	34.6	55.8
L.E.G.Ames	2	3	0	135	83	45.00	0/1	263	235	17	30.8	57.4
C.J.Barnett	3	5	0	215	126	43.00	1/0	454	450	26	28.4	47.8
D.C.S.Compton	4	6	1	214	102	42.80	1/1	349	401	35	36.8	53.4
A.Wellard	1	2	0	42	38	21.00	0	46	40	7/1	54.8	105.0
H.Verity	4	6	2	52	25*	13.00	0	176	167	6	17.7	31.1
D.V.P.Wright	3	5	2	39	22	13.00	0	97	83	6	24.1	47.0
W.J.Edrich	4	6	0	67	28	11.16	0	271	295	6	14.8	22.7
Mr K.Farnes	4	3	1	14	7	7.00	0	11	14	1	76.3	100.0
R.A.Sinfield	1	1	0	6	6	6.00	0	20	20	0	18.0	30.0
W.F.Price	1	2	0	6	6	3.00	0	28	22	1	12.9	27.3
W.E.Bowes	2	2	0	3	3	1.50	0	9	4	0	20.0	75.0

†Paynter and Hardstaff each hit one five.

AUSTRALIA BATTING

	Pld	*In*	*NO*	*Runs*	*HS*	*Ave*	*100s/50s*	*Mins*	*Balls*	*4s/6s*	*Runs /hour*	*Runs/ 100 balls*
D.G.Bradman	4	6	2	434	144*	108.50	3/1	840	851	37	31.0	51.0
W.A.Brown	4	8	1	512	206*	73.14	2/1	1169	1221	48†	26.3	41.9
S.J.McCabe	4	8	0	362	232	45.25	1/0	393	446	52/2†	55.3	81.2
S.G.Barnes	1	2	0	74	41	37.00	0	132	146	9	33.6	50.7
B.A.Barnett	4	8	1	195	57	27.86	0/1	372	399	26	31.4	48.9
A.L.Hassett	4	8	0	199	56	24.87	0/1	288	304	25/1	41.4	65.5
J.H.Fingleton	4	6	0	123	40	20.50	0	410	431	7	18.0	28.5
L.O'B.Fleetwood-Smith	4	5	3	30	16*	15.00	0	108	89	4	16.7	33.7
W.J.O'Reilly	4	5	1	60	42	15.00	0	103	86	7/2	34.9	69.8
F.A.Ward	1	2	1	9	7*	9.00	0	29	38	1	18.6	23.7
C.L.Badcock	4	8	1	32	9	4.57	0	164	169	2	11.7	18.9
M.G.Waite	2	3	0	11	8	3.67	0	58	44	2	11.4	25.0
A.G.Chipperfield	1	1	0	1	1	1.00	0	5	3	0	12.0	33.3
E.L.McCormick	3	3	0	2	2	0.67	0	19	12	0	6.3	16.7

†Brown hit two fives; McCabe hit one five.

ENGLAND BOWLING

	Overs	*Mds*	*Runs*	*Wkts*	*Ave*	*5wI*	*Best*	*NB*	*Wd*	*Runs/ 100 bls*	*Balls/ wkt*
W.E.Bowes	75.4	12	188	10	18.80	1	5-49	1	0	41.3	45.5
H.Verity	154.1	53	354	14	25.28	0	4-103	0	0	38.3	66.1
M.Leyland	8.1	0	30	1	30.00	0	1-11	0	0	61.2	49.0
Mr K Farnes	179.4	32	581	17	34.17	0	4-63	1	1	53.8	63.5
W.J.Edrich	35.2	6	139	4	34.75	0	2-27	5	0	64.1	54.3
D.V.P.Wright	120	20	426	12	35.50	0	4-153	20	1	57.6	61.7
A.W.Wellard	32	3	126	3	42.00	0	2-96	2	1	64.9	64.7
R.A.Sinfield	63	16	123	2	61.50	0	1-51	0	0	32.5	189.0
C.J.Barnett	1	0	10	0	-	0	0-10	0	0	166.7	-
Mr W.R.Hammond	33	13	67	0	-	0	0-8	1	0	33.7	-

AUSTRALIA BOWLING

	Overs	Mds	Runs	Wkts	Ave	5wI	Best	NB	Wd	Runs/ 100 bls	Balls/ wkt
W.J.O'Reilly	263	78	610	22	27.73	2*	5-56	31	0	37.9	73.1
E.L.McCormick	114	20	345	10	34.50	0	4-101	33	1	48.1	71.7
L.O'B.Fleetwood-Smith	217.5	34	727	14	51.93	0	4-34	4	1	55.4	93.6
S.G.Barnes	38	3	84	1	84.00	0	1-84	0	0	36.8	228.0
S.J.McCabe	103	19	293	2	146.50	0	2-58	2	1	47.3	310.0
M.G.Waite	92	23	190	1	190.00	0	1-150	0	1	34.4	552.0
D.G.Bradman	2.2	1	6	0	-	0	0-6	0	0	42.9	-
A.G.Chipperfield	8.4	0	51	0	-	0	0-51	0	0	98.1	-
A.L.Hassett	13	2	52	0	-	0	0-52	0	0	66.7	-
F.A.Ward	30	2	142	0	-	0	0-142	0	0	78.9	-

*O'Reilly took ten wickets in a match once.

Wicketkeeping

England

Ames 2 dismissals (both caught) for 16 byes conceded
Paynter 1 dismissal (caught) for 5 byes
Price 2 dismissals (both caught) for 5 byes
Wood 3 dismissals (all caught) for 5 byes

Australia

Barnett 5 dismissals (3 caught 2 stumped) for 36 byes

Fielding

England

Catches: Hammond 8, Compton 4, Edrich 4, Barnett 3, Verity 2, Wright 2, Paynter 2, Hutton 1, Hardstaff 1, Leyland 1.
(Paynter took 3 catches in all, one as deputy wicketkeeper).

Australia

Catches: McCabe 4, Brown 3, McCormick 3, Fingleton 2, Hassett 1, Badcock 1, Barnes 1, Waite 1.
(Waite took another catch as a substitute).

Australian Averages in First-Class Matches

Batting & fielding	Pld	In	NO	Runs	HS	Ave	100	50	Ct/St
D.G.Bradman (SA)	20	26	5	2429	278	115.66	13	5	8
W.A.Brown (Q)	25	37	5	1854	265*	57.93	5	7	14
A.L.Hassett (V)	24	32	3	1589	220*	54.79	5	6	17
C.L.Badcock (SA)	24	39	4	1604	198	45.82	4	9	14
S.G.Barnes (NSW)	13	19	2	720	94	42.35	-	5	9/4
J.H.Fingleton (NSW)	23	32	2	1141	124	38.03	4	2	17/3
S.J.McCabe (NSW)	23	33	2	1124	232	36.25	2	6	17
C.W.Walker (SA)	9	9	4	175	42	35.00	-	-	7/7
†B.A.Barnett (V)	22	29	4	737	120*	29.48	1	4	7/23
A.G.Chipperfield (NSW)	16	18	3	424	104*	28.26	1	2	12
M.G.Waite (SA)	24	30	3	684	77	25.33	-	3	14
E.S.White (NSW)	19	19	7	290	52	24.16	-	1	11
†W.J.O'Reilly (NSW)	20	17	3	224	42	16.00	-	-	2
F.A.Ward (SA)	19	17	5	162	31	13.50	-	-	8
L.O'B.Fleetwood-Smith (V)	20	20	9	99	16*	9.00	-	-	6
†E.L.McCormick (V)	18	15	4	49	12	4.45	-	-	9

†Left-handed batsman.

Bowling	*O*	*M*	*Runs*	*Wkts*	*Ave*	*5wI*	*10wM*
W.J.O'Reilly	709.4	215	1726	104	16.59	9	2
F.Ward	526.2	99	1773	92	19.27	10	1
†L.O'B.Fleetwood-Smith	555	98	1719	88	19.53	6	1
†E.S.White	375	148	708	30	23.60	-	-
A.G.Chipperfield	54.1	18	155	6	25.83	-	-
M.G.Waite	647.1	183	1454	56	25.96	3	-
E.L.McCormick	335	53	1136	34	33.41	1	-
S.J.McCabe	214	53	523	14	37.35	-	-
Also Bowled:							
A.L.Hassett	30	9	78	1	-		
S.G.Barnes	44	4	116	2	-		
C.L.Badcock	2	0	10	0	-		
D.G.Bradman	3	2	6	0			
W.A.Brown	3	0	10	0	-		

†left-arm bowler

The Australians scored 13,877 runs for the loss of 327 wickets (average 42.44 runs per wicket) off 4,158.2 overs (average 3.34 runs per over).
The Australians conceded 10,052 runs taking 442 wickets (average 22.76 runs per wicket) off 3,498.2 overs (average 2.87 runs per over).

County Championship

	P	*W*	*L*	*D*	*1st inns L*	*1st inns D*	*Pts*	*Ave*	*No Dec*
Yorkshire	28	20	2	6	0	4	256	9.14	2
Middlesex	22	15	5	2	0	1	184	8.36	2
Surrey	25	12	6	7	2	5	172	6.88	1
Lancashire	28	14	6	8	0	6	192	6.85	4
Derbyshire	25	11	8	6	3	4	160	6.40	3
Essex	26	12	11	3	3	2	164	6.30	2
Somerset	25	10	9	6	1	5	144	5.76	3
Sussex	29	11	9	9	3	3	156	5.37	3
Kent	27	8	14	5	2	4	120	4.44	1
Gloucestershire	28	8	13	7	2	4	*122	4.35	2
Worcestershire	30	9	11	10	2	3	128	4.26	2
Nottinghamshire	25	7	10	8	2	3	*106	4.24	3
Warwickshire	22	7	7	8	0	2	92	4.18	2
Hampshire	30	9	16	5	4	0	124	4.13	2
Leicestershire	22	4	9	9	1	7	80	3.63	4
Glamorgan	22	5	9	8	1	3	76	3.45	2
Northamptonshire	24	0	17	7	3	1	16	0.66	0

*Includes two points for tie on first innings in a match lost.

If the Australian first-class programme were to be subject to the same scoring system, their record would be as follows:

27	15	2	10	0	6	204	7.55	3

(For the scoring system, see *Chapter 1*).

Career Records to April 1938 of Australian Tourists and Leading English Cricketers.

	TEST					FIRST-CLASS			
	Pld	*Runs*	*Ave*	*Wkts*	*Ave*	*Runs*	*Ave*	*Wkts*	*Ave*
C.L.Badcock	3	128	32.00	-	-	3826	54.65	-	-
S.G.Barnes	0	-	-	-	-	809	50.56	-	-
B.A.Barnett	0	-	-	-	-	2272	24.42	101ct	53st
D.G.Bradman	33	4659	97.06	-	-	18022	91.94	-	-
W.A.Brown	12	812	40.60	-	-	4787	44.32	-	-
A.G.Chipperfield	13	551	34.43	5	77.20	2948	40.95	55	38.74
J.H.Fingleton	14	1066	48.45	-	-	5448	50.61	-	-
L.O'B.Fleetwood-Smith	6	24	4.80	28	30.10	371	6.87	417	20.90
A.L.Hassett	0	-	-	-	-	1390	47.93	-	-
S.J.McCabe	35	2394	46.81	34	36.41	9387	52.73	139	32.05
E.L.McCormick	9	52	8.66	26	28.23	394	10.94	144	23.84
W.J.O'Reilly	22	350	12.50	114	22.90	979	13.05	455	17.56
M.G.Waite	0	-	-	-	-	1968	27.33	76	27.85
C.W.Walker	0	-	-	-	-	1218	13.68	119ct	95st
F.A.Ward	3	27	5.40	11	39.27	433	14.43	145	24.13
E.C.S.White	0	-	-	-	-	826	20.65	80	24.70
Mr G.O.Allen	22	656	25.23	76	28.60	6761	26.51	705	20.31
L.E.G.Ames	45	2299	40.33	72ct	23st	23805	42.79	522ct	406st
C.J.Barnett	13	806	38.38	0	for 24	16938	31.54	236	34.41
L.G.Berry	0	-	-	-	-	18599	30.09	-	-
W.E.Bowes	10	23	7.67	46	23.52	1112	8.96	1254	17.18
Mr J.C.Clay	1	-	-	0	for 75	6135	15.57	960	21.02
D.C.S.Compton	1	65	65.00	2	17.00	2984	42.02	21	35.00
W.H.Copson	0	-	-	-	-	935	8.57	561	17.96
W.J.Edrich	0	-	-	-	-	3593	46.66	38	32.42
A.E.Fagg	4	111	18.50	-	-	5689	30.75	-	-
Mr K.Farnes	6	19	2.71	27	22.89	868	7.68	501	21.66
H.Gimblett	2	87	43.50	-	-	3648	28.50	-	-
T.W.J.Goddard	3	5	-	10	19.20	3426	9.65	1728	20.40
A.R.Gover	3	2	-	7	43.28	1580	9.63	1094	23.17
Mr W.R.Hammond	65	5592	59.49	80	36.32	40630	54.31	707	29.97
J.Hardstaff	11	712	39.55	-	-	11912	39.18	-	-
Mr E.R.T.Holmes	5	114	16.28	2	38.00	10376	33.04	280	33.29
L.Hutton	3	127	25.40	1	15.00	5733	40.09	63	31.85
James Langridge	7	242	26.88	19	18.36	18104	32.74	1012	21.32
M.Leyland	40	2577	43.68	5	111.00	29810	41.40	361	32.31
A.Mitchell	6	298	29.80	0	for 4	16009	36.38	-	-
T.B.Mitchell	5	20	5.00	8	62.25	2002	8.10	1270	20.64
M.S.Nichols	13	331	30.09	39	25.41	15977	27.31	1542	22.09
J.H.Parks	1	29	14.50	3	12.00	18399	30.87	663	26.75
E.Paynter	9	405	36.82	-	-	13862	38.08	-	-
R.T.D.Perks	0	-	-	-	-	2839	11.44	783	23.39
G.H.Pope	0	-	-	-	-	2812	25.33	239	19.90
W.F.F.Price	0	-	-	-	-	6857	17.76	480ct	253st
Mr R.W.V.Robins	19	612	26.60	64	27.46	8723	27.00	728	23.13
Mr A.B.Sellers	0	-	-	-	-	5111	21.29	-	-
R.A.Sinfield	0	-	-	-	-	14330	26.48	970	24.67
C.I.J.Smith	5	102	10.20	15	26.13	2642	13.76	617	18.58
H.Sutcliffe	54	4555	60.73	-	-	46924	52.54	-	-
Mr M.J.Turnbull	9	224	20.36	-	-	15518	30.48	-	-
H.Verity	30	551	22.96	109	23.39	4710	17.97	1560	14.85
W.Voce	24	289	14.45	97	26.04	5661	19.45	1278	21.88
C.Washbrook	1	17	17.00	-	-	5172	35.42	-	-
A.W.Wellard	1	5	2.50	4	27.75	8735	21.51	936	25.37
A.Wood	0	-	-	-	-	7338	21.52	515ct	189st
F.E.Woolley	64	3283	36.07	83	33.91	57379	41.04	2046	19.81
D.V.P.Wright	0	-	-	-	-	1340	12.76	268	29.63
Mr R.E.S.Wyatt	40	1839	31.70	18	35.66	30877	41.50	799	30.21

Figures partly compiled by E.L.Roberts for the *The Cricketer Spring Annual* 1938.

Epitome of the Test Series

THESE figures show that the 1938 Tests were a relatively high-scoring and relatively quick-scoring series. To underline this, and to put the matches in context, there follows a table showing the same rates for each Test series between England and Australia since 1921 played in England. In so far as a few statistics can say anything at all about the character and tempo of a Test series, the table is a fascinating portrait in figures of some historic contests. It may confirm some impressions and also challenge some assumptions about the fight for the Ashes in England in past years. The trends in the game during the period are apparent from the table and need no comment from me.

	ENGLAND						**AUSTRALIA**					
Test	*Runs*	*Wkts*	*Mins*	*Balls*	*Overs*	*Extras*	*Runs*	*Wkts*	*Mins*	*Balls*	*Overs*	*Extras*
1st	658	8	525	1,138	188	27	411	10	364	787	130.3	21
							427	6	500	1,110	184	26
2nd	494	10	434	844	137.3	24	422	10	369	737	121.4	15
	242	8	235	442	72	29	204	6	160	293	48.2	11
4th	223	10	298	598	98.1	7	242	10	315	594	98.4	5
	123	10	171	310	50.5	6	107	5	108	198	32.3	5
5th	903	7	917	2,029	335.2	50	201	8	166	318	52.1	9
							123	8	112	205	34.1	1
	2,643	53	2,580	5,361	881.5	143	2,137	63	2,094	4,242	702	93

England 49.87 runs per wicket
61.46 runs per hour
49.30 runs per 100 balls
2.997 runs per over
Australia 20.51 overs per hour
124.67 balls per hour
Australia bowled 70 no-balls (of which 27 were not hit for runs and cost 30 extras) and 4 wides.

Australia 33.92 runs per wicket.
61.23 runs per hour.
50.38 runs per 100 balls
3.044 runs per over
England 20.11 overs per hour
121.54 balls per hour
England bowled 30 no-balls (of which 15 were not hit for runs and cost 16 extras) and 3 wides.

			ENGLAND			Aus	**AUSTRALIA**			Eng
	Played	Result	Runs /wkt	Runs /over	Runs /hour	Overs /hour	Runs /wkt	Runs /over	Runs /hour	Overs /hour
1921	5	A 3-0	30.73	3.011	59.42	19.73	33.54	3.392	66.44	19.60
1926	5	E 1-0	50.63	2.585	58.53	22.64	33.33	2.404	55.97	23.29
1930	5	A 2-1	34.56	2.667	57.22	21.47	48.92	2.715	58.64	21.60
1934	5	A 2-1	34.63	2.227	49.22	22.10	40.73	3.077	61.12	19.86
1938	4	1-1	49.87	2.997	61.46	20.51	33.92	3.043	61.23	20.11
1948	5	A 4-0	29.07	2.341	46.44	19.83	48.08	2.792	55.68	19.94
1953	5	E 1-0	29.63	2.080	37.51	18.03	24.88	2.739	48.10	17.57
1956	5	E 2-1	30.86	2.344	42.59	18.17	18.52	1.790	32.17	17.97
1961	5	A 2-1	30.46	2.291	42.57	18.57	32.43	2.736	48.96	17.89
1964	5	A 1-0	32.76	2.351	42.48	18.07	36.68	2.332	44.90	19.26
1968	5	1-1	34.15	2.373	44.32	18.67	25.88	2.207	38.98	17.66
1972	5	2-2	26.75	2.408	36.44	15.14	28.95	2.634	42.29	16.05
1975	4	A 1-0	30.30	2.730	40.62	14.88	40.06	2.872	45.25	15.75
1977	5	E 3-0	34.85	2.594	39.59	15.26	25.73	2.744	40.15	14.64
1980	1	0-0	34.54	3.089	46.45	15.03	63.78	3.064	50.13	16.36
1981	6	E 3-1	26.38	2.859	40.61	14.20	26.53	2.712	40.23	14.83
1985	6	E 3-1	47.89	3.640	49.94	13.72	31.58	2.839	43.21	15.22
1989	6	A 4-0	27.71	2.956	42.24	14.29	57.87	3.123	48.55	15.54
All	87	A 26-20	32.97	2.602	45.53	17.50	33.51	2.714	47.78	17.61

Statistical Highlights of 1938

Highest Innings Total

903-7 dec, England v Australia at The Oval (highest score in England; highest score in Test cricket).
658-8 dec, England v Australia at Nottingham (4 centuries).
708-5 dec, Australia v Cambridge University at Cambridge (4 centuries).
679-7 dec, Australia v Oxford University at Oxford (7 scores over 50).
602-7 dec, Kent v Worcestershire at Dudley.
631-4 dec, Sussex v Northants at Northampton (4 centuries)
636-7 dec, Free Foresters v Cambridge University at Cambridge (rate of 104 runs per 100 balls)

Lowest Innings Totals

56, Derbyshire v Australia at Chesterfield.
52, Surrey v Yorkshire at Sheffield.
41, Warwickshire v Yorkshire at Birmingham.
56, Scotland v Yorkshire at Harrogate.

Largest Fourth Innings Total

460, Surrey v MCC at Lord's (lost by 5 runs).

Large Margins of Victory

England beat Australia by an innings and 579 runs at The Oval (largest ever in England).
Australia beat Oxford University by an innings and 487 runs at Oxford.

Highest Match Aggregates

1,496-24, England v Australia at Nottingham (62.33 runs per wicket; 7 centuries scored).
1,443-34, Middlesex v Gloucestershire at Lord's.
1,422-34, Kent v Essex at Gravesend.

Highest Individual Innings

364, L.Hutton (England v Australia at The Oval; second highest in Tests).
291, E.Paynter (Lancashire v Hampshire at Southampton).
278, D.G.Bradman (Australia v MCC at Lord's).
271, W.R.Hammond (Gloucestershire v Lancashire at Bristol).
265*, W.A.Brown (Australia v Derbyshire at Chesterfield).
258, D.G.Bradman (Australia v Worcestershire at Worcester).

Century on First-class Debut

156, M.N.Harbottle (Army v Oxford University at Camberley; his only first-class appearance).

Double Century in Each Innings of a Match

244 & 202*, A.E.Fagg (Kent v Essex at Colchester; still the only instance).
Centuries in each innings were scored by W.R.Hammond (Gloucestershire v Derbyshire at Burton upon Trent), F.S.Lee (Somerset v Worcestershire at Worcester), E.Paynter (Lancashire v Warwickshire at Birmingham) and T.S.Worthington (Derbyshire v Nottinghamshire at Ilkeston).

Leading Performers
W.R.Hammond was the leading home batsman for the sixth successive season. D.G.Bradman's average of 115.66 is still the highest in an English season.

1,000 Runs Before End of May
D.G.Bradman, 1,056 runs (average 150.86) between 30 April and 31 May.
W.J.Edrich, 1,010 runs (average 84.17) between 30 April and 31 May.

1,000 Runs in a Month
A.E.Fagg (Kent) scored 1,016 runs in July (average 72.57).

Carrying Bat Through Complete Innings
W.A.Brown, 206* out of 422, Australia v England at Lord's.
C.S.Dempster, 28* out of 62, Leicestershire v Yorkshire at Bradford.
A.H.Dyson, 110* out of 210, Glamorgan v Sir Julian Cahn's XI at Newport.
A.E.Fagg, 37* out of 127, Kent v Gloucestershire at Gillingham.
P.A.Gibb, 80* out of 163, Cambridge University v Australia at Cambridge.
F.S.Lee, 109* out of 196, Somerset v Worcestershire at Worcester (was last out for 107 in the other innings).

Fast Scoring
50 in 11 minutes by C.J.Smith (66 in 18 minutes with eight 6's, Middlesex v Gloucesteshire at Bristol).
100 in 57 minutes by H.T.Bartlett (157, Sussex v Australia at Hove. Bartlett won the Lawrence Trophy).
100 in 60 minutes by G.Cox (142, Sussex v Yorkshire at Hove).
200 in 150 minutes by M.M.Walford (210*, Oxford University v MCC at Lord's).
69 in 20 minutes by C.I.J.Smith (Middlesex v Sussex at Lord's)
75 in 30 minutes by R.T.D.Perks (Worcestershire v Nottinghamshire at Nottingham).
S.J.McCabe (232, Australia v England at Nottingham) reached 200 in 233 minutes, the second-fastest double century in Test cricket.

Century Before Lunch
A.E.Fagg (Kent v Essex at Colchester).
F.E.Woolley (Kent v Worcestershire at Tonbridge).
B.P.King (Worcestershire v Hampshire at Worcester, 2nd day).

600 Runs in a Day
Free Foresters, 636-7 v Cambridge University at Cambridge.
Kent 544, Essex 66-3 at Gravesend.

Most Runs off an Over
31 (6,6,6,6,6,1) A.W.Wellard (Somerset) off F.E.Woolley (Kent) at Wells.
28 (6,6,4,4,4,4) H.T.Bartlett (Gentlemen) off T.P.B.Smith (Players) at Lord's.
C.I.J.Smith (off R.A.Sinfield, for Middlesex v Gloucestershire at Bristol) and L.L.Wilkinson (off R.Howorth, for Lancashire v Worcestershire at Manchester) both hit three 6's off successive deliveries.
A.W.Wellard hit 57 6's in the season.

Longest Innings
800 minutes, L.Hutton (364, England v Australia at The Oval).

Monopolizing Scoring During Innings
A.W.Wellard, 73* out of 80 (Somerset v Glamorgan at Cardiff).
L.B.Fishlock, 93 out of 104 (Surrey v Australia at The Oval).
S.J.McCabe, 232 out of 300 (Australia v England at Nottingham, scoring 72 out of 77 added for the tenth wicket with L.O'B.Fleetwood-Smith).

Large Partnerships
295 (1st wicket) John Langridge & J.H.Parks (Sussex v Leicestershire at Hove).
382 (2nd wicket) L.Hutton & M.Leyland (England v Australia at The Oval).
281 (2nd wicket) John Langridge & H.W.Parks (Sussex v Glamorgan at Eastbourne).
315 (3rd wicket) C.L.Badcock & A.L.Hassett (Australia v Leicestershire at Leicester).
306 (3rd wicket) E.Paynter & N.Oldfield (Lancashire v Hampshire at Southampton).
304 (3rd wicket) W.J.Edrich & D.C.S.Compton (Middlesex v Gloucestershire at Lord's).
The following partnerships are still county records for that wicket:
283 (1st wicket) A.E.Fagg & P.R.Sunnucks (Kent v Essex at Colchester).
220 (6th wicket) H.E.Dollery & J.Buckingham (Warwickshire v Derbyshire at Derby).
239 (8th wicket) W.R.Hammond & A.E.Wilson (Gloucestershire v Lancashire at Bristol).

Century First-wicket Partnership in Each Innings
102 & 100, N.T.McCorkell & J.Arnold (Hampshire v Kent at Southampton).

Best Bowling in an Innings
9-37, M.S.Nichols (Essex v Gloucestershire at Gloucester).
9-57, G.S.Boyes (Hampshire v Somerset at Yeovil).
9-101, J.E.Walsh (Sir Julian Cahn's XI v Glamorgan at Newport).
W.K.Laidlaw took 7-70 (Scotland v Yorkshire at Harrogate) and W.J.Pershke took 6-46 (Oxford University v Glamorgan at Oxford), both on their first-class debuts.

Best Bowling in a Match
15-113, K.Farnes (Essex v Glamorgan at Clacton).
15-165, M.S.Nichols (Essex v Gloucestershire at Gloucester).

Hat-Tricks
O.W.Herman (Hampshire v Glamorgan at Portsmouth); L.L.Wilkinson (Lancashire v Sussex at Hove), D.V.P.Wright (Kent v Gloucestershire at Gillingham).

Most Overs in an Innings
87-11-298-1, L.O'B.Fleetwood-Smith (Australia v England at The Oval).
85-26-178-3, W.J.O'Reilly (same innings of above match).
A.W.Wellard took 169 wickets (average 19.24) in the season for Somerset, still a county record

All-rounder's 'Double' (1,000 runs and 100 wickets)

W.H.R.Andrews (Somerset), M.S.Nichols (Essex), G.H.Pope (Derbyshire) and T.F.Smailes (Yorks).
R.Howorth (Worcestershire) missed it by three runs.

All-round Cricket in a Match

C.J.Barnett scored 168 and took 5-63 & 6-40 (Gloucestershire v Lancashire at Manchester).
M.S.Nichols scored 159 and took 9-37 & 6-126 (Essex v Gloucestershire at Gloucester).

Fielding Records

E.P.Robinson took six catches in an innings (Yorkshire v Leicestershire at Bradford — and seven in the match).
Wicketkeeper W.F.Price took six victims (all caught) in an innings (Middlesex v Warwickshire at Lord's). W.H.V.Levett took eight dismissals (3 caught, 5 stumped) in a match (Kent v Lancashire at Dover).
N.T.McCorkell conceded no byes for Hampshire in an innings of 535-8 declared by Leicestershire at Leicester.

First to Targets

1,000 runs: D.G.Bradman (Australia) on 27 May (the earliest ever in an English season).
2,000 runs: D.G.Bradman and W.R.Hammond (Gloucestershire) on 19 July.
3,000 runs: W.R.Hammond on 8 September (only instance in 1938).
100 wickets: R.Pollard (Lancashire) on 6 July.
The all-rounder's double: M.S.Nichols (Essex) on 15 August (for fourth successive year, Nicholls was the first to achieve this).

Miscellaneous

For Warwickshire v Northamptonshire at Northampton, W.E.Hollies had bowling figures of 30-7-66-6 and 30.3-9-66-6.
At Lord's, Middlesex and Gloucestershire each scored 478 in the first innings of the match.
For the third year in a row, Northamptonshire did not record a single first-class victory.
E.L.McCormick bowled 35 no-balls in his first match in England (Australia v Worcestershire at Worcester). Nineteen of them came in his first three overs. He bowled 15 no-balls in his second match, v Leicestershire at Leicester.

Large Attendances

100,933 (four days), Second Test at Lord's.
99,614 (four days), Fourth Test at Headingley.
94,212 (four days) Fifth Test at The Oval.
89,681 (five days) First Test at Trent Bridge.

First-Class Averages for 1938

BATTING

(Qualification: 8 innings)

†Denotes a left-hand batsman. *Signifies not out.

	Innings	Not Out	Runs	HS	Ave	100s
Mr W.R.Hammond (Gloucestershire)	42	2	3,011	271	75.27	15
J.Hardstaff (Notts)	37	7	1,827	169*	60.90	7
L.Hutton (Yorkshire)	37	6	1,874	364	60.45	6
†E.Paynter (Lancashire)	52	6	2,691	291	58.50	8
†Mr H.T.Bartlett (Sussex)	31	4	1,548	175*	57.33	5
W.J.Edrich (Middlesex)	51	6	2,378	245	52.84	6
A.E.Fagg (Kent)	53	6	2,456	244	52.25	9
Mr C.S.Dempster (Leicestershire)	26	1	1,300	187	52.00	6
Mr J.R.Thompson (Warwicks, CU)	18	1	858	191	50.47	2
Mr P.A.Gibb (Yorkshire, CU)	37	3	1,658	204	48.76	4
John G.Langridge (Sussex)	54	4	2,347	227	46.94	5
D.C.S.Compton (Middlesex)	47	6	1,868	180*	45.56	5
Mr R.E.S.Wyatt (Warwickshire)	41	7	1,549	149	45.55	3
Mr J.M.Lomas (Oxford U)	21	1	908	124	45.40	1
†F.S.Lee (Somerset)	51	6	2,019	162	44.86	7
Mr B.H.Valentine (Kent)	37	1	1,593	242	44.25	6
H.H.Gibbons (Worcestershire)	55	6	2,120	178	43.26	6
†M.Leyland (Yorkshire)	47	4	1,884	187	43.81	5
Mr T.N.Pearce (Essex)	28	6	948	137*	43.09	2
L.E.G.Ames (Kent)	27	1	1,116	170	42.92	2
Mr M.M.Walford (Oxford U)	15	2	554	201*	42.61	2
N.Oldfield (Lancashire)	50	7	1,812	137	42.13	4
Mr R.H.Moore (Hampshire)	19	0	798	128	42.00	3
H.Sutcliffe (Yorkshire)	50	7	1,790	142	41.62	5
A.H.Dyson (Glamorgan)	51	5	1,885	170*	40.97	4
†L.B.Fishlock (Surrey)	53	1	2,121	165	40.78	4
†James Langridge (Sussex)	44	10	1,380	156	40.58	2
T.S.Worthington (Derbyshire)	41	2	1,573	121	40.33	5
H.E.Dollery (Warwickshire)	41	6	1,387	134*	39.62	4
C.Washbrook (Lancashire)	47	6	1,621	219*	39.53	5
J.O'Connor (Essex)	50	3	1,839	152	39.12	6
Mr A.G.Waterman (Essex)	8	1	272	103	38.85	1
H.W.Parks (Sussex)	49	6	1,658	119*	38.55	3
J.H.Parks (Sussex)	49	3	1,740	169	37.82	4
Mr R.H.C.Human (Worcestershire)	8	2	223	81	37.16	-
L.F.Townsend (Derbyshire)	46	6	1,458	167*	36.45	2
G.Geary (Leicestershire)	30	6	873	116*	36.37	3
C.J.Barnett (Gloucestershire)	51	0	1,852	168	36.31	3
A.Mitchell (Yorkshire)	39	3	1,305	133	36.25	4
J.Iddon (Lancashire)	49	3	1,667	185	36.23	2
S.H.Martin (Worcestershire)	43	3	1,449	136	36.22	3
E.W.Whitfield (Surrey)	31	3	1,005	198	35.89	3
R.J.Gregory (Surrey)	51	4	1,686	243	35.87	3
†J.F.Crapp (Gloucestershire)	51	4	1,685	137	35.85	2
Mr J.H.Human (Middlesex)	8	0	286	71	35.75	-
†M.S.Nichols (Essex)	47	6	1,452	163	35.41	3
Mr P.M.Studd (Camb U)	15	3	422	68*	35.16	-
C.B.Harris (Notts)	50	3	1,632	179	34.72	4
†Mr B.O.Allen (Gloucestershire)	53	1	1,785	104	34.32	1
W.Barber (Yorkshire)	47	4	1,455	157	33.83	3
Mr E.J.H.Dixon (Oxford U)	22	2	671	108	33.55	1
J.L.Hopwood (Lancashire)	49	3	1,520	141	33.04	3
Mr J.D.Eggar (Hampshire, OU)	17	3	462	125	33.00	1
†F.E.Woolley (Kent)	52	3	1,590	162	32.44	2
J.D.Robertson (Middlesex)	30	2	905	91	32.32	-
A.E.Nutter (Lancashire)	45	9	1,156	98	32.11	-
H.S.Squires (Surrey)	46	3	1,377	137	32.02	2
†C.Turner (Yorkshire)	24	3	671	97	31.95	-
G.Cox (Sussex)	38	2	1,134	142	31.50	4
Mr N.W.D.Yardley (Yorkshire, CU)	42	3	1,217	97	31.20	-
J.Buckingham (Warwickshire)	41	7	1,054	137*	31.00	2
E.Cooper (Worcestershire)	57	3	1,663	216*	30.79	3
†Mr G.F.H.Heane (Notts)	46	4	1,292	126	30.76	3
†J.Bailey (Hampshire)	9	0	276	69	30.66	-
G.V.Gunn (Notts)	46	1	1,360	184	30.22	2
†E.Davies (Glamorgan)	48	1	1,408	100	29.95	1
J.F.Parker (Surrey)	41	2	1,167	111	29.92	1
C.Oakes (Sussex)	26	2	717	148*	29.87	2
T.H.Barling (Surrey)	45	2	1,284	129	29.86	1
W.E.Phillipson (Lancashire)	27	7	597	55	29.85	-
W.L.Neale (Gloucestershire)	53	3	1,488	131	29.76	5
G.H.Pope (Derbyshire)	46	11	1,040	85	29.71	-
L.G.Berry (Leicestershire)	43	1	1,241	172	29.54	1
J.S.Ord (Warwickshire)	39	1	1,121	88	29.50	-
N.F.Armstrong (Leicestershire)	43	1	1,233	125	29.35	3
A.E.Alderman (Derbyshire)	47	4	1,262	150	29.34	2
Mr P.M.Whitehouse (Kent, OU)	27	5	643	72	29.22	-
Mr E.R.T.Holmes (Surrey)	28	5	670	103	29.13	1
W.W.Keeton (Notts)	53	1	1,512	109	29.07	2
Ft-Lt.A.J.Holmes (Sussex)	36	3	953	133*	28.87	2
Mr E.D.R.Eagar (Gloucs, OU)	26	1	717	147	28.68	1
†W.L.Creese (Hampshire)	54	4	1,421	103	28.42	1
G.Hill (Hampshire)	42	9	935	122	28.33	1
Mr P.Cranmer (Warwickshire)	40	4	1,014	104	28.16	1
†D.Smith (Derbyshire)	45	1	1,234	122	28.04	3
N.T.McCorkell (Hampshire)	60	3	1,586	136	27.82	1
A.E.G.Rhodes (Derbyshire)	37	4	916	107*	27.75	1
D.Brookes (Northants)	52	3	1,359	113	27.73	1
A.V.Avery (Essex)	31	1	831	138	27.70	2
F.T.Prentice (Leicestershire)	32	1	850	154*	27.41	2
G.S.Watson (Leicestershire)	43	4	1,069	81	27.41	-
H.E.Hammond (Sussex)	28	8	546	77*	27.30	-
Mr A.B.Sellers (Yorkshire)	48	6	1,143	93*	27.21	-
L.D.Thursting (Leicestershire)	30	7	625	94	27.17	-
H.Gimblett (Somerset)	51	3	1,304	112	27.16	2
†A.E.Pothecary (Hampshire)	51	1	1,357	118	27.14	2
Mr R.J.O.Meyer (Somerset)	14	4	271	76*	27.10	-
Mr G.O.Allen (Middlesex)	16	0	431	64	26.93	-
†Mr R.P.Nelson (Northants)	51	4	1,264	110	26.89	1
Mr C.H.Knott (Kent)	18	2	430	112	26.87	2
Mr W.H.Webster (Middlesex)	11	1	268	87	26.80	-
M.Tompkin (Leicestershire)	25	1	642	91	26.75	-
Mr J.P.Blake (Hampshire)	13	2	294	70	26.72	-

	Innings	Not Out	Runs	HS	Ave	100s
Mr M.A.C.P.Kaye (Camb U)	13	4	237	78	26.33	-
H.W.Greenwood (Northants)	22	0	573	72	26.04	-
Mr R.W.V.Robins (Middlesex)	41	3	989	13	26.02	1
A.Staples (Notts)	18	4	363	70*	25.92	-
Mr B.D.Carris (CU, Middlesex)	14	0	360	79	25.71	-
F.R.Santall (Warwicks)	42	3	1,001	78	25.66	-
J.H.A.Hulme (Middlesex)	34	1	843	143	25.54	1
T.W.Spencer (Kent)	31	4	688	68	25.48	-
Mr C.D.A.Pullan (Worcestershire)	23	4	479	84	25.21	-
C.Smart (Glamorgan)	43	6	933	92	25.21	-
J.Knowles (Notts)	51	4	1,179	114	25.08	1
†T.F.Smailes (Yorkshire)	43	3	1,002	117	25.05	2
†Mr A.P.F.Chapman (Kent)	8	0	200	78	25.00	-
H.Larwood (Notts)	14	2	299	87*	24.91	-
Mr R.G.Stainton (Sussex)	33	3	745	71	24.83	-
J.Y.Oakes (Sussex)	8	0	198	63	24.75	-
†E.A.Wilson (Gloucestershire)	50	4	1,138	130	24.73	1
L.C.Eastman (Essex)	43	1	1,033	90	24.59	-
R.M.Taylor (Essex)	46	1	1,099	193	24.42	1
Mr G.A.Wilson (Yorkshire)	12	4	195	55*	24.37	-
Mr D.R.Wilcox (Essex)	48	1	1,145	102	24.36	1
Mr G.R.J.de Soysa (Oxford U)	8	1	170	56	24.28	-
D.Davies (Glamorgan)	48	3	1,092	86	24.26	-
Mr S.C.Griffith (Sussex)	13	4	215	66	23.88	-
Mr R.C.M.Kimpton (Oxford U)	13	0	310	68	23.84	-
H.T.F.Buse (Somerset)	45	0	1,067	132	23.71	2
†D.F.Walker (Hampshire)	40	1	925	91	23.71	-
T.L.Brierley (Glamorgan)	51	1	1,183	116	23.66	1
A.J.Croom (Warwicks)	47	3	1,036	88	23.54	-
Mr C.G.A.Paris (Hampshire)	49	4	1,058	77	23.51	-
Mr J.D.A.Langley (Camb U)	17	0	399	119	23.47	1
K.C.James (Northants)	49	5	1,032	105*	23.45	2
E.A.Watts (Surrey)	44	12	745	69*	23.28	-
Mr H.M.Garland-Wells (Surrey)	38	3	808	94	23.08	-
W.F.Price (Middlesex)	44	7	854	69	23.08	-
Mr F.G.H.Chalk (Kent)	52	2	1,140	167	22.80	1
B.P.King (Worcestershire)	55	3	1,177	124	22.63	2
A.G.Holt (Hampshire)	15	0	339	116	22.60	1
S.M.Brown (Middlesex)	42	3	873	114	22.38	1
G.M.Emmett (Gloucestershire)	53	4	1,091	165*	22.26	1
T.P.B.Smith (Essex)	45	7	846	103	22.26	2
†Mr E.F.Longrigg (Somerset)	38	3	779	187*	22.25	1
W.H.R.Andrews (Somerset)	46	1	1,001	77*	22.24	-
C.H.Bull (Worcestershire)	27	4	497	75	21.60	-
F.Berry (Surrey)	31	3	600	104*	21.42	1
G.E.Hart (Middlesex)	19	0	404	105	21.26	1
A.V.Pope (Derbyshire)	40	6	721	103	21.20	1
V.Hopkins (Gloucestershire)	28	2	551	65	21.19	-
Hon C.J.Lyttelton (Worcestershire)	37	2	741	162	21.17	1
Mr M.J.Turnbull (Glamorgan)	34	2	673	72	21.03	-
Mr A.P.Singleton (Worcestershire)	8	1	147	47	21.00	-
W.L.Cornford (Sussex)	31	10	438	52*	20.85	-
Mr J.W.Seamer (Somerset)	14	0	291	47	20.78	-
Mr G.E.Hewan (Camb U)	9	0	187	88	20.77	-
J.Arnold (Hampshire)	42	1	849	94	20.70	-
A.Wood (Yorkshire)	37	5	661	69	20.65	-
†L.J.Todd (Kent)	49	4	921	118	20.46	1
Mr M.D.Lyon (Somerset)	42	4	777	122*	20.44	1
W.Voce (Notts)	36	4	654	111	20.43	1
†R.Howorth (Worcestershire)	54	5	997	100	20.34	1

	Innings	Not Out	Runs	HS	Ave	100s
Mr F.G.Mann (Camb U)	19	1	364	41	20.22	-
W.T.Luckes (Somerset)	43	20	464	90*	20.17	-
Mr R.A.Ingle (Somerset)	8	0	160	52	20.00	-
Mr J.N.Grover (Oxford U)	12	0	239	53	19.91	-
J.E.Timms (Northants)	51	1	993	121	19.86	1
A.W.Wellard (Somerset)	46	1	884	73*	19.64	-
Mr D.E.Young (Oxford U)	14	3	215	29*	19.54	-
Mr H.D.Burrough (Somerset)	16	0	308	64	19.25	-
R.Duckfield (Glamorgan)	30	6	462	66	19.25	-
P.R.Sunnucks (Kent)	31	1	572	82	19.06	-
Mr F.R.Brown (Surrey)	18	0	342	88	19.00	-
H.J.Butler (Notts)	13	8	95	22	19.00	-
E.C.Jones (Glamorgan)	33	5	525	132	18.75	1
G.S.Boyes (Hampshire)	55	10	842	104	18.71	1
D.Jones (Nottinghamshire)	26	3	426	60	18.52	-
C.I.J.Smith (Middlesex)	46	6	736	69	18.40	-
W.T.Nevell (Middlesex)	12	4	147	32*	18.37	-
G.O.Dawkes (Leicestershire)	34	7	493	49	18.25	-
R.A.Sinfield (Gloucestershire)	47	20	486	39*	18.00	-
W.Farrimond (Lancashire)	40	11	510	55	17.58	-
Mr A.B.Lavers (Essex)	20	0	351	39	17.55	-
A.F.Townsend (Derbyshire)	15	2	225	68*	17.30	-
Revd J.W.J.Steele (Hampshire)	22	1	362	44	17.23	-
W.L.Budd (Hampshire)	10	0	172	35	17.20	-
R.W.Haynes (Gloucestershire)	29	1	481	55	17.17	-
Mr J.C.Clay (Glamorgan)	26	11	251	48*	16.73	-
H.Verity (Yorkshire)	34	11	385	45*	16.73	-
D.V.P.Wright (Kent)	34	8	435	51*	16.73	-
J.Horton (Worcestershire)	31	3	465	70	16.60	-
R.Smith (Essex)	31	12	312	53	16.42	-
†E.P.Robinson (Yorkshire)	37	8	474	66	16.34	-
M.Dunkley (Northants)	34	2	522	70	16.31	-
†A.B.Wheat (Notts)	37	9	447	52	15.96	-
J.S.Buller (Worcestershire)	48	11	585	64	15.81	-
N.Grimshaw (Northants)	19	2	268	52*	15.76	-
F.H.Winrow (Notts)	15	1	219	69	15.64	-
Mr J.G.W.Davies (Kent)	12	0	185	49	15.41	-
E.W.Brooks (Surrey)	41	9	493	59	15.40	-
Mr C.J.P.Barnwell (Somerset)	28	3	384	49*	15.36	-
†T.H.Wade (Essex)	43	9	521	67	15.32	-
Mr A.W.Snowden (Northants)	18	0	274	64	15.22	-
F.P.O'Brien (Northants)	30	1	436	44	15.03	-
Mr W.H.L.Lister (Lancashire)	40	3	547	65	14.78	-
Mr C.H.Palmer (Worcestershire)	15	1	205	56	14.64	-
W.A.Hill (Warwickshire)	14	2	171	51	14.25	-
Mr C.R.Maxwell (Notts)	12	0	170	33	14.16	-
H.Elliott (Derbyshire)	38	6	448	50*	14.00	-
J.K.Nye (Sussex)	18	5	181	38	13.92	-
L.M.Cranfield (Gloucestershire)	17	7	138	22*	13.80	-
Mr I.A.R.Peebles (Middlesex)	17	2	207	58	13.80	-
L.H.Gray (Middlesex)	27	19	108	24*	13.50	-
J.M.Sims (Middlesex)	28	6	296	50	13.45	-
B.L.Muncer (Middlesex)	10	0	134	39	13.40	-
N.W.Harding (Kent)	32	3	388	42*	13.37	-
Mr K.C.Kinnersley (Somerset)	8	2	80	25*	13.33	-
H.G.Davies (Glamorgan)	26	3	306	40	13.30	-
Mr E.K.Scott (Oxford U)	9	1	106	31	13.25	-
H.A.Smith (Leicestershire)	35	7	371	33	13.25	-
Mr A.M.T.Jones (Somerset)	22	0	281	106	12.77	1
Mr R.F.H.Darwall-Smith (Oxford U)	13	3	126	45	12.60	-

	Innings	Not Out	Runs	HS	Ave	100s
W.Place (Lancashire)	8	0	100	40	12.50	-
†F.Warne (Worcestershire)	13	1	149	60	12.41	-
R.C.L.Court (Hampshire)	9	1	99	35	12.37	-
T.McMurray (Surrey)	11	1	122	30*	12.20	-
W.E.Fantham (Warwickshire)	15	4	134	27*	12.18	-
A.Jepson (Notts)	23	9	168	30*	12.00	-
G.A.E.Paine (Warwickshire)	29	0	348	38	12.00	-
†R.T.D.Perks (Worcestershire)	49	8	491	75	11.97	-
R.J.Partridge (Northants)	46	7	463	47	11.87	-
W.H.Flamson (Leicestershire)	19	7	140	50*	11.66	-
A.D.G.Matthews (Glamorgan)	10	2	93	32	11.62	-
Mr G.Evans (Oxford U)	10	1	103	21*	11.44	-
Mr W.J.Pershke (Oxford U)	10	5	57	17*	11.40	-
Mr J.V.Wild (Camb U)	17	0	193	34	11.35	-
F.G.Woodhead (Notts)	30	8	243	38*	11.04	-
Mr E.A.Ingram (Middlesex)	8	1	77	27	11.00	-
Mr G.B.Cuthbertson (Northants)	14	0	152	40	10.85	-
R.Pollard (Lancashire)	35	9	281	26*	10.80	-
A.R.Gover (Surrey)	32	14	194	23	10.77	-
H.Halliday (Yorkshire)	9	1	86	36	10.75	-
P.C.Davis (Northants)	24	1	247	37	10.73	-
A.Davies (Glamorgan)	16	5	118	27*	10.72	-
†C.Lewis (Kent)	28	15	139	21*	10.69	-
Mr J.N.Dennis (Essex)	10	1	96	37*	10.66	-
Mr R.J.Crisp (Worcestershire)	15	4	116	29	10.54	-
Mr R.H.R.Buckston (Derbyshire)	33	6	279	60*	10.33	-
R.O.Jenkins (Worcestershire)	18	8	102	21	10.20	-
W.E.Bowes (Yorkshire)	23	12	113	43*	10.27	-
F.G.Foy (Kent)	8	0	81	25	10.12	-
J.H.Mayer (Warwickshire)	28	11	171	52*	10.05	-
The following also batted:						
Mr M.D.P.Magill (Oxford U)	4	2	120	80	60.00	-
Nawab of Pataudi (Worcestershire)	5	1	233	121*	58.25	1
Mr V.E.Jackson (Leicestershire)	4	0	164	99	41.00	-
Mr J.H.Pawle (Essex, FF)	7	0	265	76	37.85	-
Major A.C.Wilkinson (FF)	6	1	184	93	36.80	-
Mr D.O.Hay (Oxford U)	3	0	105	96	35.00	-

BOWLING

(Qualification: 10 wickets)

†Denotes a left-arm bowler.

	Overs	Maidens	Runs	Wickets	Ave
A.D.G.Matthews (Glamorgan)	180.5	36	395	30	13.16
W.E.Bowes (Yorkshire)	932.3	294	1,844	121	15.23
†H.Verity (Yorkshire)	1,191.4	424	2,476	158	15.67
H.J.Butler (Notts)	257.1	55	648	39	16.61
Mr I.A.R.Peebles (Middlesex)	234.5	51	649	38	17.07
Mr J.C.Clay (Glamorgan)	648	150	1,639	94	17.43
Mr W.Wooller (Glamorgan)	143.2	30	374	21	17.80
E.A.Watts (Surrey)	777.1	141	2,383	129	18.47
Mr K.Farnes (Essex)	701.2	137	2,016	107	18.84
Mr E.A.Ingram (Middlesex)	114	39	227	12	18.91
J.H.Mayer (Warwickshire)	687.4	145	1,868	96	19.45
T.B.Mitchell (Derbyshire)	717	104	2,570	131	19.61
†M.Leyland (Yorkshire)	385.4	99	1,237	63	19.63
W.H.Copson (Derbyshire)	742.4	156	1,995	101	19.75
M.S.Nichols (Essex)	1,228.1	264	3,408	171	19.92
C.I.J.Smith (Middlesex)	1,153	283	2,672	132	20.24
A.W.Wellard (Somerset)	1,233.4	241	3,491	172	20.29
T.F.Smailes (Yorkshire)	912.5	243	2,355	113	20.84
F.Wilkinson (Yorkshire)	341	77	502	24	20.91
Mr D.E.Young (Oxford U)	252.3	59	732	35	20.91
R.Pollard (Lancashire)	1,231.5	252	3,216	149	21.58
†G.S.Boyes (Hampshire)	970.3	269	2,323	107	21.71
W.H.R.Andrews (Somerset)	851.2	156	2,704	124	21.80
E.P.Robinson (Yorkshire)	819	199	2,287	104	21.99
R.G.Garlick (Lancashire)	127	24	309	14	22.07
R.C.L.Court (Hampshire)	112.1	25	292	13	22.46
†C.Rhodes (Lancashire)	124.3	32	272	12	22.66
Mr J.E.Walsh (Leicestershire)	219.5	25	778	34	22.88
D.M.Smith (Sussex)	86.2	7	298	13	22.92
T.W.Goddard (Gloucestershire)	971.1	201	2,625	114	23.02
L.L.Wilkinson (Lancashire)	1,251.2	240	3,531	151	23.38
D.V.P.Wright (Kent)	768	152	2,579	110	23.44
Mr R.J.Crisp (Worcestershire)	295.3	37	1,040	44	23.63
L.H.Gray (Middlesex)	559.4	99	1,682	71	23.69
G.E.M.Heath (Hampshire)	886.3	184	2,306	97	23.77
Mr J.G.W.Davies (Kent)	147	34	334	14	23.85
†F.E.Woolley (Kent)	177.5	35	525	22	23.86
R.T.D.Perks (Worcestershire)	1,058	188	3,261	136	23.97
†W.L.Creese (Hampshire)	356.1	100	937	39	24.02
G.H.Pope (Derbyshire)	872.5	165	2,486	103	24.13
Mr R.J.O.Meyer (Somerset)	293	58	799	33	24.21
A.V.Pope (Derbyshire)	895.2	195	2,213	91	24.31
T.P.B.Smith (Essex)	1,178	219	3,509	144	24.36
A.E.Nutter (Lancashire)	879.4	189	2,243	91	24.64
R.O.Jenkins (Worcestershire)	300.1	57	863	35	24.65
R.A.Sinfield (Gloucestershire)	1,393	347	3,249	131	24.80
Capt J.W.A.Stephenson (Essex)	394	79	1,146	46	24.91
G.Geary (Leicestershire)	538.4	131	1,174	47	24.97
Mr G.O.Allen (Middlesex)	173.5	29	575	23	25.00
W.E.Hollies (Warwickshire)	981.4	225	2,503	100	25.03
Revd J.W.J.Steele (Hampshire)	393	69	1,102	44	25.04
F.G.Woodhead (Notts)	682.2	156	1,728	69	25.04
Mr R.W.V.Robins (Middlesex)	470.3	66	1,705	68	25.07
A.E.Watt (Kent)	734.4	169	1,927	76	25.35
S.H.Martin (Worcestershire)	895.1	234	2,171	85	25.54
†R.Howorth (Worcestershire)	948.5	171	2,769	108	25.63
J.F.Parker (Surrey)	581.2	107	1,719	67	25.65
R.J.Partridge (Northants)	897.5	169	2,416	94	25.70
N.F.Armstrong (Leicestershire)	116	19	361	14	25.78
J.H.Cornford (Sussex)	848.2	156	2,297	89	25.80
†E.Davies (Glamorgan)	699.2	135	1,862	72	25.86
H.A.Smith (Leicestershire)	972	224	2,409	92	26.18
A.Staples (Notts)	260.1	54	688	26	26.46
J.H.Parks (Sussex)	999.4	300	2,258	85	26.56
F.Berry (Surrey)	428.3	92	1,171	44	26.61
†W.Voce (Notts)	972	195	2,613	98	26.66
J.V.Daley (Surrey)	104.2	19	295	11	26.81
Mr W.J.Pershke (Oxford U)	249	45	752	28	26.85
A.R.Gover (Surrey)	730.2	99	2,326	86	27.04
Mr H.M.Garland-Wells (Surrey)	223	36	677	25	27.08
†D.J.Wood (Sussex)	447.1	74	1,409	52	27.09
Mr G.F.H.Heane (Notts)	518.1	129	1,445	53	27.26
†L.J.Todd (Kent)	945.1	204	2,625	96	27.34
W.H.Flamson (Leicestershire)	580.3	130	1,453	53	27.41
†G.A.E.Paine (Warwickshire)	725	179	1,777	64	27.76

	Overs	Maidens	Runs	Wickets	Ave
P.F.Jackson (Worcestershire)	433.4	80	1,294	46	28.13
J.D.Robertson (Middlesex)	134	30	373	13	28.69
L.Hutton (Yorkshire)	227.1	51	576	20	28.80
J.M.Sims (Middlesex)	514.1	66	1,675	58	28.87
L.F.Townsend (Derbyshire)	219.5	52	588	20	29.40
H.T.F.Buse (Somerset)	660	171	1,805	61	29.59
J.E.Timms (Northants)	452.2	96	1,247	42	29.69
H.E.Hammond (Sussex)	745	116	2,133	71	30.04
J.Mercer (Glamorgan)	654.2	119	1,837	61	30.11
J.Buswell (Northants)	745	115	2,400	79	30.37
E.J.Herbert (Northants)	527.1	97	1,438	47	30.59
†C.Lewis (Kent)	486.3	129	1,408	46	30.60
R.J.Gregory (Surrey)	399.2	108	1,048	34	30.82
W.E.Phillipson (Lancashire)	630.2	129	1,761	57	30.89
Mr C.J.Knott (Hampshire)	224.3	44	650	21	30.95
Mr B.D.Carris (Camb U)	83.1	11	310	10	31.00
†H.L.Hazell (Somerset)	486.5	90	1,479	47	31.46
†D.C.S.Compton (Middlesex)	130	18	504	16	31.50
R.Smith (Essex)	463.3	68	1,714	54	31.74
O.W.Herman (Hampshire)	1,098	198	3,263	101	32.30
A.Jepson (Notts)	393.3	88	1,072	33	32.48
L.C.Eastman (Essex)	531.1	142	1,303	40	32.57
A.E.G.Rhodes (Derbyshire)	183.2	36	589	18	32.72
H.S.Squires (Surrey)	553.1	120	1,542	46	33.52
Mr M.A.C.P.Kaye (Camb U)	219.1	32	845	25	33.80
Mr P.M.Whitehouse (Kent, OU)	328.3	76	890	26	34.23
Mr F.R.Brown (Surrey)	364.4	25	1,610	47	34.25
J.K.Nye (Sussex)	540.3	77	1,749	51	34.29
N.W.Harding (Kent)	417	62	1,462	42	34.80
†G.M.Emmett (Gloucestershire)	402.4	49	1,574	45	34.97
†James Langridge (Sussex)	686	161	1,757	50	35.14
H.Daer (Essex)	95	16	387	11	35.18
Mr N.W.D.Yardley (Yorkshire, CU)	269.2	59	780	22	35.45
†J.Sperry (Leicestershire)	335.4	59	961	27	35.59
A.Robinson (Northants)	165.2	23	500	14	35.71
C.J.Barnett (Gloucestershire)	327.2	60	1,009	28	36.03
Mr J.V.Wild (Camb U)	299.2	68	1,047	29	36.10
W.L.Budd (Hampshire)	121.3	19	398	11	36.18
C.Oakes (Sussex)	164	4	833	23	36.21
Mr G.E.Hewan (Camb U)	192.5	40	725	20	36.25
K.Wilmot (Warwickshire)	490.3	83	1,384	38	36.42
A.G.Tuppin (Sussex)	234.3	47	621	17	36.52
A.J.Croom (Warwickshire)	170.1	16	660	18	36.66
G.V.Gunn (Notts)	420	65	1,307	35	37.34
Mr D.H.Macindoe (Oxford U)	460.5	103	1,346	36	37.38
C.J.Scott (Gloucestershire)	422.3	51	1,430	38	37.63
Mr C.Tyler (Gloucestershire)	167.1	33	533	14	38.07
†J.Iddon (Lancashire)	269.2	56	694	18	38.55
W.J.Edrich (Middlesex)	175.4	22	587	15	39.13
C.Turner (Yorkshire)	265.5	75	587	15	39.13
G.Hill (Hampshire)	524.4	127	1,414	36	39.27
Mr R.F.H.Darwall-Smith (Oxford U)	321	63	1,025	26	39.42
C.Smart (Glamorgan)	237.1	26	819	20	40.95
W.T.Nevell (Middlesex)	161.5	26	493	12	41.08
†L.D.Thursting (Leicestershire)	116	16	452	10	45.20
G.Lester (Leicestershire)	453.3	55	1,558	34	45.82
E.C.Jones (Glamorgan)	257.5	28	840	18	46.66
Mr G.Evans (Oxford U)	173	39	515	11	46.81
W.E.Fantham (Warwickshire)	168.2	16	703	15	46.86
L.M.Cranfield (Gloucestershire)	172.4	27	593	12	49.41
Mr W.R.Rees-Davies (Camb U)	227	28	940	17	55.29
Mr W.R.Hammond (Gloucestershire)	343.2	82	847	14	60.50
†Mr R.P.Nelson (Northants)	197.5	45	639	10	63.90
F.T.Prentice (Leicestershire)	314.3	47	1,052	14	75.14
The following also bowled:					
R.Giles (Notts)	29.4	12	42	7	6.00
Mr W.K.Laidlaw (Scotland)	28.3	7	70	7	10.00
Mr C.S.Marriott (FF)	55.2	17	101	9	11.22
J.Duffield (Sussex)	28	4	71	5	14.20
Amar Singh (England XI)	32.1	3	100	6	16.66
Mr C.W.S.Lubbock (Northants)	34	6	101	6	16.83
Hon C.J.Lyttelton (Worcestershire)	49.4	3	180	9	20.00

(OU = Oxford University; CU = Cambridge University; FF = Free Foresters.)

Fielding & Wicketkeeping Victims

Unless otherwise stated figures refer to catches. Victims taken by substitutes are not included.

W.Farrimond	84	(69ct	15st)
E.W.J.Brooks	79	(70ct	9st)
J.Buckingham	78	(43ct	25st)
T.H.Wade	78	(64ct	14st)
W.T.Luckes	73	(61ct	12st)
W.F.Price	73	(51ct	22st)
Mr W.H.V.Levett	68	(51ct	17st)
J.S.Buller	67	(49ct	18st)
H.Elliott	63	(53ct	10st)
A.Wood	58	(36ct	22st)
N.T.McCorkell	56	(46ct	10st)
K.C.James	49	(41ct	8st)
G.O.Dawkes	43	(30ct	13st)
Mr B.O.Allen	42		
Mr P.A.Gibb	42	(23ct	19ct)
A.B.Wheat	42	(34ct	8st)
E.P.Robinson	41		
H.G.Davies	39	(24ct	15st)
A.Mitchell	39		
G.S.Boyes	37		
John G.Langridge	37		
D.C.S.Compton	35		
W.L.Cornford	35	(30ct	5st)
A.E.Fagg	34		
R.M.Taylor	34		
Mr W.R.Hammond	33		
T.P.B.Smith	31		
Mr N.W.D.Yardley	30		
R.J.Gregory	29		
Mr C.G.A.Paris	28		
L.L.Wilkinson	28		
H.F.T.Buse	27	(26ct	1st)
W.J.Edrich	27		
A.E.Nutter	27		
J.H.Parks	27		
A.B.Sellers	27		
E.A.Wilson	27	(18ct	9st)
R.Pollard	26		
D.F.Walker (Hants)	26	(25ct	1st)
A.Wellard	26		
C.Turner	25		
J.F.Crapp	24		
W.L.Creese	24		
R.Howorth	23		
G.H.Pope	23		
F.R.Santall	23		
A.E.Alderman	22		
Mr H.M.Garland-Wells	22		
L.J.Todd	22		
Mr M.J.Turnbull	22		
H.Verity	22		
E.A.Watts	22		
F.E.Woolly	22		
H.Gimblett	21		
D.Smith	21		
S.M.Brown	20		
G.M.Emmett	20		
Mr S.C.Griffiths	20	(15ct	5st)
Fl-Lt A.J.Holmes	20		
W.L.Neale	20		
M.S.Nichols	20		
T.L.Brierley	20	(18ct	2st)

Note that the England wicketkeeper L.E.G.Ames took only 17 victims (16ct 1st).

Bibliography

Wisden Cricketers' Almanack 1939 and subsequent years.
The Cricketer 1938, and subsequent years.
Playfair Cricket Monthly 1960-1973.
Wisden Cricket Monthly 1979 to date.
Contemporary daily newspapers, especially *The Times.*

The Australian tour
Cricket Crisis, J.H.Fingleton (Cassell 1946).
The Essential Neville Cardus, Neville Cardus, ed.R.Hart-Davis (Cape 1949).
Days Without Sunset, Denzil Batchelor (Eyre & Spottiswoode 1949).
Game Of A Lifetime, Denzil Batchelor (Werner Laurie 1953).
Australian Cricket: A History, A.G.Moyes (Harrap 1959).
Ten Great Innings, Ralph Barker (Chatto & Windus 1964).
Ten Great Bowlers, Ralph Barker (Chatto & Windus 1967).
The Bradman Era, Bill O'Reilly and Jack Egan (Willow 1984).
The Bradman Albums (Macdonald 1988) Vol 2.
The Bradman Years: Australian Cricket 1918-48, Jack Pollard (Angus & Robertson 1989).

General Reference
Cricket Between Two Wars, P.F.Warner (Chatto & Windus 1942).
Homes Of Sport: Cricket, Yardley and Kilburn (Garnett 1952).
Lord's, P.F.Warner (Harrap 1946)
Gentlemen v Players, Michael Marshall (Guild 1984).
The Guardian Book Of Cricket, ed.Matthew Engel (Pavilion 1986).
The Players: A Social History, Ric Sissons (Kingswood 1988).
Cricket's Second Golden Age, Gerald Howat (Hodder & Stoughton 1989).

County and Domestic Cricket
To The Wicket, Dudley Carew (Chapman & Hall 1946).
Gentlemen v Players, P.F.Warner (Harrap 1950).
County Champions, various (Heinemann Quixote 1982).
Oxford And Cambridge Cricket, Chesterton and Doggart (Willow 1989).
The Roses Matches 1919-1939, Neville Cardus (Souvenir 1982).
Gloucestershire Road, Graham Parker (Pelham 1983).
Mainly Middlesex, T.C.F.Prittie (Hutchinson 1946).
Sixty Years Of Somerset Cricket, Ron Roberts (Westaway 1952).
Sussex Cricket, John Marshall (Heinemann 1959).
The Family Fortune, Alan Hill (Scan 1978).
We Don't Play It For Fun, Don Mosey (Methuen 1988).
And the County Histories published by Convoy (Early 1950s); Arthur Barker (early 1970s) and Christopher Helm (late 1980s) and others

Biographies and Reminiscences
Cricket Prints, R.C.Robertson-Glasgow (Werner Laurie 1943).
More Cricket Prints, R.C.Robertson-Glasgow 1948.
The Daily Worker Cricket Annual 1948 (article by Douglas Wright).
Between Wickets, Ray Robinson (Collins, 3rd edn 1948).
Australian Bowlers, A.G.Moyes (Harrap 1953).
Australian Batsmen, A.G.Moyes (Harrap 1954).
Hit For Six, Gerald Brodribb (Heinemann, 1960).
The Playfair Cardus, Neville Cardus (Dickens 1963).

Cricket: The Great Ones, ed.John Arlott (Pelham 1967).
Cricket: The Great Bowlers, ed.John Arlott (Pelham 1968).
Cricket: The Great Captains, ed.John Arlott (Pelham 1971).
Compton On Cricketers Past And Present, Denis Compton (Cassell 1980).
Australian Cricket: The Game And The Players, Jack Pollard (Hodder & Stoughton 1982).
Who's Who Of Cricketers, Bailey, Thorne and Wynne-Thomas (Guild 1984).
The Wisden Book Of Obituaries, ed.Benny Green (Macdonald 1986).
Tours And Tests, Kenneth Farnes (Lutterworth 1940).
Cricket My Destiny, Walter Hammond (S.Paul 1946).
46 Not Out, R.C.Robertson-Glasgow (Hollis & Carter 1948).
Bradman, A.G.Moyes (Harrap 1948).
Cricket Heritage, W.J.Edrich (S.Paul 1948).
Playing For England, Denis Compton (Sampson Low 1949).
Express Deliveries, Bill Bowes (S.Paul 1949).
Cricket Is My Life, Len Hutton (Hutchinson 1949).
Cricket Campaigns, Norman Yardley (S.Paul 1950).
Farewell To Cricket, Don Bradman (Hodder & Stoughton 1950).
Sticky Wickets, Lionel Lord Tennyson (C.Johnson 1950).
Three Straight Sticks, R.E.S.Wyatt (S.Paul 1951).
Close Of Play, Leslie Ames (S.Paul 1953).
It Isn't Cricket, Sidney Barnes (W.Kimber 1953).
How's That!. Frank Chester (Hutchinson 1956).
Flannelled Foolishness, E.R.T.Holmes (Hollis & Carter 1957).
Cricket And All That, Eddie Paynter (A.Richardson 1962).
Afternoon Light, Sir Robert Menzies (Cassell 1967).
The Lindsay Hassett Story, R.S.Whitington (Heinemann 1969).
Time Of The Tiger, R.S.Whitington (S.Paul 1972).
The Hand That Bowled Bradman, Bill Andrews (Macdonald 1973).
Bradman, Irving Rosenwater (Batsford 1978)
Cricket And All That, Compton and Edrich (Pelham 1978).
'Tiger' Smith, E.J.Smith/Murphy (Lutterworth 1981).
Batting From Memory, Jack Fingleton (Collins 1981).
Bradman: The Illustrated Biography, Michael Page (Macmillan 1983).
Fifty Years In Cricket, Len Hutton (S.Paul 1984).
Walter Hammond, Gerald Howat (Allen & Unwin 1984).
'Tiger', Bill O'Reilly (Collins 1985).
Gubby Allen, Man Of Cricket, E.W.Swanton (Hutchinson 1985).
Hedley Verity, Alan Hill (Kingswood 1986).

Statistical

The Playfair Book Of Cricket Records, Roy Webber (Playfair 1951).
The Kaye Book Of Cricket Records, Bill Frindall (Kaye/Ward 1968).
The Wisden Book Of Test Cricket 1877-1984, Bill Frindall (Macdonald 1985).

Political

1938: A World Vanishing, Brian Cleeve (Buchan & Enright 1982).
Chips: The Diaries Of Sir Henry Channon, ed.R.R.James (Weidenfeld & Nicholson 1967).
Harold Nicholson Diaries And Letters 1930-39, ed.Nigel Nicholson (Collins 1966).
The Gathering Storm, W.S.Churchill (Cassell 1948).
The Life Of Neville Chamberlain, Keith Feiling (Macmillan 1946).

Video Cassettes

The Legend Of Sir Donald Bradman, narrator Bill O'Reilly (Powerplay).
1938: A Year To Remember (Parkfield Pathe 1990).